THE ART AND SCIENCE OF CHILD CARE

The Art and Science of Child Care

Research, policy and practice in the European Union

edited by
MATTHEW COLTON
WALTER HELLINCKX
POL GHESQUIÈRE
MARGARET WILLIAMS

arena

Published by
Arena
Ashgate Publishing Limited
Gower House
Croft Road
Aldershot
Hants GU11 3HR
England

Ashgate Publishing Company
Old Post Road
Brookfield
Vermont 05036
USA

British Library Cataloguing in Publication Data

Art and Science of Child Care: Research, Policy
and Practice in the European Union
I. Colton, M.J.
362.7094
ISBN 1-85742-285-6

Library of Congress Cataloging-in-Publication Data

The art and science of child care: research, policy and
practice in the European Union / edited by Matthew Colton
... [et al.]
p. cm.
Includes index.
ISBN 1-85742-285-6: $42.95 (approx.)
1. Child care – European Union countries. 2. Child care – Research – European Union countries. 3. Child care – Government policy – European Union countries. 4. Child care services – European Union countries. I. Colton, M.J., 1955– .
HQ778.7.E88A78 1995 94-35598
362.7'14'094–dc20 CIP

Typeset by Pol Ghesquière, Vesaliusstraat 2, B-3000 Leuven (Belgium)

Printed and bound in Great Britain by Hartnolls Limited, Bodmin, Cornwall

Contents

Preface

Matthew COLTON
Pol GHESQUIÈRE
Walter HELLINCKX
Margaret WILLIAMS

It is some centuries now since mathematics had much to do with mysticism: but for Pythagoras, who was a religious prophet as well as a mathematician, numbers were the reflection of an ideal world, revealed through mystic contemplation. The Greeks believed that thought alone was the road to truth, that mind was superior to matter, that a spectator at a game was more important than a player. Even in more modern times, knowledge belonged to the aristocrats who had the leisure for speculation, to the church which endorsed the virtue of contemplation, and to the academics, whose lives were dignified by the ideal of abstract truth.

Throughout our history, we have separated mind from matter, the physical from the spiritual, the abstract from the actual, the empirical from the contemplative. The value we place on the separate ends of the spectrum may have altered - we value empiricism now where once we despised it - but the separateness itself is little changed. Wars still rage between the qualitative and the quantitative, between pure and applied research, subjectivism and objectivism, intuition and measurement, theory and practice. Many of us still believe that the human creativity which we call "art" is somehow diminished or even extinguished by the emphasis on logic, observation and repetition which is the heart of "science".

The purpose of this book is to close the gap between art and science in the field of child care. The most fundamental task of any society is raising its children to maturity, and this task is an art, requiring judgement, intuition and creativity. It is also a science, based on knowledge of what works best with what type of child in what kind of situation. It demands a unified and coherent child-care policy - based on the experience of practitioners and the knowledge derived from research - which sets goals, points to methods and establishes these within the wider context of national and international legal, social, political and economic systems. We are a long way from such a policy and such policies as we have rarely seem to be informed by knowledge derived from either practice or research - perhaps, in part, because we have separated these from one another.

The scholars who have contributed to this book come from different disciplines and different countries. They view the field of child care from different professional perspectives: but they would all agree that the integration of art and science in research, policy and practice and the establishment of links between them is one of the most vital contributions we can make to the future of our children and our society.

The theme of this book concerns just such an integration. Its plan takes us from the general to the particular, beginning with a discussion of childhood itself and moving on through an exploration of the ways in which research, policy and practice *might be* linked to specific studies in which research, policy and practice *have been* linked. The book describes these linkages in the areas of developmental research, evaluative research, residential care and foster care, focusing on keys to integration such as the application of theoretical models to practice, the dissemination of research findings to a wide variety of actors, the utilization of the results of research studies by practitioners and policy makers, and the involvement of practitioners in research endeavours. These integrative keys are placed in the context of issues important in the child-care field, such as the outcomes of short-term and long-term extrafamilial care, the development of assessment instruments, the design of evaluative studies, the treatment of delinquency, educational attainment, the return home of separated children, the affective relationships between children and carers, and the differing perspectives of children and parents.

In the first chapter, *Feran Casas* discusses the development of the concept of childhood and of social research into the problems of childhood. He addresses the existing dichotomy between theoretical paradigms and practical action, and examines attempts in various European countries to achieve the convergence between research, policy and practice which is the focus of the book.

In a similar vein, *Roger Bullock* and *Michael Little* in Chapter 2 explore the background to the current divisions between research and practice and between pure and applied research. The relationship between research and development is considered through a description of the recent history of research and development at the Dartington Social Research Unit. The terms "research" and "development" are clarified and are integrated into the concept of research development work. This concept is illustrated through a discussion of work undertaken following the completion of the *Going Home* research project, which involved disseminating findings in an attractive way, getting practitioners to apply results to cases, using scientific methods to test the power of predictive factors, and relating the difficulties of implementation to the wider structural and organisational aspects of agencies.

Sonia Jackson, in Chapter 3, continues with the theme of practice-oriented research through a discussion of the development, testing and application of an assessment instrument for children. Recent British legislation has attempted to introduce a new philosophy of care for children, aiming to actively promote their development, whenever possible in partnership with their parents. Evidence is growing that this has not happened in the past, and outcomes for children growing up in residential or foster care have been very disappointing. The chapter identifies some of the difficulties in providing good quality care for children separated from their families, and describes a scheme which is being widely implemented in the United Kingdom and several other countries. The *Looking After Children* programme takes as a model the childrearing practices of successful parents in the community and uses them as a basis for assessment and action in relation to seven developmental dimensions. Early findings are reported from evaluation studies in four local authorities and from the use of the assessment instrument with children in their own families.

Ko Rink takes a somewhat different approach to the assessment of children's problems and the development of appropriate methods of care. In Chapter 4, he discusses a number of related reaction pattern research studies concerning the attitudes of juveniles to social limits. This chapter looks at the development and use of a standard reaction instrument (SRI) to identify juveniles who tend towards delinquent behaviour and to suggest appropriate treatment methods for delinquent juveniles based on their attitudinal flexibility towards social limits.

In Chapter 5, *Matthew Colton, Anthony Health* and *Jane Aldgate* address the assessment of children from another perspective. They examine the possible relationship between educational attainment and behaviour, basing their discussion on a longitudinal study of foster children and a 'comparison group' of children receiving social work support while remaining with their birth families. After a brief summary of the methodology used in the study, the overall levels of attainment and progress of the two groups are reported. This is followed by an account of the incidence of behavioural problems among the children. Finally, the third part of the chapter considers whether the study data support the commonly-held view that behavioural problems and low educational achievement among separated children are linked.

Nicola Madge, in Chapter 6, turns to the short-term and long-term outcomes of extra-familial care, citing research studies which focus on the outcomes of residential, foster and home-on-trial provisions, and stressing the need to know more about the process as well as the outcomes of care. *Eric Scholte* takes up the topic of outcomes in relation to the effectiveness of care-services for juveniles. In Chapter 7 he discusses the application of longitudinal research studies to three major trends in care services in West European countries. These trends are: the establishment of a continuum of care; an increasing awareness of the complexity of the problems of children at risk; and an increasing demand for outcome evaluation. Through meta-analysis of a number of research studies, Scholte explores the links between the child's problems at intake - assessed on the basis of a socio-ecological model - the type of care provided, and the outcomes of care as reflected in the degree of resolution of the assessed problems.

It is logical then to pass on to the matter of quality in child care, a topic which is of great current concern. In Chapter 8, *Walter Hellinckx* and *Benedikte van den Bruel* explore quality evaluation in residential care, describing why such evaluation is needed, the various meanings of the term and the different methods employed to measure the process, effects and environment of care. Paying specific attention to the resources required and the target groups at whom the care is aimed, the authors examine the reasons for the general lack of systematic quality evaluation in residential care.

Continuing with the subject of evaluation in Chapter 9, *Frits Harinck* and *Monika Smit* consider process evaluation in residential care. In doing so, they discuss six types of evaluation: component analysis; monitoring; underlying process evaluation; implementation evaluation; clarifying practitioners' concepts; and formative evaluation. They stress the need for relating the type of evaluation undertaken to the programme's developmental stage, drawing examples of each evaluation type from the field of residential care, which was the focus of previous chapters.

In company with *Erik Knorth*, *Monika Smit* continues the discussion of quality and evaluation in Chapter 10 with an exploration of the need for a systematic approach to residential child care, and a particular focus on goal-oriented care in the context of individual treatment plans. The authors present a model in which key decision-making steps are integrated with a systematic child-care cycle comprising initial assessment, decision-making, planning, implementation and evaluative assessment. Short case studies illustrate the application of the model to the formulation, implementation and evaluation of treatment plans for children.

In Chapter 11, we leave the area of residential care, moving on to an evaluation of family support services and the difficulties surrounding the implementation of child-care policy. Recently, in the United Kingdom, the 1989 Children Act brought together in a single code of law all the public and private laws concerning the care, protection and upbringing of children and the provision of services to them and their families. In Chapter 11, *Matthew*

Colton, Charlotte Drury and *Margaret Williams* highlight key dilemmas in the implementation of the Act and the conflicts facing local authorities. The three issues considered are definitions of need, identification of children in need, and family support services.

The subject of support services is continued in Chapter 12 by *Pol Ghesquière, Walter Hellinckx* and *Herman Baartman* who examine the meaning of the term "multi-problem family" with particular attention to the client perspective. The authors describe a study to explore the support services offered to multi-problem families as a function of the different ways that the families and helping professionals respectively view themselves, each other, and the relationship between them. Information is derived from the content analysis of interviews with families and relevant literature.

The client perspective is examined further by *Paul Durning* in Chapter 13 through an exploration of parenting roles. Durning looks at the processes involved in bringing up children in residential institutions, with a focus on the ways in which research into residential settings increases understanding about the child-rearing process. Questions about what parenting means, both privately and professionally, are clarified through a description of a research study into the roles and tasks of carers in families and institutions. Comparisons are made between the child-care philosophies and activities prevalent in France and Great Britain, with attention given to the difficulties of linguistic and conceptual translation.

We thus travel from a general discussion of the concept of childhood and the theories underpinning child-care to specific issues such as parenting and family support. The concluding chapter by *Matthew Colton, Pol Ghesquière, Walter Hellinckx* and *Margaret Williams* summarises what has gone before, drawing attention to the suggestions made by the contributing authors as to how research, policy and practice in the child-care field might be more effectively linked.

1 Social research and policy making

Ferran CASAS

The emergence of childhood

The historical perspective

Throughout history, different peoples in different places have adopted special policies to deal with the problem of children who, for some reason, have been separated from their families. In Ancient Rome, such children were brought together in the Asylum of Mount Eldus and trained to swell the ranks of the Roman legions. During the Middle Ages, public authorities almost always entrusted responsibility for orphan children to charitable institutions. In most European countries, over the centuries, there has been a growing interest in developing regulations to ensure that children without families are cared for in an appropriate manner: that is, in a manner fitting to the material standards and spiritual and moral values of the period. Regulatory provision has varied widely at different times in different countries. However, generally speaking, responsibility for care has gradually progressed up the hierarchy of public authority: from local authorities, to regional authorities, and finally to central administration. The trend towards centralisation has also applied to charitable institutions as the amount of money handled by these bodies has become increasingly more substantial.

Many historians have demonstrated that the process of regulating care has been influenced by two primary factors (Platt, 1969; Martinez Shaw, 1986). First, those involved in caring for children in need have generally demonstrated a desire for moral control of the socially deprived.

Second, various systems have traditionally been developed to categorise and prioritise different levels of need. These systems have involved the philosophical, and often physical, separation of people identified as belonging in different categories. Children have been separated from adults, boys from girls, those who exhibit unacceptable behaviour patterns from those who do not, those who are in some way deficient from those who are not, and so on.

At a political level, interest in children resulted in part from the gradual spread of compulsory schooling, which was instituted in some countries at the end of the last century and in others after World War II. Industrial legislation to prevent the exploitation of working children and new special criminal legislation for minors (Thernborn, 1992) also excited political interest in issues affecting children.

The awareness of children *as a population group* did not emerge in many industrialised countries until the second half of the twentieth century. At this time, attention began to focus on the need to give overall coherence to the wide range of social actions aimed at children as a whole, or at subgroups of children. In other words, genuine *childhood policies* began to appear. A childhood policy, in this sense, may be defined as a set of actions endorsed by public authorities and undertaken for the purpose of improving the living conditions of children.

During the last few decades, emerging childhood policies have generally run counter to the former tendency to classify, separate, and institutionalise children. In the Scandinavian countries, in particular, the wide acceptance of the principle of "normalisation" (Nirje, 1969; Bank-Mikkelsen, 1973) marks a crucial historic moment. The belief that all children should be provided with a normal family life whenever possible constitutes a root principle from which modern policies, practices and research efforts have sprung. The wealth of scientific study stemming from this principle has yet to be adequately appraised.

The belief in normalisation has also had a profound effect upon regulatory frameworks. Some countries, such as Norway, already have a Ministry specifically identified as "Childhood". Others countries have designated officials who are charged with the defence of children's rights (Ombudsman) (Flekkoy, 1990). Realistically, it must be acknowledged that policies relating to children are often considered to be of minor importance compared to policies on other issues. Nevertheless, such policies are in place and are being implemented to varying degrees with respect to protecting and providing services for children. As nations become increasingly globally aware and increasingly interlinked, it becomes more necessary to relate any social action concerning children to an international framework, encompassing both policies specific to children and social policies in general.

Although policies and practices relating to children differ widely throughout Europe, there is a common denominator in that almost all European countries have a far-reaching social welfare system which covers the child population as a whole and provides a wide variety of services and benefits. In every industrialised country without exception, this welfare system is linked to a structured system for the protection of children. Within such systems, as a rule, the principle of avoiding the separation of children from their natural families has gradually taken precedence. For example, children are no longer removed from their homes merely because their families are poor, although, towards the beginning of the century, poverty was a primary reason for breaking families apart. In the present day, other services designed to support the family can be brought into play when poverty poses a threat to the welfare of the child.

Nevertheless, there are sometimes circumstances where separation cannot be avoided. Parents may be unwilling or unable to care for the child, or the child may be experiencing emotional or behavioural difficulties which can be more effectively addressed outside the home. Historically, children who could not be cared for by their families were often boarded out with a paid individual or sent to live with others in a children's home. These two traditional methods of child care - foster care and residential care respectively - have been incorporated into modern welfare and child protection policies at local, regional and national levels (Casas, 1990). However, they are now commonly regarded as services of "last resort", reserved for cases where less intrusive methods have proven unsuccessful.

The importance of the convention on children's rights

The Convention on Children's Rights, 1989, marked a major historical change in the way that "childhood" is conceptualised. Many people continue to perceive a child as a fragile being, who is "in the process of becoming", who will eventually achieve the status of adulthood and is meanwhile in need of protection and civilly passive. The Convention acknowledged the child, at the highest international level, to be an individual with rights. In other words, children now have not only the right to be protected but also the right to be autonomous, to express their opinions and desires in matters that affect them, and to participate in social life as leading and active figures, as citizens in the profoundest sense. It is no longer enough to talk of child protection policies. It is now necessary to consider social policies for the promotion of childhood and its quality of life.

The Convention confirmed what many research studies have already demonstrated: that children are social actors who interact with their environment and modify it, right from the tenderest age. In the strictest sense, the quality of life of social actors can only be improved if they feel themselves to be at the centre of any change affecting them (Casas, 1991), and if they participate in determining the nature of that change (Hart, 1992).

As a direct outcome of the Convention, a World Summit of Heads of State and of Government was convened on behalf of children. The Plan of Action passed at this Summit explicitly recognises the need to conduct more research into the real situations in which children live and to exchange results in order to promote courses of action that are more effective in enhancing child welfare. The Convention marked the start of a New Era for children: a "new childhood" with greater participation by the social actors concerned.

Involvement of international agencies

The initial action of the United Nations in recognising childhood has apparently revitalised other processes of recognition, which either did not hitherto exist or had lain dormant in the headquarters of other International Agencies. Thus, in the last few years, as part of the co-ordinated research programme, the Council of Europe has initiated exploratory research into childhood, particularly in connection with street children. The Council has also approved an ambitious Project on Childhood Policies (III.8) within its Social Policy Steering Committee (CDPS: *Comité Directeur de la Politique Social*), which is coordinated by a Committee of Experts from different countries. Committee members include not only those knowledgeable about children but experts from other Steering Committees in fields related to children.

An agreement between the Austrian Government and the United Nations has resulted in the institution of the European Centre in Vienna. This Centre has developed a Childhood Programme, promoting the drafting of "Childhood Reports" in many of the countries of the so-called U.N.-European Region, as well as the production of new national statistics about children. The Childhood Programme has adopted a predominantly sociological approach (see Journal Eurosocial, especially 36/1 to 12/1990, and Qvortrup, 1990).

The O.E.C.D. (Organisation for Economic Cooperation and Development) has also shown an increasing interest in some of the issues associated with childhood. One of these issues is child care, particularly the care of young children since parents can only work if child-care services are of high quality, readily available and financially accessible.

Finally, it should be pointed out that the European Community has hitherto been reluctant to concern itself with childhood issues since these are not included in the Treaty of Rome. However, studies carried out by the European Commission Childcare Network, coordinated by Peter Moss, marked a break with this tradition. The European Parliament has also recently approved a proposal by the member José M. Bandrès on the need for a European Convention on Children's Rights.

Social research into the problems of childhood

Research and its social impact

It is not common for discoveries and advances in the social and human sciences to have such an immediate and resounding public impact as do technological advances in the biological and physical sciences. However, if knowledge gained in the course of the twentieth century, and especially in the second half, is compared with prior knowledge, there can be no doubt that advances in the social sciences have been spectacular. In recent times, great strides have been made in the knowledge and understanding of human needs pertaining to social development. For example, there has been a growing appreciation of children's learning capabilities and of ways of fostering the acquisition of knowledge. Increasing importance has been attributed to the natural need of every child to discover, explore, act, be responsible, and be autonomous.

There are a number of reasons for the fact that technological innovations tend to have a larger impact on public opinion than advances in the social sciences. The dearth of economic investment in social research is probably the most crucial reason. However, two other important factors must also be considered. First, studies in the social sciences are often fragmented into countless schools and theoretical paradigms. This means that, when controversies are aired, they tend to turn into endless abstract discussions, far removed from the ordinary concerns of the man on the street. Second, and paradoxically, discoveries in the social sciences often raise direct questions about issues most relevant to the man on the street: questions about relationships, value systems, rights and obligations. Such questions are uncomfortable, possibly leading to doubts about the assumptions underlying traditional and cherished life-styles. It is understandable that many people avoid these questions by oversimplifying, categorising everything as black or white, and refusing to give mature consideration to the disturbing and complex issues of modern society.

When a commercial product appears on the market with clear advantages over an earlier product, the production and sales of the later model quickly and noticeably increase. There may be some initial opposition because new commercial products can change people's lives in radical and sometimes unanticipated ways, but the opposition is usually rapidly overcome. Resistance to social change is more determined and implacable. Challenges to stereotyped opinions, bad habits and erroneous belief systems tend to be ignored or treated with outrage; and change comes slowly if it comes at all. Thus, when different behaviour patterns are discovered which could greatly enhance human inter-relations or the quality of daily life, theoretical acceptance may be forthcoming but practical implementation often is not.

The major studies carried out by Spitz and Bowlby on institutionalised children provide an excellent example. Spitz (1945; 1958) and Bowlby (1950) were able to demonstrate, with a high level of certainty, the negative effects of large institutions on the developmental processes of children, especially the youngest children. Although the World Health Organisation publicised these studies widely in 1951, large institutions did not begin to be re-organised until much later: for example, in Spain, the process did not begin until 1977. Furthermore, the re-organisation process in Spain affected only a small part of the country and is threatened with termination even today (Casas, 1988). Non-utilisation of even the most rigorous research findings is a common and frustrating phenomenon about which much has been written. The situation in Spain demonstrates almost conclusively that scientific evidence is insufficient to instigate change in the provision of public services for children at the rate that sheer logic would demand.

Research resources and the researcher's status

In most European countries, maybe with the exception of Scandinavia, the study of the social problems of childhood seems to have a dual common denominator: a low budget and a low status for the researcher engaged in the field. Low status and limited resources are naturally associated with the low popular impact of scientific achievements in the childhood field, even though these achievements are obviously of the greatest importance.

Some 15 years ago, in Spain, pioneering researchers showed that many of the social and family problems of children in Spanish institutions were similar to those revealed by researchers in other countries. The solutions to these problems called for special financial allocations. Basic research, evaluative research and structural changes in the system of child protection all had to be paid for.

Often, funding was not made available, with the result that necessary aspects of evaluation research were never undertaken. For example, some very important changes were instituted in regional and local systems without any type of prior research to permit the collection of baseline data. In many cases, outcome research was undertaken solely to determine the effectiveness of social policies in meeting highly inflexible programme goals. No attempt was made to review the goals themselves, or to look for possible alternatives which might better serve the interests of the child.

Insufficient funding and the controversies sparked by the hasty implementation of programmes of social action have resulted in difficulties for researchers, at both a sociopolitical and a personal level. Indeed, many who had combined research into childhood with research in other areas abandoned their exploration of childhood and focused their attention elsewhere.

At a sociopolitical level, conflict sprang from the ideal of a Welfare State, contrasted with the low political priority given to children. On the one hand, the goal was to develop efficient and coherent social service networks which would result in increased equality of opportunity, greater social justice and more solidarity, thereby enabling deprivation, poverty and social exclusion to be overcome. On the other hand, due to the low political priority accorded to children, the money necessary to develop such networks could not be made available.

At a personal level, researchers found that, although they were highly motivated to work in the childhood field, the real possibilities for rigorous research work were limited. Lack of research rigour gave rise to countless criticisms in the academic world, which is not always fully committed to applied activities. In other words, the mere fact of working on the social problems of childhood seemed to confer a lower status on the researcher, and this has been a contributary factor in the considerable "burning out" that has occurred amongst them.

A second, related factor has doubtless been frustration. Researchers who have made heroic efforts to achieve a reasonable standard of scientific rigour while still accommodating practitioners' need for flexibility may be understandably frustrated when, as often seems to happen, policy makers disregard their findings. Policy makers, naturally enough, would take the view that they are not disregarding findings. Research results are only one of the many factors which must be considered when a social policy is formulated. Nevertheless, one consequence of the difficulties faced by researchers is that there are often insufficient data available to guide the politicians in making their decisions.

Availability of basic data about childhood

The paucity of basic data about childhood is not solely due to the sociopolitical and personal problems faced by researchers. When attempts have been made to conduct comparative studies into the problems of children in different geographic areas, methodological problems have often been encountered.

In some cases, the researchers themselves have been at fault. Data-collection protocols have not always been properly co-ordinated, with the result that information from one region has not been strictly comparable with that from another. However, there are other problems, often less apparent, which greatly impede broad studies of a comparative nature, not only at the international level, but also often within a single country. One of the most basic difficulties concerns the lack of systematic collection of *statistical data from the child's perspective*. For example, saying that four children live in one family unit is not the same thing as saying that a child lives in a family unit with two of his four brothers and sisters and with a stepbrother.

Statistical data on children are often diverse and are collected from other people's perspectives: the family, the school, the mother's activities, and so on, may all be points of interest. Once a national or regional statistical institute has begun to collect these kinds of data, the same data will continue to be collected, even though they are not the right data for comparative studies from the child's perspective. Authors who have made the most in-depth analyses of this situation have stated that the actual data available suffer from a kind of "cult of adultism" (Edgar, 1986). This means that it is not possible to obtain a coherent view of the activities or welfare of the children of a specific area from the perspective of the children themselves (Qvortrup, 1990).

An additional consideration is that the legal systems of child protection vary widely from country to country. The combination of these two factors forces analysts to be cautious when making comparisons. Nevertheless, comparisons are essential if a consistent framework relevant to child care is to be sufficiently well developed to be acceptable to those responsible for formulating social policies.

Convergence between research and practice

The rise in evaluative research

Lack of collaboration, and indeed antagonism, between pure researchers and professional social workers is unfortunately a widespread and well established phenomenon. Confrontations between the two camps have often coincided with the frequent "crises" arising in the human and social sciences. Professional practitioners are commonly accused of lacking theoretical rigour, while theorists are accused of lacking social relevance.

However, efforts have been made to draw the sides together. Some epistemologists, such as Bunge (1980), have pointed out that both pure and applied studies in the social sciences can contribute to knowledge. In Bunge's own words, pure research and applied research:

> *"besides being methodologically similar, are both goal-oriented; it is only that the goals are different. The goal of pure research is **truth for truth's sake**; the goal of applied research is **truth that is useful** to someone."*

Evaluative research, which represents a crucial point of convergence between both interests, began to assume increasing importance in the 1970s, especially after the work of Struening and Guttentag (1975). Suchman (1967) has defined evaluative research as the application of social research techniques to the study of human services programmes on a large scale.

However, evaluation research itself is prey to the different, and often antagonistic, perspectives of researchers, practitioners and politicians. The so-called "social indicators movement" is an excellent example of the crisis-ridden dialectic between basic research needs and the informational needs of political decision makers. Plessas and Fein (1972) have discussed the "fundamental dispute over social indicators", referring to the difficulties inherent in reconciling the pressing political need to identify and define social goals for immediate, short-term action, with the rigorous and often lengthy scientific research necessary to achieve these ends. Basically, the problem is one of timeframes. The speed required by policy makers and the cautious rigour considered necessary by scientists are diametrically opposed.

The unsatisfactory relationship between research and social policies

Between the 19th and 23rd of June 1991, a European seminar took place in Madrid on "applied research and social policies for childhood in Europe in the 90s", with representatives from 20 countries participating (M.A.S., 1991). The contributions to this seminar revealed considerable general dissatisfaction with the link between research and social action programmes. A very few countries, such as Sweden, presented the research-social action relationship as wide-ranging and long-lasting. A number of countries, like the United Kingdom, presented it as partial, generally focused on certain specific topics. In almost half the countries represented, it was considered that there is practically no stable link. Some countries - Poland for example - stated that there was a lot of quality research but it had no impact on social policies. Others, such as Greece, pointed out that social action programmes were rarely preceded by research. Still others, like Austria, pointed to their lack of an evaluative tradition.

In short, the European picture with regard to research-social action links is highly heterogeneous. A Finnish representative mentioned the feeling in her country that too much research is undertaken in relation to the results achieved. A representative from France remarked that the results of research into the social problems of childhood are seldom exchanged and publicly compared; and, therefore it is generally believed that research is something of "no practical use". This belief is so prevalent that no advantage is taken even of the discoveries made in fieldwork (M.A.S., 1992).

Dissatisfaction is apparently felt not only by researchers towards politicians, but also vice versa. The question to be answered is, therefore, "Are there ways of producing mutual satisfaction?" Rosenczveig (1991) comments that there is often a reciprocal failure to listen and a lack of appreciation on both sides of the other's needs. Politicians should realise that the pacing and autonomy required by researchers necessitate considerable independence from political considerations. However, researchers must also realise that politicians cannot make their decisions purely on the basis of research, since social development involves other, non-scientific values.

Research and public opinion

The idea of "childhood" may exist as a theoretical concept but it will make no impact in the real world until a sufficient number of people believe that "childhood" is a real state, significantly different from "adulthood". Ariès (1960) has shown that the notion of childhood regarded as self-evident today has not always existed; rather, it is a recent invention which only finally emerged after the industrial revolution. As previously mentioned, the idea that the child is an "individual with rights", just like other human beings, had no formal international recognition until the plans made at the Convention on Children's Rights came into force in 1990.

Throughout history, the social context in which children grow up has changed along with changing physical conditions. However, the social representations of adults about children, in different societies at different times, have had effects which are just as large, if more intangible and subtle. Study of these representations is made more difficult by their very intangibility. In all European countries, the systematic and rigorous collection of data on psychosocial aspects of the dynamics of society has very rarely included data that affect the child population, perhaps with the exception of phenomena regarded as particular problematic, such as delinquency and drug abuse.

However, lack of such data and lack of practice in their collection may be viewed as a relatively minor problem. Far more important is the existence, and even predominance, of negative attitudes and mistaken *social perceptions* towards children and adolescents on the part of adults. Certain qualities may be wrongly attributed to children on the basis of *stereotypes* and *prejudices*; unfortunate *social reactions* in the face of needs or conflicts may result in a lack of *support* for the child, or the wrong type of support. Ideas about children's capacities and development often do not reflect reality and tend to constitute shared social stereotypes rather than shared objective knowledge (D'Alessio, 1990).

In short, there is still a lot to learn about the ways in which adults in different cultures represent children, their problems and their quality of life. Such knowledge is not only of theoretical interest, but is also directly applicable to problem solving. For example, the way in which the adults of a society perceive and define childhood will determine their expectations of their children at different ages, their behaviour towards their children and their aspirations for their children in the future (Casas, 1992).

In the modern age, the perceptions of both adults and children are moulded by the media to a very large extent. Television and radio shows about family life deal with current social issues and provide easily assimilated, if simplistic, guidelines on acceptable parenting skills and attitudes. Children may expect their parents to behave as parents do on television and feel disappointed, or even betrayed, when the parents do not. Parents, similarly, may follow the model presented on television when dealing with a problem and discover, to their bewilderment, that the television approach is ineffective with a real-life child. Nevertheless, media representations generally have more effect than a library of text books, and it cannot be assumed that writers, any more than policy makers, are familiar with the results of research into the topics portrayed. However, inaccuracies aside, the media do serve to bring to the public attention facts and informed opinions which might otherwise be lost to the dust of academia. In addition to shows about family life, there are also interviews, documentaries and public debates in which expert opinion is canvassed for public consumption. In so far as public opinion dictates social action, it would seem that the media, at present, have a greater influence than research results.

However, given the historical dichotomy between research and policy, it is only to be expected that the process of convergence will be slow, sustained by the courage and persistence of policy makers and researchers who are prepared to accommodate each other and work together towards "the new childhood" so recently envisaged.

The search for coherence between research and action

The process in some countries

The most significant changes that have taken place in Spain in the last ten years in relation to residential and foster care for children have usually followed the sequence set out below:

1. A growing interest emerges amongst a few professionals in improving some aspect of child care. Agreement is reached among the professionals about the need for change.
2. A small group of politicians takes an interest in the subject. The first political decisions are made to invest resources to address the need for change.
3. Co-operation is established or increased between researchers and child care professionals.
4. Some of the media take an interest in the subject and offer to report it and facilitate discussion.
5. Pressure groups appear in support of some proposals or in reaction to them.

6. Processes of social change accelerate. A growing number of political decisions are made in connection with the question. New research proposals appear.

In other words, at least in Spain, the processes of change in relation to the care of children with serious social and family problems involve a growing interaction between five main groups of social actors: researchers, politicians, professionals of social intervention, the media and the public.

Support for the attainment of knowledge through research must stem precisely from this interaction. As Figure 1.1 shows, the ultimate goal of increased knowledge is to promote attitudes and behaviour which will lead to an improved society.

Countries with specialised centres

The relationship between research and the development of social action programmes is facilitated by the existence of a few channels of communication. Some European countries have one or more centres engaged in research into the realities of childhood and the practical consequences of social policies concerning children. Some countries, such as Norway and Spain, have a single government centre which co-operates with the universities. Others, such as the United Kingdom and France, have both government and non-government centres; and in others, such as Germany and Holland, there are various centres which are not devoted exclusively to childhood but also explore a number of related subjects. In countries such as Sweden and Denmark, such centres are closely associated with the universities. Qvortrup (1992) has just published a guide to the most important centres in E.C. countries engaged in research work relating to the family, young people and childhood.

A large number of these centres are involved in training professional social workers and most of them issue specialised publications of some kind. Centres of this type play an important role in bringing together representatives of the five main groups of social actors previously mentioned - researchers, politicians, professionals of social intervention, the media and the public - by offering them wide-ranging support, particularly with respect to information and training.

Conclusions

If research and practice are ever to form a coherent unity, the glue that binds them together must be social policy. In order to be effective in

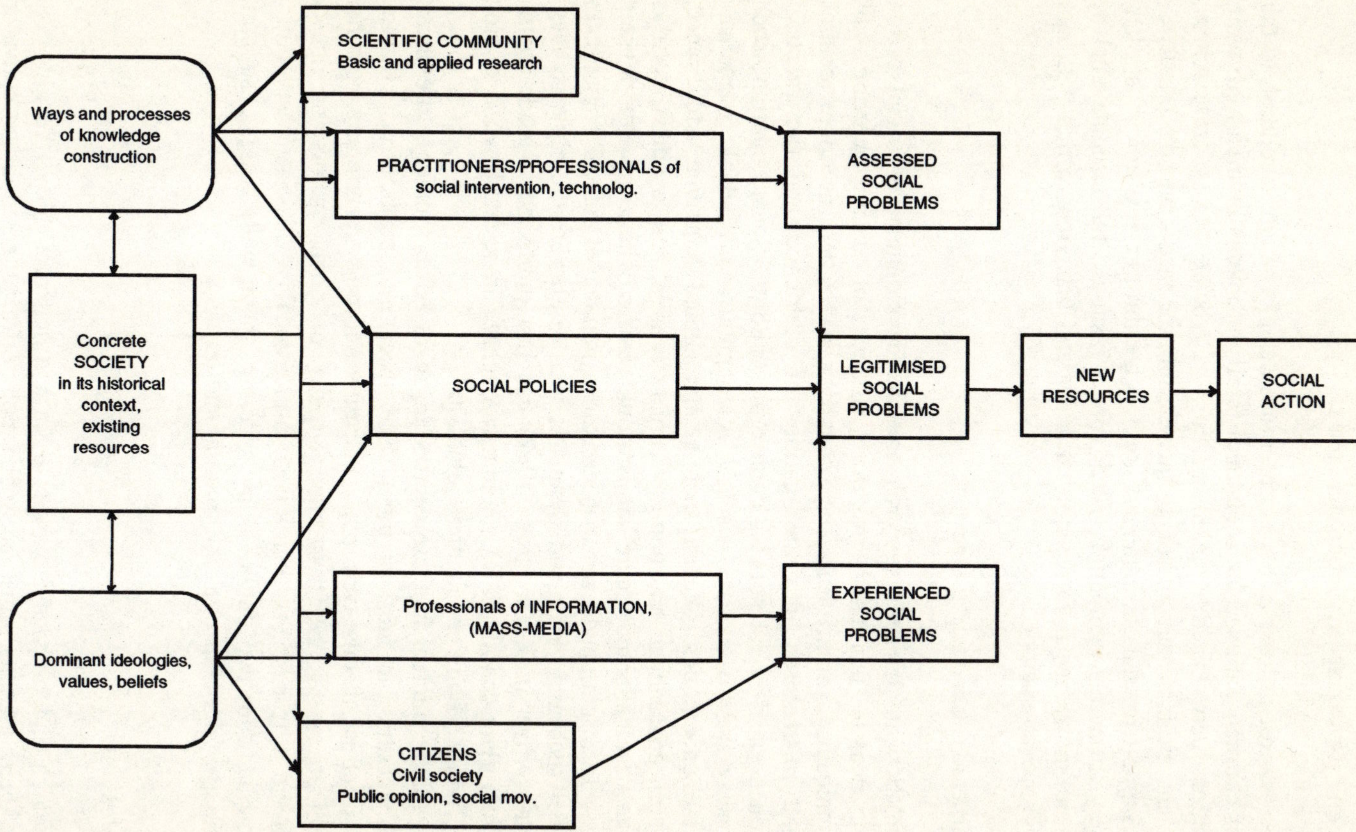

Figure 1.1: Determinants of social action

human, social and economic terms, policies must be informed both by theory derived from research and by practical input from those professionals working in the field. In addition, no policy, however well informed, can be effective without the support of the children and families whom it is meant to serve; and without the support of the media who are so influential in shaping public opinion. The convergence of research and practice may therefore best be served by providing a forum where representatives of these five key groups of social actors can come together, at national and international levels.

The difficulties and antagonisms which have existed and continue to exist between the groups may stem, in part, from the fact that each group approaches the issue of childhood from a different perspective. Professionals in the field focus on solving the practical problems presented by individuals, communities and other specific groups. They tend to be wary of politicians, defensive about research and suspicious of the media. The researcher's focus is on truth, approached cautiously and slowly through accurate and meticulous measurement, careful observation and continuous verification. Information professionals need novelty: dramatic and spectacular events and issues which will capture the public attention. The public themselves need information of a human, immediate kind which will be relevant to them in their daily lives. In addition, they need to feel that they are participating, that they are being listened to, that their opinions, needs and wants are receiving attention. The politician's task is to formulate a coherent, legal framework of service, establishing priorities, standards and procedures which embrace, as far as possible, the different and often conflicting needs of all the other players.

These five different perspectives on the issue of childhood are inherently difficult to harmonise. Perhaps the best tool for the task is the ability to listen, with no feeling of superiority, no desire for domination, and no thought of assigning blame for past mistakes. Children and their families can never be adequately served unless a genuine attempt is made, on the part of all the actors, to communicate with purpose and with honesty, to appreciate each other's viewpoints, and to compromise.

References

Ariès, P. (1960), *L'enfant et la vie familiale sous l'ancien régime*, Paris, Librairie Plou.

Bandrés, J.M. (1992) (Rapporteur), *Projet de Rapport sur une Charte européene des droits de l'enfant*, Commission juridique et des droits des citoyens, European Community.

Bank-Mikkelsen, N.E. (1973), 'La normalización como objetivo en las actividades de la vida diaria', *Boletín de Estudios y Documentación del Inserso*, vol. 15, 31-39.

Bowlby, J. (1950), *Maternal Care and Mental Health,* Genève, WHO.

Bunge, M. (1980), *Epistemología*, Barcelona, Ariel.

Casas, F. (1988), 'Las instituciones residenciales para la atención de chicos y chicas en dificultades socio-familiares: apuntes para una discusión', *Menores,* vol. 10, julio-agosto, 37-50.

Casas, F. (1989), *Técnicas de investigación social: Los indicadores sociales y psicosociales,* Barcelona, P.P.U.

Casas, F. (1990), 'Infancia y política social municipal', *Infancia y Sociedad,* vol. 4, 25-34.

Casas, F. (1991), *El concepto de calidad de vida en la intervención social en el ámbito de la infancia,* Lecture in the III Jornadas de Psicología de la Intervención Social, Madrid, novembre 1991.

Casas, F. (1992), 'Las representaciones sociales de las necesidades de niños y niñas, y su calidad de vida', *Anuario de Psicología,* vol. 53, 27-45.

D'Alessio, M. (1990), 'Social representations of childhood: an implicit theory of development', in G. Duveen & B. Lloyd (eds.), *Social representations and the development of knowledge*, Cambridge University Press.

Edgar, D. (1986), 'New family policy issues', *Australian Institute of Family Studies Newsletter,* vol. 16, August.

Flekkoy, Malfrid G. (1990), *Working for the rights of children*, Innocenti Essays, no. 1, Florence, I.C.D.C. UNICEF.

Hart, R.A. (1992), *Children's participation. From tokenism to citizenship,* Innocenti Essays, no. 4, Florence, I.C.D.C. UNICEF.

Martinez Shaw, C. (1986), 'L'assistència pública a la Barcelona moderna', *L'Avenç*, març, 30-35.

M.A.S. (Ministerio de Asuntos Sociales), *European Seminar on Applied Research and Social Policies for Children in Europe in the 90'*, Madrid, M.A.S., Junio 1991 (in press).

Morales, J.F., Blanco, A., Huici, C., Fernández, J.M. (1985), *Psicología Social Aplicada. Introduction*, Bilbao, Desclée de Brower.

Moss, P. (1990), *Childcare and equality of opportunity*, Brussels, Commision of the European Communities.

Nirje, B. (1969), 'The normalization principle and its human management implications', in R. Kugel & W. Wolfensberger (eds.), *Changing patterns in residential services for mentally retarded,* Washington, D.C., U.S. Government Printing Office.

Platt, A.M. (1969), *The child savers: the invention of delinquency,* The University of Chicago.

Plessas, D.J., & Fein, R. (1972), 'An evaluation of social indicators', *Journal of the American Institute of Planners*, vol. 38, no. 1.

Qvortrup, J. (1990), 'Childhood as a social phenomenon - An introduction to a series of National Reports', *Eurosocial*, vol. 36/1990.

Qvortrup, J. (1992), *Family, youth, childhood. Inventory of Research Institutes in the EEC - 1992*, University Center of South Jutland, Denmark.

Rosenczveig, J.P. (1991), *Políticas en favor de la infancia en Francia: Situación del País y perspectivas,* Contribution to the Seminario sobre Investigación Aplicada y Políticas Sociales para la Infancia en Europa, en la década de los 90, Madrid.

Spitz, R.A. (1945), 'Hospitalism', *The psychoanalytic study of the child,* vol. 1, 53.

Sptiz, R.A. (1958), *Le premier Anné de la Vie de l'Enfant,* Paris, P.U.F.

Struening, E.L., & Guttentag, M. (eds.) (1975), *Handbook of evaluation Research* (2 vol.), Beverly Hills (Calif.), Sage.

Suchman, E. (1967), *Evaluation research*, New York, Russell Sage.

Thernbon, G. (1992), *What is the place of childhood in politics?* Lecture presented in the International Conference "Childhood as a social phenomenon", Billund, Denmark, septembre 23-27, 1992.

2 Linking research and development: return home as experienced by separated children

Roger BULLOCK
Michael LITTLE

In applied social studies, research and development are a familiar coupling. It is almost impossible to imagine one without the other. Yet this has not always been the case. Theoretical scholarship has long been pursued for its own sake, seeking to improve our understanding of the human condition. Logicians and philosophers would claim to have made significant contributions by such intellectual activity. Even when faced with pressing social problems, in many countries, such as France, there is no tradition of seeking remedies by reviewing empirical evidence.

However, it is not insignificant that in the last 20 years, social policy researchers in the United Kingdom have increasingly sought to include practical dimensions to their work. This can be seen in government departments as well as universities. The Home Office Research Unit had the words "and Development" inserted into its title in the early 1980s. At the Department of Health, the head of research is no longer called the Chief Scientist but the Director of Research and Development. In universities, too, "applied" has often been added to the names of departments once content with being just social sciences. At Bristol, for instance, the former department of social administration is now called social policy and social planning.

There are several reasons for these changes. Politically, there has been pressure on the social sciences to justify their value and fulfil claims of contributing to knowledge about major social problems. Similarly, the major funding bodies seem increasingly to want findings from the research they commission to be effectively disseminated and adopted by policy makers. In the past, too much research remained unread or was restricted to a few cogniscenti. It represented poor value for money. Today, government departments, charitable foundations and the Economic and Social Research

Council (whose name was changed from the Social Sciences Research Council, again in the early 1980s) all allow time for dissemination and development in the projects they commission.

These changes reflect wider tensions between pure and applied research. Theoretical work has always had high status in the academic community while empiricism and applied research tend to have been relegated. "Just collecting a few figures for a Royal Commission", was the comment of one distinguished professor on hearing that a neighbouring research team had obtained a large government grant. But, equally, the failure of social scientists to gain much influence on, and even to invite rebuke from those dealing with social problems in the frontline, such as police and social workers, has been disappointing, especially to the veterans of the 1960s social science boom who hoped for so much. Some, in their defence, attribute more sinister motives to recent concerns with the application of research results. Tenured university staff, for example, have argued against government plans to introduce fixed-term contracts by stressing the necessity of job security for radical social inquiry at the cutting edge. Research is part of the wider political agenda and knowledge is ammunition. The changes we have discussed are part of an inevitable struggle for control over activity and information.

Whatever the significance of these wider contexts, there can be little doubt about the strength of the general trend to add development to pure research. This seems to appease funders and win over recipients. But what does this change actually mean? Development is such a vague term that almost anything seems possible.

In this chapter, we wish to consider the relationship between research and development by looking at a recent child-care study undertaken by the Dartington Social Research Unit. The Unit has done a considerable amount of work in the area of social, educational and employment services for children and families and it is significant that its most recent projects have all had a developmental component. This change clearly reflects the shifts in thinking just described. However, before illustrating this, we need to clarify the terms research and development, for both cover a number of different activities.

Research and development

Social policy research can take several forms each of which is different in its time and resource implications as well as in its functions. In broad terms, such research falls into three groups. First, there is research which is theoretical and fashions concepts and combines them into perspectives; this is usually part of an academic discipline or sub-discipline. Second, there is large scale empirical work which provides new information based upon reliable data. Such studies review situations and provide evidence on hypotheses. Third, there are evaluations of particular situations, client needs or professional practice. These studies are usually brief and limited but can be extremely useful if placed in a wider knowledge context.

At Dartington, we have at various times undertaken each type of research. However, experience has taught us that categorising research in this way can be somewhat artificial because each is closely linked to the others. Large-scale empirical studies need to be guided by well considered theories. Similarly, theoretical work which involves no data collection draws heavily upon knowledge produced by empirical studies if its conclusions are to stand. Likewise, although short-term evaluations, such as scrutinies of particular interventions, have limited value when read alone, they are an important component of our knowledge about services built up by theoretical and empirical work.

Similarly, development work can have several dimensions. It can involve drawing out policy and practice implications from research results and making recommendations about guidance and procedures. A code of practice is the likely outcome of such activity. Development work can also produce indicators or checklists to help those making decisions. These can be limited in scope, such as aide memoires, or have predictive possibilities in that they enable decision makers to be more aware of the consequences of their actions. Finally, the dissemination of research findings in a new and attractive way can be a legitimate developmental enterprise. Clearly, different types of research will have different relevance for different types of development work, and vice versa. The recent history of research and development at the Dartington Social Research Unit indicates changes in this relationship.

Recent research and development at Dartington

In 1983, the Dartington Unit began the study *Foster Home Breakdown*, which examined the factors associated with disruption in foster care. For this project, it seemed sufficient to produce a book, along with a few articles elaborating specific points in professional and academic journals. Conferences and training courses provided further opportunities to publicise the findings in the hope that those responsible would take note of the evidence and incorporate it into practice. This was a very traditional approach to research; findings are produced, reviewed and left to seep into accumulated wisdom. As nearly all social workers and foster parents are likely to be involved with a placement breakdown that leads to the precipitate departure of a child in their care, it seemed reasonable to assume that professional concern and natural curiosity would sufficiently motivate intended audiences to obtain, read and assimilate the research.

Yet, by the mid-1980s, evidence was emerging that this approach was inefficient. It relied too much on the expectation that social workers read journals and research reports, an assumption that is unfounded. Also, contract researchers were too busy pursuing their next project to worry about the effects of the last one. Neither was there any mechanism in social work by which intermediary bodies, such as the Royal Colleges in medicine, could co-ordinate and publicise research findings. Thus, links between research, policy and practice were varied. There was a system of research liaison which ensured discussion between researchers and policy makers in central government, but at local government level the relationship was far more tenuous.

Research links with local practitioners were even weaker, exacerbated not only by the failure of staff to read studies, as already described, but also by the lack of any tradition in which practitioners undertake investigations as part of their work. Thus, even if research findings were available, they were often viewed as irrelevant and alien. More serious still was the patchy adoption of research evidence in child-care training courses. The reasons for this are complex but partly stem from the difficulties of incorporating material that seems agnostic and critical into courses which seek socialisation and concensus. Committed writings tend to be preferred to competing theories and inconclusive results.

A sea change occurred in 1985. The Department of Health, a major research funder in the child-care field and anxious to improve the dissemination of findings among practitioners, produced *Social Work Decisions in Child Care*. This summarised the results of nine recently completed child-care projects and was circulated to every child welfare agency in the country, publicity that was followed up by a series of national seminars for social workers at all levels of seniority. This gave official, government approval to dissemination and successful exercises have been undertaken for subsequent research programmes.

This changed emphasis coincided with the completion of the Dartington study which followed *Foster Home Breakdown*, an explanation of the problems of maintaining links between children in care and their families. This was published as *Lost in Care*. Given the new situation, it seemed natural that development work should follow. The Unit's original plans were to prepare guidance on managing access between children absent in care and their families, but this was somewhat pre-empted when the Government department published its own Code of Practice: *Access to Children in Care*. As this Code had been informed by the research taking place, it fulfilled the need for a practice guide based on academic studies, the first of the three types of development work discussed earlier.

In view of these developments, it was decided that it would be most useful to go a stage further and get a group of practitioners to consider the new Code in detail and see how it could best be implemented. Refinements and new recommendations would be suggested. A group was duly convened and the report on its discussions, *Access to Children in Care: Practitioners' Views* gives their conclusions. It demonstrates the benefits of this kind of development work. For example, when considering the needs of long-stay children in care, the Code highlights the dangers when parents move to the periphery of a child's life. A complaints procedure is specified as an effective check on this tendency. To prevent such drift, the Code recommends regular monitoring as to whether access arrangements are working as intended, whether any problems have arisen in the interim, and any changes to arrangements which are needed. The professional group commenting on this emphasised that the term "careful monitoring by social workers" is too vague and should include the frequency, quality and significance of parental visits to the child, thus adding detail to a recommendation in the Code. They also emphasised that complaints should not in any way be allowed to prejudice the child or the family's situation, so qualifying a general proposal.

This kind of developmental exercise was useful in that it provided further amendments and refinements to the Code, many of which were incorporated into the more extensive guidance that accompanies the 1989 Children Act. It highlights ambiguities, offers practice tips and adds sophistication to a publication designed to link theory, research findings and practice. Although the meetings of professionals provided a useful forum to explore these links, there was a limit to what could be achieved. The ultimate product was a perfect *Code of Practice*, but there was no indication of how well it would be used and little motivation for practitioners to adopt its recommendations, particularly as it did not carry the full force of law.

This experience of the developmental work for *Lost in Care* alerted us to the shortcomings of this approach. We were not happy with its theoretical underpinning, nor could we be sure that it was having any effect on the practitioners it was trying to influence. Because of the way in which we organised the work, it did not always reach a wide audience and could not easily be replicated elsewhere. Moreover, some groups, such as those training social work professionals, managed to avoid our attentions altogether.

New approaches to development work

The focus of the *Lost in Care* development work was on applying and conveying the empirical results of the research, not on the theory which underpinned it. This meant that, while we had sought to ground the research project on sound middle-range theory, we did not apply the same rules to the developmental work. In the next project to be described, the *Going Home* study, we tried to remedy this weakness. For example, in the research report, we stress the continuities in family life which affect decision-making in respect to separation and return and show how they frequently influence the success of child-care plans. In the various developmental instruments arising from the study, we likewise incorporated ideas of continuity and the need for professionals and family members to re-consider regularly the effects of separation and return.

This new approach to developmental work also fills another gap in that the exercise is tested against clear criteria to see whether or not it is effective. Frequently, in the past, it has been sufficient to produce reports on the applications of research findings and it mattered little that some simply gathered dust on the shelves of social work offices. The *Going Home* project has an experimental design to measure what works and why.

In addition to these two improvements, we have increased the scope of our developmental work. Previously, in order to ensure high quality, we frequently worked in a narrow geographical area, for example in setting up a Family Support Group in a local city or designing leaflets for the parents of children in a particular residential home. However, it proved difficult to extend this work and replicate it elsewhere. In the current project, we have tried to achieve a better balance between our investment in the study and the audience we are trying to reach: hence the practical materials derived from the *Going Home* research are being tested in 15 local authorities.

Finally, the increased vigour with which we have pursued work in this area has taught us that the audience we hope to reach gets its information from several sources and, in order to influence practice, several developmental exercises are required. For example, we have been surprised in the *Going Home* work that many parents read - and are influenced by - the decision-making tool prepared for social workers. Indeed, some practitioners found it helpful to complete the booklet with parents and, where appropriate, children. But we have also found that social workers have been reading - and may be influenced by - the booklet designed for parents. Research information is therefore conveyed in very different ways and frequently reaches an audience wider than that targeted. We are learning much more about who reads what and why. Our commitment to broadening the scope and increasing the quality of the media we use is evidenced by our decision to employ a designer/journalist for the exercise and by the range of materials we now produce.

Let us now look more closely at the example of the research development work we have undertaken following the completion of the research published in *Going Home: The Return of Children Separated from their Families.*

The *Going Home* study

This research had several aims. These were:

i. to clarify the concept of return through an exploration of relevant literature;
ii. to chart the processes and return avenues experienced by all children in care;
iii. from these data to identify groups of children particularly vulnerable to return difficulties, such as re-abuse, placement breakdown, behaviour problems and family rejection;
iv. to scrutinise the return experiences of these children, concentrating particularly on different household situations to which children return and different styles and levels of social work support;
v. to highlight factors significantly associated with successful returns;
vi. to inform social workers about the most effective ways of preparing and managing children's returns.

Part of this research was to discover factors associated with a child's likelihood of return at different points in a care career and with the success of the return once it occurred. Multi-variate analysis of the extensive data combined with qualitative scrutiny of a small number of families allowed us to establish the factors that were not only significant but whose influences were also independent of others.

Results from the extensive study were obtained by analysing follow-up information on three groups of children. These factors were derived from quantitative and qualitative evidence scrutinised in earlier research projects: (i) a five-year follow-up of 450 children entering care; (ii) a 12-month follow-up of 321 children returned home "on trial", and (iii) a five-year follow-up of 102 young people leaving Youth Treatment Centres and other specialised provision. Although these studies were originally undertaken prospectively, and so provided reliable data, the analysis for this research was retrospective in the sense that it derived the significant factors by working back from known outcomes. The intensive study, in contrast, looked closely at 31 children in 24 families followed up for two years from the point that return became an issue.

It was found that different predictive factors apply at different points in the child's care career. One checklist of factors is applied at the initial separation and estimates the likelihood of return within six months, whilst another is relevant six months later and estimates the likelihood of return in the coming 18 months. If the child is still away from home after two years, then another checklist can be used to predict the chances of return within the following three years. Once the child is back home, a further set of factors indicates conditions associated with success of placement. The content of each Checklist is not relevant to this chapter, but each posed some 15 questions based on the key variables obtained from the research. From these answers, an estimate of the likely outcomes can be calculated.

To confirm the predictive power of these factors, we had to apply them prospectively to a new study group of children for whom the outcome was unknown. We needed social workers to use the checklists at the key moments identified in the study. To gain their interest, we carefully prepared a decision-making instrument which contained the checklists of factors, any of which could be completed in a few minutes by those familiar with the case. We complemented the checklists with a commentary that discussed the research findings and provided definitions of the terms used. We felt it was important for respondents to understand the wider context of children's reunions, so for example, information is given on patterns of return over time. It is important that social workers, parents and carers understand that 87 per cent of children looked after return home and that the chances of this happening remain high during their stay away. Indeed, return is always the most likely thing to happen to a child.

Other parts of this instrument are devoted to more sensitive information. There are quotations from some of the parents and children who helped us with the research and a page of excerpts from literature dealing with questions of separation and return. We could not be sure what professionals would read and hypothesised that one social worker would be more influenced by the "Prodigal Son" than a statistical finding, whilst another would turn to the tearful insights of a mother whose child has gone away.

Great care was taken with regard to the presentation of the booklet. Colour printing and photographs have been used to stimulate interest in new research findings. Social worker professionals are inundated with forms and research documents, most of which are drab and bureaucratic. In presenting our work we attempted to do something different. For example, we decided to make it more attractive by printing it side-on rather than as a traditional book, efforts that seem to have been appreciated by social workers.

As well as validating the significance of the factors already included in the checklists, others might be identified for inclusion, some already included might be rejected and the wording of others might be revised. Moreover, the relevance of the factors to the care careers of sub-groups of children can be more fully explored. The Children Act 1989, for instance, brings children with disabilities into the category of "children in need" while making respite care, once their sole preserve, an option for all. The factors derived for an in-care population under previous legislation may not apply to those looked after under the new Act.

An additional methodological benefit of the exercise is to clarify the role of prediction in child care, and indeed social work research generally. There is a need to establish what can and cannot be predicted and with what degree of certainty. We believe that the study is methodologically interesting because the factors have been derived from a mix of qualitative and quantitative evidence; however, the precise value of such an exercise remains unknown. Even if statistical outcomes are good, in terms of predictive power, there are still difficulties in applying them to individual cases and getting social workers to think in terms of probabilities. This mathematical perspective is not an integral part of their intellectual tradition and sits uneasily alongside case work, management and therapy. Nevertheless, no research instrument can cover all eventualities and professional judgement must prevail in the end. We have made every effort to remind practitioners who are insecure and anxious for guidance on matters of reunification that the tools produced by this part of the research take the form of aids to decision-making rather than substitutes for it.

We hope that the product of this part of the research will be used in several ways. For example, the *Going Home* booklet might form part of the child's case file, to be completed by social workers and carers at reviews. Hopefully, it will keep everyone mindful of return possibilities and alert them to work that needs to be done to ease the child's transition. While some of the messages in the checklists are fairly obvious, many are not and the booklet may indicate issues that have been missed. For example, while risks of abuse will almost certainly be high on the agenda, difficulties that the child might have in negotiating role and territory in the family home are likely to be less discussed.

Additional products of the developmental work

Although the testing of the factors is the kernel of the development work in the *Going Home* project, this part of the research seeks to do more than refine the predictive instruments. For example, the data collected provide new information about children who are looked after. As the testing involves all children separated in several local authorities within a given time period, it generates material which can be compared with earlier studies undertaken in the early 1980s, such as *Lost in Care* and *Who Needs Care?* This enables us to highlight changes in policy and practice resulting from recent legislation, particularly the Children Act 1989. Hence, we can see whether certain reforms, such as making respite care available to all children in need and promoting voluntary arrangements for looking after those who need to live away from home, have been achieved. We can also see how the new legal orders and powers that apply to separation and return are being used. As well as this, more information will be forthcoming about important research areas, such as the success and duration of children's sojourns.

In order to extend the circulation of the research findings to parents and other family members, we are also working with the Family Rights Group to prepare a booklet summarising the important research messages. Expressing ideas simply, without condescension, for people who perceive themselves to be "failed parents" has been challenging. The preparation of this document has required collaboration between the research team, parents, lawyers and social workers.

We are also preparing a computer disk which contains the key research messages on the return of children long separated from home. The principal audience for this product are team leaders or social work supervisors. As well as giving information to the users, the package will invite them to enter data about each of the children looked after in their team. This will allow team leaders to compare the profile of separated children in their geographical area with those from other regions. It will also help to identify those children for whom plans have drifted and highlight any cases where return could be a priority. This package is being designed in collaboration with an experienced programmer who is himself a foster parent.

Finally, inspired by medical marketing to doctors, we shall prepare an attractive flier to alert wider audiences to the research and its findings. Many professionals concerned with child care, such as guardians *ad litem*, judges and court clerks, work in isolation and are not part of the networks, weak as they are, in which social work research findings are disseminated.

Understanding the process of implementation

In seeking to improve general knowledge about children's return from care, we have been struck by variations in the ease with which the instrument has been implemented in different agencies. This has revealed much about the wider issue of changing social work practice and the abilities of large bureaucracies, such as social services departments, to adapt to new ideas. We are making special studies of the implementation process and are seeking to relate this to wider value systems and organisational structures. For example, social workers everywhere are eager for guidance on returning children as this is difficult and sensitive work. However, their anxieties may lead them to over-identify with the findings in the booklet and accept them uncritically, a well-established technique for shifting responsibility. On the other hand, it is noticeable that those local authorities which already have elaborate and sensitive monitoring systems seem less keen to use our material than those whose evaluative schemes are less developed.

We have a long-standing interest in why social workers find it difficult to incorporate guidance into practice and these examples provide a useful case study. Working closely with those making return decisions on children helps us decide the best ways forward regarding further development of this research material.

Conclusion

It can be seen that the aims of the developmental phase of the *Going Home* project are various. They are:

i. to test prospectively the factors associated with return outcomes as found in the retrospective scrutiny;
ii. to provide up-to-date comparative information on the backgrounds and care careers of children being separated and returned before and after the implementation of the 1989 Children Act;
iii. to develop a number of different methods of disseminating research findings and to evaluate their use and effectiveness; and
iv. to estimate the effect of the Unit's involvement in local authorities upon child-care practice generally.

These objectives go beyond the traditional models of developmental work, such as that described earlier where working groups of professionals and carers interpreted findings, drew out practice implications and made recommendations for changes in official guidance.

The approach adopted in the *Going Home* project is more research development work. We believe it takes things forward by disseminating findings in an attractive way, getting practitioners to apply results to cases, using scientific methods to test the power of predictive factors and relating the difficulties of implementation to the wider structural and organisational aspects of agencies. A welcome addition to all this is the generation of new information in important practice areas and the opportunities this provides for pre- and post- 1989 Act comparisons.

We believe that this type of developmental work strengthens the relationship between child-care research, policy and practice. As the following diagram (Figure 2.1) shows, some links, such as those between research and central government policy, are relatively strong, but in other areas, for instance, social work training and practitioners' own work, we have made little headway.

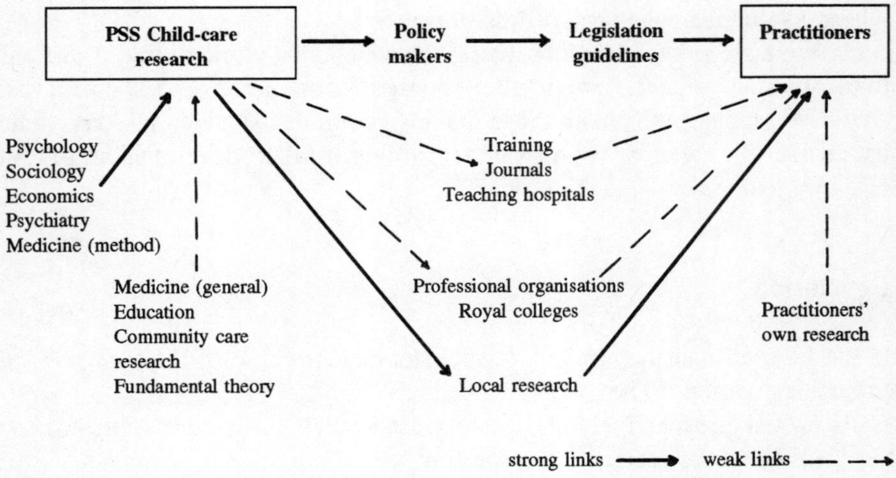

Figure 2.1: Links between research, policy and practice

Links between research, policy and practice: the current situation in the United Kingdom

The model of developmental work we have described also seems a better way of understanding the impact of the *Going Home* research on social work policy and practice. Has it made any difference and, if so, what? Having undertaken several studies of children's separation and return in the mid 1980s, the Unit is in a good position to assess changes. We have been too long in the business of expecting wonders from research or claiming great things for it, but evidence suggests that our efforts might not have been in vain. Ideas have certainly changed since *Lost in Care* tentatively asked the question, almost unthinkable today, "Are links important?".

References

Berridge, D. & Cleaver, H. (1987), *Foster Home Breakdown,* Oxford, Blackwell.

Bullock, R., Little, M., Hosie, K. & Millham, S. (1990), *Access to Children in Care: Practitioners' Views,* University of Bristol, Bristol Paper in Applied Social Studies, no. 15.

Bullock, R., Little, M. & Millham, S. (1993), *Going Home: The Return of Children Separated from their Families,* Aldershot, Dartmouth.

Department of Health and Social Security (1983), *Access to Children in Care,* London, HMSO.

Department of Health and Social Security (1985), *Social Work Decisions in Child Care: Recent Research Findings and their Implications,* London, HMSO.

Millham, S., Bullock, R., Hosie, K. & Haak, M. (1986), *Lost in Care: The Problems of Maintaining Links between Children in Care and their Families,* Aldershot, Gower.

3 Better outcomes from residential and foster care: the 'Looking After Children' programme

Sonia JACKSON

Introduction

There is a long tradition in the UK of research into the care of children separated from their families, but until recently it has been more concerned with the service provided than with the outcomes for the children themselves. Decision-making and the stability and continuity of placement have been the overriding concern. What happens to a child within the placement and the implications of the quality of care received for his or her development and life chances have received rather little attention.

Three factors have coincided to change this situation. The first was the enactment and implementation of the Children Act, 1989, "the most comprehensive piece of legislation, which Parliament has ever enacted about children" (Department of Health, 1989). The Act aimed to introduce a new set of principles into the substitute care of children whose families were unable to provide adequately for them, and required substantial changes in the way that services for separated children were provided. The second factor was the evidence building from research and various public scandals of serious weaknesses in the child welfare system and the damaging consequences for children growing up within it. The third was the government's ideological commitment to market principles in the delivery of social services. Cost-effectiveness, quality assurance and performance monitoring were not ideas that had previously been given much prominence in the field of child care. Almost for the first time the question was asked, what is the *outcome* of all the resources of money and professional time invested in the provision of care for separated children? One further factor in this shift of perspective was the growing emphasis on consumers' rights, including the right to have their opinions heard and taken into account. Symptomatic is the change in the terminology of British social work, from "client" to "service user" and the idea of working in partnership with people who need help.

All these elements came together to stimulate the development in the UK of a scheme designed to assess and improve outcomes for children in residential and foster care. The *Looking After Children* programme has been developed and piloted over six years by a team of researchers based at Bristol and Swansea Universities and the Dartington Social Research Unit. It consists of a package of materials: three administrative documents - an Essential Facts Sheet, a Plan and a Review form; and six Assessment and Action Records, colour-coded by the age of the child. A computerised version is in process of development together with an associated video and training pack.

The core of the scheme and the means through which its philosophy is expressed is the set of Assessment and Action Records, which are designed to provide a method of recording and evaluating outcomes of residential and foster care that can feed back directly into practice. In relation to individual children, they enable supervisors and managers to assess in detail the quality of care being offered and to identify problems. When the data are aggregated, they provide evidence for policy formation and strategic planning.

The programme developed in parallel with the enactment and implementation of the 1989 Children Act, and the work of the development team had considerable influence on the content of the Guidance and Regulations issued in association with the legislation (DH, 1991). The materials that make up the scheme are designed to help social workers and carers to fulfil the requirements of the Act. Among many other changes, the Act altered the vocabulary of child welfare in Britain, so that children are no longer "in care" unless they are subject to a court order, but are rather "looked after" by local authorities: hence the title of the programme.

This chapter discusses the theoretical rationale for the scheme, its design, implementation and evaluation so far. It also considers the question of how far the scheme is culturally specific and the potential for applying its principles in different countries and contexts.

Origins and development

The foundations of the programme were laid in a meeting called by the government department responsible for child welfare and attended by most of the active UK researchers in the field. The aim was to review all currently available evidence on outcomes of public care for children, to identify gaps in knowledge, and to consider ways of measuring and assessing the impact of care on children's development.

A previous round of government-sponsored research had already produced much important information. For example, while the age profile of children in care had changed markedly, with a much higher proportion of older adolescents, many residential units continued to operate regimes better suited to young children (Parker, 1988)). Most care episodes were relatively short, but children who did not return home within six months were likely to stay long and were in great danger of losing contact with their families and community networks, finding themselves completely alone on leaving care (Millham, Bullock, Hosie and Haak, 1986). Important aspects of children's development seemed to be overlooked both by researchers and by social workers, notably health and education (Jackson, 1987). Other signs that the care system was not meeting children's needs effectively were the instability of placement (Berridge, 1985; Rowe, Hundleby and Garnett, 1989) and the inconsistency of planning and decision-making. Vernon and Fruin (1986) showed that there was a large element of chance in determining whether children remained in care or went home to their families. Packman, Randall and Jacques (1986) found that there was often little difference in the circumstances of children who came into care and those from similarly disadvantaged families who did not. These findings strongly influenced the drafting of the new legislation.

As already mentioned, research on outcomes tended to focus on continuity of placement, especially in foster care (Berridge and Cleaver, 1987). Apart from a few retrospective accounts (e.g. Kahan, 1979), there was a surprising lack of recent evidence on the impact of the care experience, positive or negative, on the children themselves. There were, however, some worrying indicators. For example, it was known that nearly a quarter of the adult prison population had been in care, and 30 per cent of homeless 16 and 17 year olds had a care background. These facts suggested that the care system was failing at least some of the children for whom it was responsible quite badly, and research was urgently needed to find out why. There seemed to be two main reasons for the lack of information on outcomes. One was that local authorities made no attempt to follow up or keep in touch with young people who had left care; the other was the absence of any generally acceptable means of assessment or monitoring.

Clearly, there was a need to develop an effective assessment instrument, and a smaller group of those who attended the initial meeting agreed to take on this task, with the idea that whatever was produced should be of use to social workers, carers and managers, not simply to researchers. As a first step it was necessary to define the concept of outcome and to unravel the many complex issues which were raised as soon as the attempt was made. It is only possible here to give a brief account of some of those issues and how they were resolved. They are described and discussed more fully in the book, *Looking After Children: Assessing Outcomes in Child Care* (Parker, Ward, Jackson, Aldgate and Wedge, 1991).

Developing a model of outcome assessment

The most basic question is: what is an outcome in the context of public care of children? Having defined it, how do we measure it? By what criteria do we evaluate it? When does it occur? Whose perspective do we take? Are we simply concerned with the outcome for the child or should it be for the family as a unit? Should we attempt to assess outcome in relation to the reason why care was provided for the child in the first place or in relation to some general standard of wellbeing?

Some of these dilemmas can be illustrated by taking a relatively simple example, such as placement of a child with foster carers following a substantiated allegation of abuse. Should this be seen as an outcome or a beginning? Since the object of the intervention was to protect the child, do we only need to decide if this has been achieved, or should we attempt to assess the impact of the whole experience on the child's development and functioning? If the latter, at what point should this be done?

How do we evaluate a whole experience, given that the outcome will look very different depending on whose perspective we take? For the general public, the outcome is that a child has been rescued, which is obviously good. For the service providers, it is not quite so simple. A scandal has been avoided but additional costs will be incurred. The child's social worker may be disappointed by the failure of her plan to support the child within the family, or relieved to have found an acceptable foster placement. The parents could see the outcome as good in so far as it relieves the strain on the family, or more likely experience it as punitive and stigmatising. The child may welcome escaping from the ill-treatment but see separation from the family as a negative outcome, especially in the longer run.

This raises the second question of which outcomes to assess. In this case, should the assessment simply ask if the placement has protected the child from further abuse or consider how the agency's intervention has affected the child's subsequent development and life chances?

The third matter to decide is: when has an outcome occurred? Admission to the foster family could be considered a beginning in the sense that day-to-day responsibility for the child's care has been transferred, but for the child and the family, and probably also the social worker, it is the culmination of a long series of events. Should assessment begin when the first contact was made with the child-care agency, when the suspicion of abuse was confirmed, when the child joined the foster family, or only after a period of settling in? Should it be continuous or take place at the point of leaving care? Leaving care might seem the logical point, but this could be misleading, coinciding with a period of adolescent turmoil and disaffection. In any case, to postpone the assessment until then might provide some information on how well the care system had done its job but could only have limited impact on practice.

In the course of many long hours of discussion spread over a two year period, these issues were gradually resolved. It was decided that the focus of assessment should be on the individual child, in line with the Children Act principle that the welfare of the child is paramount. The aim should be to assess children's general wellbeing, not simply whether the immediate purpose of accommodating or looking after them had been met. The assessment scheme should balance long-term and short-term objectives, looking at children's overall development rather than concentrating, as social workers often do, on critical events.

If the purpose of the scheme was to lead to improved practice it would need to adopt a formative as opposed to a summative style of evaluation (Patton, 1978). This implied an assessment instrument that could monitor a child's progress at regular intervals and produce information of direct use to practitioners, not a score or scale designed to measure some endpoint state which would need interpretation by an expert.

A further requirement of the instrument was that it should contribute to a better understanding of the connection between child-care interventions and outcomes by establishing a theoretical framework in relation to which the outcome could be evaluated. Two theoretical perspectives which influenced the development of the *Looking After Children* scheme were the "production of welfare" approach developed by the Personal Social Services Research Unit at the University of Kent (Knapp, 1984) and the notion of competence as a dynamic concept embodied in the work of Maluccio (Aldgate, Maluccio and Reeves, 1989). Both these models acknowledge in different ways the complicated interconnections between the factors determining a particular outcome, but stress the value of examining the intervening processes to provide relevant data on the strengths and weaknesses of services. Thus, it is never possible to be sure that a particular long-term outcome for a child was directly attributable to a social work intervention, but a method of assessment which adopts an interactional perspective can determine how far the care or service offered contributed to the *likelihood* of success.

But what do we mean by success? What is the appropriate standard by which to judge the care provided for children by public bodies? In the past, this standard was defined as providing for their basic physical needs at a level no better than that of children of a similar social background (Jackson, 1987). More recently, concern with their emotional experiences has claimed the attention of social workers, especially in Britain and the United States, but this has sometimes been at the expense of attention to more practical matters. The 1989 Children Act sets new standards, relating them closely to what might be expected of an average parent. Although the definitions tend to be somewhat circular, the intention is clear. "Parental responsibility", a key concept in the Act, is defined as "a collection of powers and duties which follow from being a parent and bringing up a child" (HMSO, 1989). Earlier grounds for care and supervision orders are replaced with the question, "Is the child receiving that care which it would be reasonable to expect a parent to give?" This implies some consensus on what is reasonable parenting and assumes that the outcome of it will be the achievement of a satisfactory quality of life for children. It fits well with an interactional theoretical framework and with the idea of focusing on intermediate rather than final outcomes in designing a method of evaluation. This substantially reduces the difficulty of making connections between child-care interventions and their effects. The extent to which a child-care agency is successfully carrying out its responsibilities can be judged by the extent to which it mirrors the practices of the "reasonable" parent.

It might be pointed out that the needs of children who come to the attention of public bodies are likely to be far more complex and demanding than those growing up in their own families, and to that extent the care provided should go beyond what the ordinary reasonable parent would (or could) do. On the other hand, parents whose children have special needs also go beyond what would normally be done by seeking advice, help or special treatment.

A multi-dimensional view of child development

Adopting an active view of child care as the promotion of welfare rather than the prevention of harm implies a move away from the one-dimensional view of outcome, preoccupied by what concerns social workers rather than the overall development of the child. Children's lives may be as deeply affected by the actions that child-care workers fail to take as by what they actually do (Fisher et al., 1986). It is therefore important that a comprehensive assessment scheme should cover all the aspects of development which are informally monitored and promoted by "reasonable" parents. The choice of dimensions for inclusion in the *Looking After Children* scheme was based on a theoretically derived view of what parents might think significant, which has since been confirmed by the empirical study described later in the chapter.

Seven dimensions are incorporated in the *Looking After Children* assessment scheme, all of which need to be assessed if the adequate fulfilment of parental responsibilities is regarded as the ultimate purpose of child-care interventions. These seven dimensions are: health; education; identity; family and social relationships; social presentation; emotional and behavioural development; and self-care skills. The rationale for the choice of these dimensions is explained fully in the report on the first phase of the research (Parker et al., 1991). Not only are they self-evidently important, but in most cases there are clear research findings to show that they are especially problematic for children in residential and foster care.

Identifying the dimensions was the first stage in the process of constructing the assessment instrument. Since it was intended to assess outcomes for all children and young people from birth to leaving care it was clearly necessary to divide the population for assessment into age groups, and these correspond with developmental and social expectations. The complete scheme comprises six Assessment and Action Records for age bands Under 1, 1-2, 3-4, 5-9, 10-15 and 16 and over.

The 'Looking After Children' model

The Assessment and Action Records in their final form follow a model which is set out in Figure 3.1. They start by asking what would be the aims of a reasonable parent for a child of this age on a particular dimension. They then ask what would a reasonable, adequately-resourced and well-informed parent do in order to maximise the chances of achieving those aims? This approach produces a series of what might be called "quality of care" questions. Each main question triggers a series of subsidiary questions. For example, on the Education dimension (for all age groups over 5) the aims are that "the child's educational attainments are average or above and that s/he acquires special skills and interests and takes a full part in school activities". Since we know that school attainment is closely related to reading competence, one of the quality of care questions is "How often does the child go to a library or bring a book home from school?" If the answer is less than once a week, the subsidiary questions are asked "what further action will be taken" and "who will take it"? The person completing the Record is asked to explain lack of information (a "don't know" answer) or no action. At the end of each section, the question is asked if the specified aims have been achieved. A negative answer to this question should lead to closer scrutiny of the preceding questions to see what more might be done to achieve the aims.

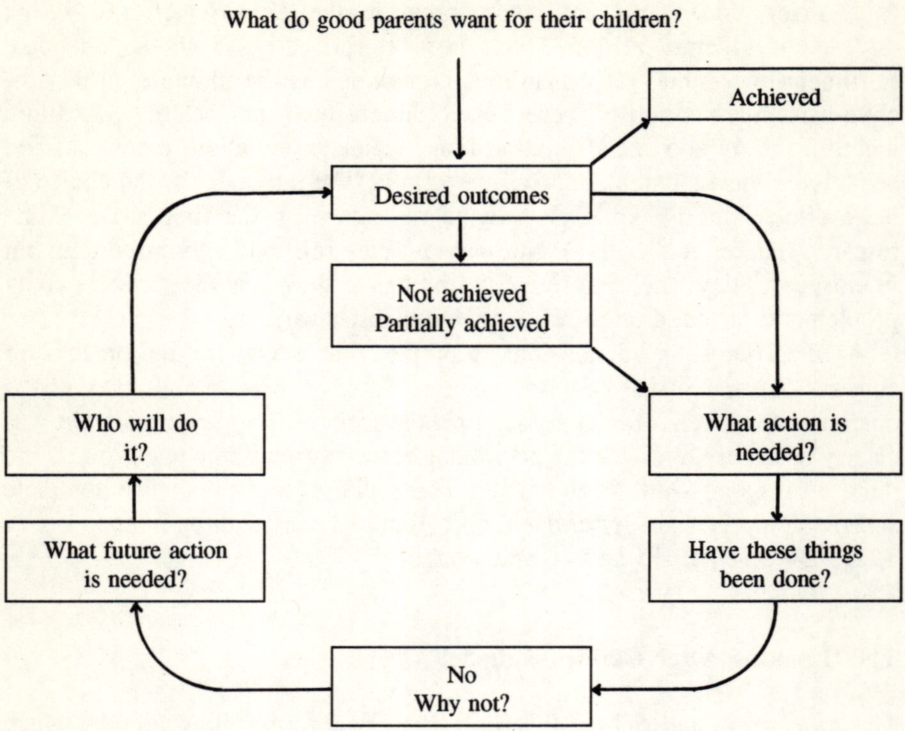

Figure 3.1 The 'Looking After Children' model

Evaluating the model

This model has been evaluated in two stages. The first stage was a feasibility study designed to discover if the monitoring schedule (not at that point called an Assessment and Action Record) would be acceptable to social workers and what impact if any it would have on their practice. Only two age groups were included in this study: 3-4 year olds and over 16s. Thirty two social workers from four local authorities took part, and the schedules were also used in two residential units. The results were generally encouraging. They showed that the assessment scheme could be used by social workers and was very effective in drawing attention to overlooked aspects of child development, although many shortcomings were identified in the design of the schedules. The findings of the pilot study are reported in detail elsewhere (Ward and Jackson, 1991; Ward, Jackson and Parker, 1991).

On the basis of feedback and comments from the social workers, foster carers and young people who took part in this exercise, the monitoring schedules were completely redesigned, and forms for four other age groups were added. It was also clear that there was little chance of the scheme being used on a regular basis unless it was incorporated into the mainstream of local authority child-care systems. This led, in the revised version of the programme, to the addition of three administrative documents, to form a complete package for recording information, planning, and reviewing arrangements for looked after children. This package was launched at the end of 1991 as one of the companion documents to the Children Act. All the materials were then available for sale and could be used by any local authority or child-care agency that wished to do so.

The second stage of evaluation had two main aims: to refine and improve the administrative documents and the Assessment and Action Records and to see if their use could be shown to improve child welfare practice and outcomes. Assessments were carried out on 200 children in four different areas. In addition, although the materials are still technically at an experimental stage, their adoption has been encouraged by the Social Services Inspectorate through a series of seminars and circulars. As a result, the formal evaluation has been supplemented by evidence from questionnaires distributed to many local authorities and agencies who have joined the advisory network for the project. Some have set up independent appraisal exercises and fed back the results.

It was decided not to impose a tight research design, even on the four core authorities, because we were interested not only in results from use of the Assessment and Action Records, but also in testing the circumstances in which they were most likely to be completed (non-completion was a serious problem in the feasibility study). As a result of this flexibility, each area used the programme in a different way. Two authorities concentrated the research in a particular area office or team of social workers, two others chose to assess selected children across the whole area, and the fifth had already decided to adopt the complete package to replace their reviewing system before they were approached to participate in the research. In each area, social workers were asked to assess a set number of children on two separate occasions. Persuading social workers to complete the Records, especially for the second time, presented some difficulties, but since two areas did more than their quota the target number of 200 was exceeded.

As before, there were many suggestions for improving the questions, as well as a more fundamental criticism, that the assessment scheme was unsuited for use with children with disabilities. (This point has been addressed by adding a supplementary form when the assessment relates to a child with a severe disability). However it was clear that the basic model was sound and had the potential to fulfil its objectives. Completing an Assessment and Action Record provides a focus for collaborative work between social workers, foster carers, birth parents, young people and sometimes other professionals (not all at the same time). Carers find that it makes their work more visible and puts them on a more equal basis with social workers, since they have the detailed knowledge needed to complete the form. Social workers reported that using the forms made them aware of aspects of the child's development that they had previously overlooked, and of precisely those parental actions which are liable to be omitted in the case of looked-after children.

There were important findings about the circumstances in which the assessments were most likely to be completed: if the project had the unequivocal support of management, if there were clear, attainable timescales, and if there was a specific requirement for all members of any staff group who worked closely together to take part. For instance, in Birmingham all social workers in one area team agreed to assess a selected sample of children and young people over the age of ten within a six-week period. Not only did they succeed in assessing their agreed quota of 30 children and young people, but they repeated the process with them all a year later. However, in other areas initial enthusiasm was not so well sustained. Residential workers found it hard to find time and space to undertake the work, even though the content of the assessments that were completed made clear the value of their use in residential settings. For example, the neglect of education in many residential units was clearly evident (cf. Jackson, 1988\9).

The evaluation study produced evidence that use of the assessment scheme stimulated as well as recorded good practice, particularly with respect to encouraging collaborative work and involving the children and young people themselves. It also identified instances where important information about a child was unavailable, for example names and addresses of close family other than parents, and serious omissions in the care provided. One example was the reluctance of some social workers to explore identity issues unless the child was black, so that children were left with no sense of their past history or help in developing a positive self-image. Twenty-eight per cent of 10-15 year olds in the core sample group, for instance, had never discussed with an adult what they should say when asked questions about their family background or care situation. Consumer studies, such as the survey carried out by the Who Cares Trust and the National Consumer Council (Fletcher, 1993) make it clear that this is a constant preoccupation for many children in the care system who experience bullying and discrimination.

Some social workers who were sensitive to the feelings of looked-after children unfortunately translated this into a reluctance to answer questions on educational attainment for fear that it would reinforce the children's negative self-image. Generally, the study confirmed previous findings about the curious educational unawareness of social workers. One in ten of the children in the core sample was not attending school at the time the assessment was completed, but there seemed to be little attempt to organise compensatory educational help for them. A small number of social workers actually saw this as a reason to leave the education section blank, not regarding it as part of their "parental responsibility" to find out what educational experiences the child was receiving while out of school.

Setting standards for parenting

During the phase when the Assessment and Action Records were being piloted, some social workers expressed doubts about their content on the grounds that the standards of child-care practice which they implied were far beyond those of ordinary parents. As already described, the seven developmental dimensions, the aims or desired outcomes associated with them for children of different ages, and the parental actions likely to lead to those outcomes were based on the best available evidence. However, the team was not on very firm ground here as there is surprisingly little objective information on the behaviour of "ordinary" parents with their children, and even less on variations associated with different ethnic backgrounds and cultures. On some dimensions there is no published evidence at all, and we were obliged to rely on personal and professional experience.

As part of the second phase of the research, therefore, it was decided to use the materials to assess a comparison group of children not looked after by child-care agencies. During 1993, Assessment and Action Records were completed with 400 children and young people living with parents or relatives, one hundred from each of the four older age groups. The object was to discover to what extent the developmental dimensions and aims identified by the research team corresponded with those of parents in the community, and if the questions asked about ways of achieving aims reflected what parents do for and on behalf of their children. This is the largest and most detailed study of parenting behaviour in Britain to have been undertaken in the past twenty years. Analysis of the data is not complete at the time of writing but it is possible to draw some general conclusions.

First, the study found that, without exception, all four hundred parents considered the seven dimensions included in the Assessment and Action Records to be important in their children's development. Second, it confirmed that the aims which parents have for their children are very similar to those specified in the Records, though they sometimes express them rather differently. There was also a remarkable congruence in the ways in which they thought those aims might be achieved and what they as parents should do to make this more likely. They often considered that they fell short of the standards they set for themselves, but this was almost always due to lack of resources or other pressures on them, not lack of awareness. For example, all those interviewed knew that it was important to read to young children, though not all were sufficiently well organised to do it on a regular basis. Parents generally knew that smoking was bad for their children's health, and hoped that their children would not take it up, even if they were smokers themselves.

It is interesting to note that the questions about education and diet which were often criticised by social workers during the evaluation phase as "middle class" were not seen in this way by the working class families in the survey. One question that particularly came under attack was whether looked-after children were learning to play a musical instrument. Some child-care workers and managers suggested that this was an aspiration irrelevant to the families of children in the care system. In fact 31 per cent of 5-9 year olds in the looked-after sample and almost half of 8 year olds from all social classes in the comparison group were learning to play musical instruments. In the comparison group, this was found to depend more on the quality of the school music service than on social class. This is only one of many instances where assumptions made by social workers about what people in a different social class from themselves might want for their children serves to depress expectations and limit opportunities.

The researchers found no evidence that the expectations about "reasonable" parental behaviour implied by the questions in the Records were unrealistic in any way. They were impressed by the efforts made by parents, including those living on low incomes in difficult circumstances, to do their best for their children.

A greater difficulty occurred with older children. Asking young people of 16 about their use of alcohol or their knowledge of sexually transmitted diseases with their parents present took considerable tact, and some of them clearly found such questions intrusive. This is one reason why it is essential for social workers to be thoroughly familiar with the content of the Assessment and Action Records before attempting to use them with young people looked after by local authorities.

On the other hand, as with social workers and foster carers, using the Assessment and Action Records with parents and children tended to highlight problem areas and provide a trigger for the discussion of difficult issues. This suggests that they may have value as a therapeutic tool as well as for purposes of assessment and research, and not only with children who are separated from their parents.

Implementation and training

The research team, with strong backing from the Department of Health, adopted a policy of disseminating information about the programme while it was still in the stage of evaluation and development. As a result, in addition to the four local authorities participating in the research study, many others have adopted the materials for use with part or all of their care population. Many of these have provided regular feedback and advice. In return, the project publishes a newsletter, of which over a thousand copies are distributed bimonthly. In parallel with the evaluation of the materials, therefore, a great deal of experience is building up of the most effective ways of introducing and using the package.

Although some social workers who are already in sympathy with the ideas behind the scheme find little difficulty in using it as intended with no more than a brief introduction, it is clear that the best results are achieved with a well-planned training programme. This needs to be combined with a commitment from senior management to support the use of the system and to ensure that it replaces previous documentation rather than being added to it.

Without training, there is a risk that the programme will be treated simply as a form-filling exercise to be rushed through as quickly as possible, an attitude typified by the social worker who said "If I weren't doing this I could be getting on with some real work". Evidently she saw the Assessment and Action Record as an interruption to this "real work" instead of as a way of identifying what needed to be done with the young person and his carers. A number of separate problems were revealed by the process of evaluation.

First there is the question of time. The assessment forms are substantial documents, and the more effective they are in raising matters for discussion, especially when several people are involved, the more time they take to complete. It is not intended that this should be done in a single session, and for a social worker with already high standards of professional practice, the AAR could simply be seen as a way of systematising work that would be done anyway over a series of visits or meetings. However, in most cases, use of the forms reveals significant gaps and actions needing to be taken, which means more work for the social worker. Only if this is acknowledged by managers committed to providing high quality care for children will social workers be prepared to devote the necessary time to use the forms as intended.

Secondly, the forms may be completed in a perfunctory way, either by a social worker sitting in an office or, in the worst case, by handing them over to young people to complete unaided. It is possible that the presentation of the schedules, which for the two oldest age groups are addressed directly to the child or young person, may have contributed to this misuse, although the schedules make it clear that the young people will need help from their social workers or foster carers. In cases where it seemed that the AAR has been given to the young person to fill in alone, only a few of the questions had been answered. Clearly, the task was far too daunting. One of the objectives of the system is to engage the efforts and imagination of *all* those concerned with the child's welfare to find ways of promoting his or her development and overcoming obstacles. It is therefore essential that it should be seen as a collaborative exercise.

As already explained, "quality of care" questions designed to find out if necessary "parental" actions are being taken to make it likely that aims for different dimensions of development will be achieved are followed by three or four subsidiary questions. These ask respondents to make further plans where necessary actions have been omitted and to decide who should carry them out. The final subsidiary question asks for reasons if no plans have been made to remedy shortfalls. From a practice viewpoint, this question is clearly crucial. There may be good reasons why it would not be appropriate to take a particular action in relation to a specific child. More often, it reveals exactly the kind of passive acceptance of an unsatisfactory situation that young people in care so often complain about (Fletcher, 1993). For instance, one social worker said there was nothing to be done about the fact that a 10-year-old had no books because in the residential unit where he lived there would be nowhere to read them anyway. Sometimes the question was left blank when action was clearly needed: for example, when a vaccination record had been lost or a child had been excluded from school with no alternative plans made for her education or use of time.

Training is needed to help social workers distinguish between genuine reasons and excuses for inaction. "The child is not old enough" might be an acceptable reason for doing nothing more if a child of 5 has not yet learnt to swim, but not for a 9-year-old. Similarly, "We are waiting for a change of placement" is not a good reason for failing to arrange a dental appointment. Often the real reason for inaction when a problem is identified is that no one can think of what to do about it. One of the objectives of training is to help those completing the Assessment and Action Records to recognise when they need to seek advice from others, not necessarily from within their own organisation.

When social workers can be persuaded to provide reasons for inaction, their answers provide the data that can be used to improve services. Quantifiable information from social workers can be crucial in managerial decisions about allocation of resources. For example, if lack of transport, or no money to pay fees is the reason why 4-year-olds in foster care are not getting any kind of pre-school experience, this should be evident from scrutiny of a series of AARs for this age group. The agency would then have to decide how important it considers pre-school education for children which it looks after and allocate funds to remove the practical or financial difficulties if necessary. It seems that some social workers are apprehensive about being too explicit in revealing deficiencies of the service in case they attract criticism themselves. A training pack in process of development aims to overcome this kind of attitude by helping participants in training to understand the thinking behind the programme and the research which underpins most of the questions. The training pack consists of a video, materials for two half days of training and a Reader, which summarises in brief chapters the key research findings relevant to the seven dimensions and more general concepts, such as outcomes and parenting.

The first training session is designed to familiarise participants with the materials, which they will already have had in advance, and with the philosophy of the programme. The video shows Assessment and Action Records being used with children of different ages and circumstances, with foster carers, residential workers, social workers and parents. There is an emphasis on working in partnership, collaboration between professionals, listening to children, and linking assessment to action. Following some role play exercises and discussion the participants go away, and in the course of the next week or two complete an Assessment and Action Record with a child or young person on their caseload. The second session is mostly taken up with analysis and discussion of the completed records, after which participants work on their personal development plans. These two half days should be followed up and reinforced through the supervision system, and ideally by a further day or half day's training.

Use of the scheme outside the UK

From an early stage in its development, the *Looking After Children* programme aroused interest among people from other countries. It is now being used in Canada, Australia, New Zealand, Norway, Brazil, Belgium, and Israel and has already been translated into Flemish, Norwegian, Hebrew, Croatian, Slovenian and Ukrainian. It seems to have something to offer countries which already have well-established provision for separated children and high aspirations for them and, at the other extreme, those which are struggling to set up a system of care to provide for basic needs. The model is sufficiently adaptable to be applicable in many different circumstances.

Israel, for example, has a long tradition of good quality residential institutions for young people, and in contrast to many other countries, no stigma is attached to living in one. They tend to have stable, well-qualified staff groups and give great importance to health and education. However, when introduced to the Assessment and Action Records, many Israeli child welfare workers and directors saw immediate possibilities for developing their work. Some were shocked to discover how many questions they were unable to answer about children with whom they had lived for several years. The reason seemed to be that the emphasis on the group and the value of collaboration and mutual support within it could, however admirable, lead to the needs of individuals being overlooked. This was a problem that had already been recognised - one group director required each care worker once a week to come and discuss with him a particular child, irrespective of whether any problems had arisen - but the *Looking After Children* scheme provides a structure to ensure that the progress of each individual is looked at in detail at regular intervals.

Although not all the questions are appropriate in different national and cultural settings, the developmental dimensions appear to have wide applicability. That does not mean that they have always been recognised as important previously. For example, in one institution a staff member remarked that she had never thought specifically about self-care skills. She had assumed young people just picked them up. On reflection, though, she thought that when children lived as a group, the competence of one or two might mask the incompetence of others, allowing them to leave residential care very ill-equipped for independent living.

Suggestions made by colleagues from other countries have been particularly interesting because they expose assumptions and values of which the team was not necessarily fully aware in constructing the assessment materials. For example, in Belgium it was suggested that greater prominence should be given to leisure skills by making them a separate dimension rather than splitting them between Health and Education. This perhaps reflected the much better provision of youth recreational facilities in Belgium by comparison with Britain. In Israel, the questions relating to ethnic identity sparked off a fierce debate. Since the country's whole existence rests on the amazing survival, through centuries of dispersal, of the sense of *Jewish* identity, is it desirable to encourage children to retain a potentially divisive attachment to a different identity? With successive waves of immigration from Ethiopia and Russia, including many unaccompanied children and young people, this is becoming an increasingly urgent question. Working through the Assessment and Action Record obliged the staff group to confront a crucial issue which they had previously either avoided or denied. It illustrates the point that we cannot always assume a consensus on what are desirable outcomes, but if there is disagreement at least it is brought out into the open.

In some countries, such as Brazil, where international agencies require programmes which they fund to be evaluated, there is interest in the capacity of the *Looking After Children* scheme to produce aggregated factual data on the progress of children as well as on the service being provided for them. In the United States and Canada, the scheme is being used to evaluate specialist programmes, some of which involve high per capita costs. The scheme has the merit of producing a variegated picture, providing evidence of good points as well as weaknesses. It can demonstrate where there are strengths to be built on and which inputs are associated with good outcomes. It is therefore a more sensitive indicator than traditional types of evaluation and a more effective aid to the decision-making of funding agencies.

The Department of Health now issues a license with attached quality standards (on payment of a modest fee) to enable agencies within the UK and overseas to produce versions of the *Looking After Children* materials using the existing framework but adapted to their own particular circumstances, and including the right to translate them into other languages.

Conclusion

This chapter has described a new approach to monitoring the progress of children in public care. Parenting one's own or other people's children is essentially an art in so far as crucial qualities of sensitivity, responsiveness, unqualified affection and selflessness are hard to measure and occur rather unpredictably in relationships between children and adults. This is precisely why a more scientific approach is required in respect of those aspects of parental behaviour that can be observed and assessed.

The *Looking After Children* programme provides a model for ensuring that, when the care of children has to be shared between their parents and a number of different professionals, vital aspects of their development are not overlooked. It cannot guarantee that the outcome will be favourable. There are many factors in the lives of young people in the care system which are outside the control of their carers or social workers. However, if the programme is used as intended, it does make it much more likely that problems will be identified and addressed at an earlier stage, that the work of carers will be better valued, supported and guided, and that communication between all the different people with an interest in the child will be much improved.

The *Looking After Children* programme is still evolving, with revised materials due to be published in 1995, together with a computer programme and training pack. Further evidence will emerge from analysis of results of the use of the materials in practice, both in the UK and in other countries. The use of the assessment scheme for systematic study of parenting behaviour in the general population offers fascinating possibilities for cross-national research. Present indications are that the model and the principles on which it is based are adaptable to many different circumstances and hold real promise of better care and better outcomes for children in residential and foster care.

Note: *The Looking After Children: Assessing Outcomes programme is funded by the U.K. Department of Health and is based at Dartington Social Research Unit (Director Professor Spencer Millham), part of the University of Bristol. Present members of the team are Dr Harriet Ward, Sonia Jackson, Sue Kilroe, Sue Moyers and Anne Mason, with field consultants Hilary Corrick and Debby Jones.*

References

Aldgate, J., Maluccio, A. and Reeves, C. (1989), *Adolescents in Foster Families*, London, Batsford

Berridge, D. (1985), *Children's Homes*, Oxford, Blackwell.

Berridge, D. & Cleaver H. (1987), *Foster Home Breakdown*, Oxford, Blackwell

Biehal, N., Clayden, J., Stein, M. & Wade, J. (1992), *Prepared for Living: A survey of young people leaving the care of three local authorities.* London, National Children's Bureau.

Department of Health (1989), *An Introduction to the Children Act, 1989*, London, HMSO

Department of Health (1991), *The Children Act, 1989, Guidance and Regulations, Vol.3, Family Placments*, London, HMSO.

Fletcher, B. (1993), *Not Just a Name*, London, Who Cares?/National Consumer Council.

Fisher, M. Marsh, P. & Phillips, D.. (1986), *In and Out of Care: the Experiences, of Children, Parents and Social Workers,* London, Batsford.

Garnett, L. (1992), *Leaving Care*, London, National Children's Bureau.

Jackson, S. (1987), *The Education of Children in Care*, Bristol Papers, No.1, University of Bristol School of Applied Social Studies.

Jackson, S. (1988/9), 'Residential Care and Education', *Children and Society*, vol. 2, no. 4.

Kahan, B. (1979), *Growing Up in Care*, Oxford, Blackwell.

Knapp, M. (1984), *The Economics of Social Care*, London, Macmillan.

Millham, S., Bullock, R., Hosie, K. & Haak, M. (1986). *Lost in Care: the Problem of Maintaining Links between Children in Care and their Families,* Aldershot, Gower.

Packman, J. Randall, J. & Jacques, N. (1986). *Who Needs Care? Social Work Decisions about Children*, Oxford, Blackwell.

Parker, R. (1988), 'Residential care for children', in I. Sinclair (ed.), *Residential Care, the Research Reviewed*, London, HMSO.

Parker, R., Ward, H., Jackson, S., Aldgate, J. & Wedge, P. *Looking After Children: Assessing Outcomes in Child Care*, London, HMSO. 1991

Patton, M.Q. (1978), *Utilization-focused Evaluation*, Beverley Hills, Sage.

Rowe, J., Hundleby, M. & Garnett, L. (1989), *Child Care Now: a Survey of Placement Patterns*, London, BAAF.

Vernon, J. and Fruin, D. (1986), *In Care: a Study of Social Work Decision-Making,* London, National Children's Bureau.

Ward, H. and Jackson, S. (1991). 'Developing outcome measues in child care: a research note', *British Journal of Social Work*, vol. 21, no. 4, 393-399

Ward, H., Jackson, S. and Parker, R. (1991), *A Feasibility Study on the Assessment of Outcomes in Child Care*, Interim Report to the Department of Health, University of Bristol.

4 Reaction pattern research

Ko RINK

The purpose of reaction pattern research

Since 1980, the Northern Institute for Orthopedagogical Research (NIVO) of the Orthopedagogics department of the Rijksuniversiteit of Groningen (RUG) has been conducting research into the attitudes of juveniles with respect to social limits. In this particular context, the term *social limits* refers to laws, rules, and the expectations of others about behaviour.

The research originated from the need to provide more effective supervision for delinquent youngsters in prisons and better care for juvelines with serious behavioural problems in residential institutions. It was found that juveniles confronted with social limits react in one of four main ways: that is, they display one of four reaction types, A, B, C, or D. They may try to adjust their own behaviour in order to conform to the limits set (reaction type A). They may ignore or overstep the limits (reaction type B). They may attempt to change the limits by entering into negotiations with parents, group leaders or teachers (reaction type C). Finally, they may withdraw from the situation (reaction type D) because they are unable to cope with the stress of a conflict between what they want to do and what they are allowed to do.

These four kinds of reaction are perceived in different ways by different people. Some of those directly concerned with the care of juveniles are prepared to tolerate only reaction type A: that is, attempts on the part of the juvenile towards conformity and adjustment. Others will sometimes tolerate reaction B (overstepping limits) on the grounds that "the youngsters are still learning how to deal with rules". Still others actively prefer reaction C (changing limits through negotiation) because they consider that such behaviour shows responsibility and maturity. On the other hand Kok, Menkehorst, Naayer and Zandberg (1991), among others, point out that some group leaders find the negotiation type of reaction "troublesome" and view it as undesirable because it creates more work. The result of these different perceptions is that youngsters may meet with responses from authority figures which are inconsistent, inappropriate, or both. For example, a juvenile who appropriately tries negotiation may be praised by one authority figure but blamed later by another in an almost identical situation. Similarly, an inappropriate overstepping of limits may be condemned by one group leader but condoned by another, who perceives it as normal for the youngster's developmental stage.

The difficulty here is that very little is known about the ways in which juveniles of different ages in different situations normally react to social limits. The Reaction Pattern Research described in this article has attempted to develop a standard picture of the attitudes of juveniles towards social limits. Further, a reliable and valid Standard Reaction Instrument (SRI) is in process of being constructed. This instrument measures attitudes towards social limits and can be used as a diagnostic aid to determine whether, in what respects, and to what degree, the response patterns of a particular group of juveniles differ from the norm. Juveniles at one particular school, for example, may show less regard for social limits than juveniles at a different school, and may thus engage more often in criminal activities.

However, diagnosis of current problems is not the instrument's only use. It can also be used as a preventive tool to determine whether certain youngsters have a greater tendency towards delinquent behaviour than other, similar youngsters. If those with delinquent tendencies can be identified before the delinquent behaviour has become a reality, early specialised attention may prevent future difficulties. The instrument might be administered to children attending school, so that education pertaining to social values and organisations may be more effectively designed and presented. One of the functions of education is to socialise the young, and an extra dimension can now be added to that function.

The reaction pattern research study

The Reaction Pattern Research study involved four phases. In this article, the first phase will be discussed in detail and a brief summary provided of the other three phases.

Phase 1: a provisional standard picture for Dutch juveniles

In Phase 1 of the study, the Standard Reaction Instrument (SRI) was administered to 1,294 Dutch youngsters with no known behavioural problems[1] from eleven comprehensive schools scattered all over the Netherlands (Rink, Vos, van Lokven and Slagveer, 1989). This population group was termed the RPR1 group and constituted a reasonable sample of Dutch juveniles who were attending school at that time (Rink, et al. 1989, p. 153). The results of Phase 1 yielded a provisional version of a standard picture concerning Dutch youngsters' attitudes with respect to social limits. The most important aspects of this standard picture are summarised below.

Known reactions, self-willed reactions and motivations for self-willed reactions. The Standard Reaction Instrument presented the youngsters with ten situations or critical incidents. For example:

> "You are in a supermarket. You've got only one purchase. You go to the cash-desk and nobody is there."
>
> or: "You're watching an exciting film on TV. You had promised your mother to tidy up your room. She insists on your doing it now."

The youngsters were asked the following questions about each incident:

1. What could *one* do in such a situation? (known reactions)
2. What would *you* do in such a situation? (self-willed reactions)
4. *Why* would you do that? (motivations)

Known reactions. The youngsters responded to the question, "What could *one* do in such a situation?" in various ways. For example, one youngster may have responded to the "watching TV-tidying up your room" conflict by suggesting that one could: (1) obey mother and tidy up the room now; (2) disobey mother and watch TV now; or (3) negotiate with mother to watch TV now and tidy up the room later. The same youngster may not have thought of the option that one could withdraw from the situation, neither watching TV nor tidying up the room, and ignoring mother. Each suggestion made was categorised as reaction type A, B, C, or D (adjustment, overstepping limits, negotiation or withdrawal respectively) and overall percentage figures were obtained for the frequency with which each category occurred. These frequencies indicated the degree to which each reaction type occurred to, or was known to the youngsters. The results are shown in Table 4.1, including proportional relationships which have been rounded.

Table 4.1: Known reactions

Sequence	A	>	B	>	D	>	C
Frequencies	41.3		39.2		11.6		7.9
Proportional Relations	5	:	5	:	2	:	1

As shown in Table 4.1, reaction type A (adjustment) occurred most often to the youngsters (41.3 per cent), followed by reaction type B (overstepping limits). Reaction type D (withdrawal) came a poor third while C (negotiation) was fourth. Reactions A and B occurred to the youngsters approximately 5 times as often as Reaction C and two and a half times as often as Reaction D.

Self-willed reactions. As discussed, youngsters were next asked what they would personally do in each particular situation: that is, which of the reaction types they would select. The frequency with which each reaction type was selected is shown in Table 4.2.

Table 4.2: Self-willed reactions

Sequence	A	>	B	>	C	>	D
Frequencies	58.6		29.0		8.4		4.0
Proportional Relations	15	:	7	:	2	:	1

Table 4.2 shows that youngsters were more than twice as likely to choose obedience (A) rather than disobedience (B) and 15 times more likely to choose obedience than withdrawal. Comparison between Tables 1 and 2 shows some marked differences between youngsters' knowledge of the four reaction types and their preferences when it came to a personal choice. To begin with, the sequence is different: the positions of negotiation (C) and withdrawal (D) are reversed in Table 4.2 as compared with Table 4.1. The proportions are very different: for example, knowledge of A and B are approximately equal (Table 4.1) but A is twice as likely as B to be actually selected (Table 4.2). In addition, negotiation (C) is only half as well known as D (Table 4.1) but is twice as likely as D to be selected (Table 4.2). However, Table 4.2 is similar to Table 4.1 in that C and D are both considerably less well known and less frequently selected than either A or B. Youngsters seem to be more prone to choose between

obedience and disobedience rather than to seek alternative solutions to problem situations.

Motivations for self-willed reactions. When youngsters had been asked what they would do in each of the ten situations presented on the instrument, they were next asked why they would do that. The motives they gave were classified according to the following typology:

a: I-directed motives, placing self-interest at the centre;
b: Other-directed motives, placing other people or society at the centre;
c: Now-directed motives, oriented towards immediate gratification;
d: Future-directed motives, oriented towards considering the consequences of one's own behaviour.

This typology includes a social dimension (I versus society) and a temporal dimension (now versus future). In addition, motives a and c (I and now) together indicate a tendency towards the concrete while motives b and d (society and the future) tend towards the abstract.

Table 4.3 shows the sequence, frequencies and proportional relations for the motives underlying the self-willed reactions.

Table 4.3: Motives for self-willed reactions

Sequence	a	>	c	>	b	>	d
Frequencies	36.2		30.6		20.0		13.2
Proportional Relations	3	:	2	:	2	:	1

As Table 4.3 shows, the youngsters were almost twice as likely to choose themselves over society (a as compared to b), and more than twice as likely to focus on immediate gratification rather than future consequences (c as compared to d). With respect to concrete and abstract dimensions, concrete "I-now" motives (a and c) predominate quite markedly over "society-future" motives (b and d). The tendency towards abstraction can generally be qualified as weak (b: 20.0%; d: 13.2%).

Correlations between known and self-willed reactions and motivations with satisfaction. A youngster's response to a given situation will be determined not only by his general attitudes towards social limits but also by the specifics of the situation. For example, a child who is asked by his mother to tidy the bedroom is more likely to tidy the bedroom if he gets on well with his mother than if he does not. Similarly, he may be more willing to tidy the bedroom if the mess in the bedroom is all his own, not his own mess and his brothers'. Accordingly, it was assumed that the attitudes towards social limits of the 1,294 Dutch younsters studied would be partly determined by their perception of the circumstances in which the limits were set.

In order to elicit their perceptions, the youngsters were asked to indicate their satisfaction with a number of environmental factors, classified as ecological, strain and bond factors. These factors were drawn from the criminological work of Luttikhuis (1990, p. 13) who found correlations between environmental factors and deviant behaviour in juveniles and adults. The ecological factors included in the Standard Reaction Instrument are the number of residents in the youngster's home, their ages and ethnicity. Ecological theory correlates deviant behaviour with a socially disorganised living environment: and dissatisfaction with factors such as the number of people living in the house indicates that the environment is socially disorganised from the youngster's perspective.

The strain factors included in the SRI are: financial situation, social status, employment status and access to material facilities. It is theorised that a difference between the youngster's aspirations and the actual possibilities open to him may produce personal frustration or stress (strain) which may influence his attitude with respect to social limits. The bond factors included are: reference persons, reference groups, atmosphere, the attitude of significant adults towards children or juveniles, lifestyle, and the way in which problems are tackled in the home. A youngster who is bonded to loving parents, for example, may feel more inclined to keep to the limits set by them; and if the problem-solving technique prevalent in the home is negotiation, the youngster may be more liable to apply this technique elsewhere.

An analysis of the statistical correlations between measured satisfaction on the one hand and results with respect to known reactions, self-willed reactions and motives on the other hand yielded the following two clusters of combinations:

1. An increase in the tendency towards adjustment or obedience (A) co-occurs with:
   - an increase in the tendency towards negotiation (C);
   - a decrease in the tendency towards overstepping limits (B);

- a decrease in the tendency to withdraw (D);
- an increase in future-directed motivation (d);
- a decrease in concrete motivation, directed towards self-gratification in the present (a/c);
- an increase in familiarity with reaction types and motivation types; and
- an increase in satisfaction.

2. An increase in the tendency towards overstepping limits (B) co-occurs with:
   - a decrease in the tendency to negotiation (C);
   - an increase in the tendency to withdraw (D);
   - an increase in concrete motivations (a/c);
   - a decrease in the future-directed motivation (d);
   - a decrease in familiarity with reaction types and motivation types; and
   - a decrease in satisfaction.

A comparison between these two clusters of combinations shows that juveniles with a strong tendency towards overstepping limits (B-reaction) have less flexible attitudes to social limits than juveniles with a strong tendency towards adjustment (A-reaction). In addition, the "B-juveniles" show less future-directed motivation (that is, less regard for the consequences of their own actions) a greater tendency towards withdrawal, more motivation directed towards themselves in the here-and-now situation and a lesser tendency to negotiate. The "A-juveniles" generally showed a profile that was opposite in every respect.

The remaining phases of the RPR

The aims and progress of the other 3 phases of the Reaction Pattern Research project will be only briefly discussed here. Further information is available in the publications about the research noted in the references.

In the second phase of the RPR, Vos (1991a) administered the SRI to a population of detained juveniles, termed the RPRII-population. He developed a separate SRI profile for this group and compared this profile to that of the RPRI-population. Based on the differences between the RPRI and RPRII populations, he made recommendations to the Boards of the Detention Centres regarding the training and treatment of the detained juveniles, with respect to their attitudes towards social limits.

In the third phase of the RPR, the SRI was administered to a different set of school-attending juveniles from cultural minority groups, termed the RPRIII population (Sanches and Vos, 1991). A separate SRI profile was constructed for this group, and this profile was compared with the profiles for the RPRII and RPRI populations respectively.

In the fourth phase of the research, the differences between the profiles of the RPRI, RPRII and RPRIII populations were used to modify the SRI so that the instrument could be used not only with groups of juveniles but with individual juveniles to determine the degree to which each personally differs from the standard picture.

New initiatives and possibilities with respect to reaction pattern research

As discussed earlier in this chapter, one of the original purposes of Reaction Pattern Research was to improve treatment strategies for *groups* of juveniles exhibiting deviant behaviour (see, for example, Vos, 1991a and 1991b). The development of a standard picture for nondeviant juveniles with respect to their attitudes towards social limits has contributed towards this aim; and so has the construction of an instrument - the SRI - designed to measure attitudes towards social limits. Mention has also been made in this chapter of the possibility of using the SRI to predict possible future deviant behaviour among groups of juveniles: those attending a particular school, for example. Once the possibility of future deviance has been established, preventive efforts can be initiated through special education. In addition, modification of the SRI will enable it to be used with individual juveniles to measure actual and potential deviance from normal attitudes towards social limits.

In the meantime, discussions with colleagues in the field of (ortho-)pedagogics have resulted in a number of new, internationally-oriented initiatives with respect to Reaction Pattern Research. The remainder of the chapter will consider these initiatives.

Towards a standard picture at the European level

Together with Schlee and Neukäter (Orthopedagogics department at the University of Oldenburg), Hellinckx (Orthopedagogics department at the Catholic University of Leuven), Broekaert (Orthopedagogics department at the University of Gent), Mutzeck (Orthopedagogics at the university of Leipzig), Mertin (Head of the Education Advisory Service of the City of Prague and attached to the Faculty of Psychology of the Prague University) and Wittzock (Orthopedagogics at the university of Rostock) the present author has submitted a request for a research grant to the European Committee. The initial request for a grant in this area came from the

President of the European Association for Residential and Foster Care for Children and Adolescents (EUSARF). The grant now being considered would enable comparative Reaction Pattern Research to be undertaken in three German federal states (N ± 1500), in the Belgian state of Flanders (N ± 1000), in Prague, the Czech capital, (N ± 300), and in Holland (N = 1,294). For this purpose, the SRI has been translated into Flemish, German and Czech.

At the time of writing, initial consent, as required by the European Committee, has been received from the governments of Holland, of the German states Schleswig-Holstein and Nedersachsen and from the Flemish government. The research envisaged has a dual purpose. First, it would compare the attitudes towards social limits of juveniles without behavioural problems in the participating countries. Second, it would contribute towards a standard picture at European level.

Possible connections between reaction patterns, parenting style and discipline problems at school

Together with Ott and Watt from the Faculty of Education of the University of New Brunswick in Fredericton (Canada), an investigation was undertaken into the connection between the attitudes towards social limits of juveniles at junior and senior highschools in Fredericton and Oromocto, the discipline problems experienced by teachers regarding these juveniles, and the parenting style of the juveniles' parents, as perceived by the juveniles themselves. If it could be established, for example, that some juveniles have disciplinary problems because of inflexible attitudes towards social limits, the problems might be ameliorated through attempts to change the attitudes. On the other hand, if it is established that the disciplinary problems are due to other factors - both parents working outside the home, for example - a different approach to problem-solving will be needed. Teachers might be guided in their approach by an indication of the sources of the problem.

In order to undertake this research, the Dutch version of the SRI was adapted to the Canadian social reality: for example, critical incidents which would be relevant to Canadian students were developed. Approval was obtained from the Ethics Committee of the University of New Brunswick, and the parents or guardians of the juveniles to be involved in the study were asked for written consent.

So far, the Canadian version of the SRI has been administered to approximately 500 youngsters. This version includes questions about:

- the extent to which the parents are available to the youngsters at home;
- parental child-rearing styles;

- any abuse or neglect experienced at home, including sexual abuse;
- existing, serious problems as perceived by the youngsters (for example, poor relationships with parents or teachers, lack of spending money, concerns about sexuality, and so forth); and
- the extent to which the youngsters are already certain about their future profession. (This last item has to do with current research being undertaken at New Brunswick).

A second instrument has been prepared to elicit information from teachers about the extent to which they have experienced discipline problems with the youngsters involved in the study. The data will be analysed and the results published through a joint effort by RUG (Rijkuniversiteit of Groningen) and the University of New Brunswick.

Transgenerational connections between reaction patterns

Together with Broeckaert (Orthopedagogics department at the University of Gent-Belgium) an investigation is being considered into the connection between juveniles' attitudinal flexibility towards social limits and that of their parents and grandparents. Theoretically, such a connection may be anticipated. If this connection does exist and is found to be significant, then lack of flexibility on the parents' part may be countered by a suitable educational program for their children.

Other possibilities for reaction pattern research

Staff and researchers in the Department of Orthopedagogics at RUG are considering the possibilities of RPR research in the following areas: learning disabilities; care for the handicapped; and children with conduct disorders.

With respect to learning disabilities, the SRI could be used to determine whether there is a connection between the attitudinal flexibility of secondary-school students and their academic achievement at school. The so-called "B-type" youngsters have a lower attitudinal flexibility with respect to social limits, know fewer reaction and motivation alternatives, and show less capacity for temporal abstraction than the "A-type" youngsters. If B-type youngsters also have poorer academic records than A-type youngsters, the question arises as to whether attitudes towards social limits and academic achievement have a common root. Possibly the concept "learning capacity" or "learning ability' needs to be defined not just in terms of academic skills but in a broader context, including attitudes and social values as well as cognitive ability.

The Canadian research mentioned earlier also raises the question of whether there is any relation between the way a child is raised, attitudinal flexibility with respect to social limits, discipline problems at school, and academic achievement. An enquiry into the connection between the way a child is raised and his or her academic achievement has already been undertaken. Stevens (1983) of the Rijksuniversiteit of Utrecht has pointed out the importance of that relationship with respect to the development of learning problems. In addition, Van Peer (1991), affiliated with the RUG, has recently completed a doctoral thesis on the extent to which parents of children with learning disabilities teach their children problem-solving skills differently from parents of children without learning disabilities. Van Peer did not find any significant difference between the instructional methods of these two groups of parents. However, it should be noted that Van Peer asked parents to teach their children in a room at school. Had the instruction taken place at home instead, differences between the two groups may have been found.

The SRI could also be used to investigate the relationship between the development of aggression in children and their attitudinal flexibility with respect to social limits. In his recently concluded doctoral study of detained juveniles (RPRII-population), Vos (1991a) points out that these juveniles have a lower attitudinal flexibility with respect to social limits than the juveniles belonging to the RPRI-population: that is, the Dutch juveniles with no known behavioural problems. For example, the RPRII-population is less well acquainted with the alternatives of negotiation (C) and withdrawal (D) than the RPRI-population. In addition, the RPRII-population shows less capacity for temporal abstraction (motivation type d) than the RPRI-population.

From the results obtained with the RPRI population, it appears that a decrease in these aspects of attitudinal flexibility is associated with an increase in the tendency towards overstepping limits (reaction type B). The question now is whether this relationship also holds good with regard to aggression as a subtype of the B reaction type: and whether, if it does, it differs from (for example, is stronger than) the relationship found with the remaining B-reactions. As mentioned earlier, Vos made recommendations to the Boards of Detention Centres concerning the most effective treatment strategies for detained juveniles, based on the results of his research. He advised that juveniles should be taught to think in terms of future consequences and also taught to consider alternative responses to a command other than just obedience or disobedience. If decreased attitudinal flexibility turns out to be also related to aggression, Vos's advice might be expanded to include specific treatment strategies for detained juveniles known to be aggressive.

Finally, staff and researchers in the Department of Orthopedagogics at the RUG have been considering the possibilities of "translating" the SRI so that it could be used to develop a standard picture for mentally retarded people with serious behavioural disturbances. The Department has been interested in the treatment of this population for many years (see, among others, Van Gemert, 1985 and 1991). As is the case with normal juveniles, "behavioural disturbance" in mentally retarded people is a phenomenon that is difficult to define and interpret unequivocally. Decisions about diagnosis and treatment differ depending on the personal opinions of the particular professional involved, with the result that some of the mentally retarded may not be given the most effective or appropriate treatment. Using an adapted version of the SRI, a standard picture for mentally retarded people without behavioural disturbances might be developed, so that there would be an objective basis for comparison. Treatment strategies could then be devised based on the relationship between certain behavioural problems and ways of reacting to social limits.

Notes

1. In this chapter the addition "with no known behavioural problems" means that during this investigation these youngsters did not have any officially registered contacts with a judicial authority (for instance police or court) as the result of a (suspected) lawbreaking activity.

References

Kok, J.M., Menkehorst, G.A.B.M., Naayer, P.M.H. & Zandberg, Tj. (1991), *Residentieel gedragstherapeutisch behandelingsprogramma. Ontwikkeling, invoering, effectmeting,* Assen, Dekker & Van de Vegt.

Luttikhuis, G. (1990), *Jongeren met afwijkend gedrag en hun leefwereld. Een literatuuronderzoek naar de waarderingen van jongeren met afwijkend gedrag ten opzichte van hun leefwereld,* Groningen, Vakgroep Orthopedagogiek RUG (dissertation).

Rink, J.E., Vos, R.C., Van Lokven, H.M. & Slagveer, C.M. (1989), *Grensgevallen. De houding van jongeren t.a.v. sociale grenzen. Deel 1. Nederlandse jongeren. Algemeen,* Leuven/Amersfoort, Acco.

Rink, J.E. (1991), 'Het reaktiepatronenonderzoek bij adolescenten: Interdisciplinaire aspecten', *Bulletin Nederlandse Vereniging voor Adolescentenzorg,* vol. 9, no. 1/2.

Sanches, M.R. & Vos, R.C. (1991), 'Primäre Prävention von Verhaltensstörungen bei Jugendlichen ethnischer Minderheiten', in H. Neukäter (ed.), *Verhaltensstörungen verhindern. Prävention als Pädagogische Aufgabe,* (pp. 217-229) Oldenburg, Universität Oldenburg, Zentrum für pädagogische Berufspraxis.

Stevens, L.M. (1983), 'Leerproblemen als opvoedingsproblemen', *Tijdschrift voor Orthopedagogiek*, vol. 22, no. 12, p. 695-704.

Van Gemert, G.H. (1985), *'Gedragsgestoordheid' bij zwakzinnigen*, Lisse, Swets & Zeitlinger (Doctoral dissertation).

Van Gemert, G.H. (1991), *Zorg voor ernstig geestelijk gehandicapten* (public lecture at the RUG).

Van Peer, D.R. (1991), *Sociale ondersteuning van kinderen met leerstoornissen*, Lisse, Swets en Zeitlinger (Doctoral dissertation).

Vos, R.C. (1991a), *De houding van jongeren in detentie ten opzichte van sociale grenzen*, Groningen (Doctoral dissertation).

Vos, R.C., (1991b), 'Prävention von Eskalation - sekundäre Prävention von Verhaltensproblemen bei verhaltensgestörten Jugendlichen in der Heimerziehung', in H. Neukäter (ed.), *Verhaltensstörungen verhindern. Prävention als Pädagogische Aufgabe*, (pp. 217-230) Oldenburg, Universität Oldenburg, Zentrum für Pädagogische Berufspraxis.

5 School attainment and behaviour of foster children: a longitudinal study

Matthew COLTON
Anthony HEATH
Jane ALDGATE

Introduction

Research over the past three decades suggests that children "looked after" by local authorities are not well served by the education system. It is now well-established that the attainment of such children tends to fall below national norms for their age groups (Essen et al., 1976; St. Claire and Osborn, 1987; Jackson, 1988; Heath et al., 1989; Colton et al., 1991). Moreover, one of the major findings consistently resulting from studies on children in public care has been the high incidence of behavioural problems among this group compared to the general population (Colton et al., 1991).

This chapter examines the possible relationship between educational attainment and behaviour. It is based on a longitudinal study of foster children and a "comparison group" of children receiving social work support while remaining with their birth families. After a brief summary of the methodology used in the study, the overall levels of attainment and progress of the two groups are reported. This is followed by an account of the incidence of behavioural problems among the children. Finally, the third part of the chapter considers whether the study data support the commonly-held view that behavioural problems and low educational achievement among separated children are linked.

Methodology

The sample comprised 49 foster children (26 boys and 23 girls) who were attending ordinary state schools in one county and were of approximately Middle-School age (8-14 years) when the study began. Each child had been in care for a minimum of six months and many had lived with their foster families for several years (mean length of placement = 6 years; median = 7 years).

It seemed worthwhile to compare the foster children, not only with the general population through the use of standardised tests, but also with children from similar backgrounds to those of the foster children's birth families. Therefore, a comparison group was chosen comprising children who had never been in care but whose families were receiving preventive social work support in the community at the start of the study. Thirty four boys and 24 girls within the same age band and attending similar schools were recruited to this comparison group. As with the foster children, virtually all of the second group were of white/European ethnic origin.

The children's educational attainment was assessed through standardised tests in reading (the Suffolk reading test and NFER's EH2 test for older children), vocabulary (the BPVS) and mathematics (NFER's BM test). The reading and vocabulary tests were administered by members of the research team in Autumn 1987, 1988 and 1989, but the maths test (at the request of the local Department of Education) was administered by school teachers, first in 1987 and again in 1989. The children's scores were age standardised and thus show how well the child was performing relative to the national average for children of the same age.

Two parallel questionnaires - one for children's parents, the other for their teachers - devised by Rutter were used for assessing the children's behaviour. The questionnaires are quick and simple to use, have established reliability and validity, and discriminate, within limits, between children who show disorder and those who do not. The questionnaire for parents consists of 31 questions presented under three headings: health problems, habits, and behaviour. The teachers' questionnaire contains 26 statements about the child's behaviour, 18 of which are identical to the items constituting the behaviour section of the parents' questionnaire. A total score of 13 or more for the parents'scale (possible range 0-62) and 9 or more for the teachers' scale (possible range 0-52) indicates disorder.

The teachers' questionnaire was completed by teachers who knew the individual children reasonably well - for example, class or form teachers. Those concerned were free to confer with their colleagues when filling in the questionnaire. Rutter's parents' questionnaire was completed by the children's current carers, usually the foster or birth mother, during visits to the children's homes by a member of the research team. The parents' questionnaire was used once only, at the start of the study, while the teachers' questionnaire was applied on three occasions in conjunction with the three rounds of attainment tests (for further details see Colton et al., 1991).

In addition, the children's carers were interviewed at the beginning of the study, the children and teachers during the course of the study, and the social workers towards the end of the study. Information was also obtained about the children's social work histories from their social work files (for further information about data and methods, see Heath et al., 1993).

Educational attainment and progress

By the time three rounds of testing had been completed, six subgroups of varying size had emerged from the original two groups. Four subgroups derived from the original foster group: (1) children whose foster placements broke down; (2) children whose legal status changed, giving greater legal security to their caregivers through adoption and custodianship orders; (3) children who were reunited with their families of origin; and (4) children who experienced no such changes. The remaining two subgroups comprised children from the original comparison group: (5) children who went into care; and (6) children who remained at home throughout the study. As there were some missing data on the later rounds of testing, analyses are confined to those children for whom there were no missing data on a given test. Table 5.1 compares the average scores of the six subgroups for each round of attainment tests.

It was expected that evidence would be found of educational progress among the children who remained with their foster families throughout the study. However, on none of the three tests is there any evidence for relative progress on the part of the "no-change" foster subgroup. On the reading test, for example, their average score was 94 in the first round, 93 in the second and 92 in the third. It should be emphasised that this shows lack of progress relative to national norms for their ages. The children were of course making absolute gains in their reading ability, vocabulary and maths, and indeed were making much the same absolute gains as the nationally average child. It had been hoped, however that they would be catching up with the national average; or, in other words, that their age-standardised scores would be improving. This clearly did not prove to be the case.

Table 5.1: Educational attainment and progress

Scores on the reading test				
	1st round	2nd round	3rd round	N
Foster Group				
No change	94 (16)	93 (12)	92 (10)	29
Custodianship	92 (12)	89 (9)	91 (12)	8
Residential care	96 (8)	97 (4)	90 (3)	3
Returned home	83 (16)	90 (13)	90 (10)	4
Comparison Group				
No change	89 (16)	90 (15)	91 (15)	39
Went into care	105 (30)	96 (23)	103 (25)	3

Scores on the vocabulary test				
	1st round	2nd round	3rd round	N
Foster Group				
No change	94 (13)	94 (15)	94 (14)	28
Custodianship	98 (12)	95 (18)	89 (10)	8
Residential care	98 (17)	105 (9)	93 (5)	3
Returned home	86 (20)	84 (24)	92 (14)	4
Comparison Group				
No change	91 (16)	91 (17)	96 (19)	39
Went into care	96 (27)	98 (34)	115 (17)	3

Scores on the maths test				
	1st round	2nd round	3rd round	N
Foster Group				
No change	88 (14)	-	88 (13)	24
Custodianship	90 (9)	-	84 (11)	6
Residential care	95 (4)	-	93 (3)	3
Returned home	85 (13)	-	90 (9)	3
Comparison Group				
No change	94 (13)	-	88 (14)	26
Went into care	97 (25)	-	92 (19)	3

* Figures in brackets give the standard deviations

The group of foster children who were in perhaps the most favourable circumstances, at least with respect to a sense of permanence, was the group who became the subject of custodianship or adoption during the course of the study. It seemed reasonable to expect that the increased sense of security for caregivers and children conferred by the custodianship and adoption orders might be reflected in the educational attainment of the children concerned. Again, the data give no support to this hypothesis. Indeed, on the maths and vocabulary tests there was a decline in performance.

The other subgroups are too small to warrant any conclusions, although there are hints that the children who returned home improved relative to the others over the course of the study. The improvement occurred on the vocabulary and maths tests as well as on the reading test. However, the children who went home scored particularly badly on all three tests in the first round (perhaps due to transitory factors), and their improvement merely brought them up to the average for the foster group as a whole. There are also hints that the children who moved into residential care made less progress than the others. These children showed a decline in their scores on all three tests but, given the tiny numbers involved, no firm conclusions should be drawn. In addition, it had been expected that children from the original comparison group who were taken into care might show a deterioration in performance. However, complete data were only obtained on three children and, as can be seen, there is no consistent pattern in their progress.

In sum then, it is not possible to reject the null hypothesis that changes in placement or legal status during the course of the study were unrelated to educational progress. The results reveal that even those foster children who were in the most favourable situations, with settled and long-term placements, were performing well below national norms for their age group.

Behavioural problems

Initial findings on the foster children's behaviour were consistent with previous research showing relatively high rates of behavioural problems among children looked after by local authorities. The first administration of the Rutter behaviour questionnaires yielded evidence of emotional or behavioural disorder at home or at school, and sometimes in both places, among 42 per cent of the original group of foster children. However, the same was true for a startling 64 per cent of the original comparison group. The application of Rutter's method for calculating the "true prevalence of disorder" indicated that 31.4 per cent of the original foster group were manifesting emotional or behavioural disorder against 45.5 per cent of the comparison group. The difference between the two groups is not statistically significant. Even so, both estimates are very high compared with the figure of 6.8 per cent obtained by Rutter and his colleagues for the general population on the Isle of Wight (see Colton et al., 1991).

Although the average scores for male foster children were significantly higher than those of female foster children on both questionnaires, the differences between the foster and comparison groups remained directionally the same when gender differences were controlled for. Overall differences between male and female members of the comparison group were not statistically significant for either questionnaire (Colton et al., 1991).

Table 5.2 shows the numbers of children in each of the six subgroups at or above the cut-off for disorder on the three rounds of the teachers' questionnaire.

Table 5.2: Numbers at or above cut-off for disorder on teachers' questionnaire

	1st round	2nd round	3rd round	N
Foster Group				
No change	3	4	4	24
Change of status	2	0	1	4
Residential care	2	1	2	3
Returned home	0	1	0	4
Comparison Group				
No change	9	8	14	29
Went into care	1	3	1	4

Some 48 per cent of children in the no-change comparison group (that is, the group for which data are available on all three rounds of the teachers' questionnaire) were manifesting behavioural problems at school by the third round of tests. This compares with 17 per cent of the no-change foster group. The other subgroups are too small to warrant conclusions.

Table 5.3: Average score on teachers' questionnaire

	1st round	2nd round	3rd round	N
Foster Group				
No change	4 (4)	5 (4)	5 (4)	24
Change of status	6 (5)	3 (2)	3 (4)	4
Residential care	9 (8)	11 (12)	8 (5)	3
Returned home	5 (3)	4 (4)	1 (1)	4
Comparison Group				
No change	7 (7)	7 (6)	9 (6)	29
Went into care	8 (9)	14 (14)	8 (10)	4

* Figures in brackets give the standard deviations

Table 5.3 reveals that the means for each of the no-change subgroups are similar for all three rounds of teachers' questionnaire. The means for the no-change comparison group are higher than for the no-change foster subgroup. In fact, the mean for the no-change comparison group reaches the cut-off for disorder (9) on the third round of the teachers' questionnaire. Other subgroups are too small to warrant conclusions. It is worth noting, however, that the differences between any two subgroups for the three rounds of the teachers' questionnaire are not significant at the .05 level or less (Scheffe multiple comparison test).

Attainment and behaviour

As previously indicated, behavioural problems among separated children have been linked with their generally low level of educational attainment (Colton, et al., 1991). Therefore, it was expected that foster children for whom there was no evidence of behavioural problems would make greater overall progress than those manifesting emotional or behavioural disorder. Table 5.4 presents results derived from the first round of the teachers' questionnaire, the single application of the parents' questionnaire, and the three rounds of the reading tests.

Table 5.4: Behaviour and reading progress

Parents' scale				
	1st round	2nd round	3rd round	N
Foster children Below cut-off for disorder	95 (14)	94 (10)	93 (9)	32
At or above cut-off for disorder	87 (15)	88 (10)	88 (11)	12
Comparison Group Below cut-off for disorder	93 (18)	94 (16)	95 (17)	23
At or above cut-off for disorder	86 (16)	87 (13)	88 (14)	19
Teachers' scale				
	1st round	2nd round	3rd round	N
Foster children Below cut-off for disorder	91 (17)	90 (13)	91 (11)	28
At or above cut-off for disorder	97 (9)	94 (6)	93 (9)	10
Comparison Group Below cut-off for disorder	95 (16)	95 (15)	97 (15)	25
At or above cut-off for disorder	82 (16)	85 (13)	84 (14)	17

* Figures in brackets give the standard deviations

Table 5.4 shows that, in general, children below the cut-off points for emotional or behavioural disorder had higher average reading scores than those on or above the cut-offs for disorder. Whilst the reverse applies to the foster children in relation to the behaviour questionnaire completed by teachers, the differences between the two groups of foster children are not significant at the 0.05 level or less (two-tailed t-tests).

With regard to the parents' questionnaire, differences between the two groups of foster children on the first round of the reading test are statistically significant at the 0.05 level, but just fall short of being statistically significant at the 0.05 level on the second and third rounds (one-tailed t-tests, direction of differences specified in advance). Differences between the two groups of comparison children are not statistically significant at the 0.05 level for any of the three rounds of the reading test (one-tailed t-tests).

Differences between the two groups of comparison children in relation to the teachers' questionnaire are significant at the 0.01 level or less for all three rounds of tests (two-tailed t-tests). Nevertheless, the fact remains that the reading scores of children who are *below* the cut-off points for emotional or behavioural disorder are consistently below the national average. This applies to both behaviour questionnaires, and all three rounds of the reading test.

Similar conclusions were reached from the application of the vocabulary and maths tests. Tables 5.5 and 5.6 show that children who were below the cut-off points for emotional or behavioural disorder generally scored higher on the vocabulary and maths tests than those on or above the cut-off points: but the scores of the children *without* serious behavioural problems still tended to be below average. Conversely, children in the comparison group below the cut-offs for disorder on both questionnaires achieved overall scores of 100 (parents' questionnaire) - the national average - and 103 (teachers' questionnaire) for the third round of the vocabulary test.

It is important to note that differences between the two groups of foster children remain in the same direction when the second round of the teachers' questionnaire is used in conjunction with the reading test: that is, children above the cut-off for disorder achieve higher averages on the three rounds of the reading test than those below the cut-off. However, the reverse is true when the third round of the teachers' questionnaire is used with the reading test.

Discrepancies were also found between the results produced for the foster children by the different rounds of the teachers' questionnaire with regard to both vocabulary and maths. The differences between the two groups of foster children reported in Table 5.5 are in the opposite direction when the second and third rounds of the teachers' questionnaire are used in conjunction with the maths test; that is, children below the cut-off for disorder obtain higher average scores than those at or above the cut-off. The same is true when the second round of the teachers' questionnaire is used with the vocabulary test: and this is the reverse of the results reported in Table 5.6, which involve the first round of the teachers' questionnaire. However, when the third round of the teachers' questionnaire is used in conjunction with the vocabulary test, the differences between the two groups of foster children are in the same direction as those presented in Table 5.6: that is, children above the cut-off for disorder unexpectedly achieve higher average scores for the three rounds of the vocabulary tests than those below the cut-off for disorder.

Table 5.5: Behaviour and progress in maths

Parents' Q.				
	1st round	2nd round	3rd round	N
Foster children Below cut-off for disorder	90 (11)	-	90 (13)	27
At or above cut-off for disorder	86 (15)	-	84 (9)	10
Comparison Group Below cut-off for disorder	99 (10)	-	91 (12)	13
At or above cut-off for disorder	91 (16)	-	86 (16)	16
Teachers' Q.				
	1st round	2nd round	3rd round	N
Foster children Below cut-off for disorder	88 (14)	-	88 (13)	26
At or above cut-off for disorder	91 (8)	-	88 (10)	9
Comparison Group Below cut-off for disorder	97 (15)	-	92 (14)	19
At or above cut-off for disorder	91 (11)	-	82 (10)	10

* Figures in brackets give the standard deviations

These results suggest that caution should be exercised in interpreting findings for the foster children which involve the teachers' questionnaire. Perhaps greater confidence can be placed in the results produced by the parents' questionnaire. Because carers know their children rather better than do teachers, it may well be the case that they were able to provide more accurate assessments of their children's behaviour.

Table 5.6: Behaviour and vocabulary

Parents' Q.				
	1st round	2nd round	3rd round	N
Foster children				
Below cut-off for disorder	96 (12)	97 (13)	93 (10)	31
At or above cut-off for disorder	89 (18)	86 (20)	90 (18)	12
Comparison Group				
Below cut-off for disorder	95 (17)	94 (16)	100 (19)	24
At or above cut-off for disorder	88 (16)	89 (19)	94 (19)	20
Teachers' Q.				
	1st round	2nd round	3rd round	N
Foster children				
Below cut-off for disorder	91 (15)	90 (17)	90 (13)	27
At or above cut-off for disorder	99 (13)	98 (10)	94 (10)	10
Comparison Group				
Below cut-off for disorder	96 (17)	95 (18)	103 (16)	26
At or above cut-off for disorder	85 (14)	87 (15)	87 (19)	18

* Figures in brackets give the standard deviations

It was decided to test whether a slightly more refined classification of the children with respect to behaviour would yield significant differences in reading scores. The results of this exercise are presented in Table 5.7, which concerns behaviour at home and school, measured by the parents' and teachers' questionnaires and the third round of the reading test.

Table 5.7: Behaviour at home and school and reading attainment

	Home	N	School	N
Foster children				
Low	95 (8)	15	93 (11)	18
Medium	91 (10)	17	86 (10)	10
High	88 (11)	12	93 (9)	10
Comparison Group				
Low	100 (15)	11	96 (13)	14
Medium	90 (17)	12	97 (18)	11
High	87 (14)	19	84 (14)	17

* Figures in brackets give the standard deviations

Children from the original foster and comparison groups are subdivided into three groups according to their behaviour scores: low (0-3 on the teachers' questionnaire; 0-6 on the parents' questionnaire), medium (4-8 on the teachers' questionnaire; 7-12 on the parents' questionnaire) and high (9 - the cut-off for disorder - and above, on the teachers' questionnaire; 13 - the cut-off for disorder - and above, on the parents' questionnaire). It was anticipated that the lower the behaviour scores, the higher would be the reading scores. However, Table 5.7 shows that this was not the case for the teachers' questionnaire where the pattern of scores is mixed and the differences within the foster and comparison groups are not significant at the 0.05 level or less (Scheffe multiple comparison procedure). Conversely, the pattern of scores for the parents' questionnaire are in the direction predicted. Although the differences within both the foster and comparison groups are not significant at the 0.05 level or less (Scheffe multiple comparison procedure), it is worth highlighting that the comparison subgroup with the lowest overall level of behaviour problems had an average reading score of 100.

Finally, analyses were carried out to ascertain whether there were significant differences in attainment between children manifesting behaviour problems at either home or school, on the one hand, and those for which there was no evidence whatsoever of behavioural problems. Table 5.8 summarises the results obtained. The third rounds of the reading, vocabulary and maths tests are employed. Cases included are those for which data are available for all three rounds of a given attainment test.

Table 5.8: Behaviour and attainment

	No behaviour problems			Behaviour problems		
Foster children		(SD)	N		(SD)	N
Reading	93	(10)	21	93	(10)	4
Vocabulary	93	(11)	20	99	(15)	4
Maths	90	(14)	19	88	(10)	3
Comparison Group						
Reading	100	(14)	15	84	(13)	9
Vocabulary	105	(17)	16	85	(18)	10
Maths	95	(10)	9	82	(14)	6

* Figures in brackets give the standard deviations

Table 5.8 indicates that both groups of foster children have below average scores. The differences between the two groups are not significant for any of the three attainment tests. In contrast, the comparison group for which there is no evidence at all of behavioural problems achieved average scores of 100 on the reading test and 105 on the vocabulary test; they also obtained the highest mean of scores on the maths test. Moreover, the differences between the two groups of comparison children are statistically significant for all three tests - behaviour and reading, behaviour and vocabulary, and behaviour and maths (0.05 level or less, one-tailed t-tests).

Thus, the link between educational attainment and behaviour is clearly visible in the scores of the comparison group. Overall, children in the comparison group who showed no evidence of disorder either at home or at school were attaining at levels on, or just above, the national average in reading and vocabulary. However, the relationship between attainment and behaviour is markedly less apparent among the foster children. The overall attainment scores of the foster children in reading, vocabulary and maths are consistently below the national average, irrespective of whether or not there is evidence of emotional or behavioural problems.

Discussion

This chapter has explored the relationship between the educational progress of a group of 8-14 year olds in long-term foster care and their behaviour.

The results with respect to the children's attainment confirm previous research documenting the low educational attainment of children in care. Thus, they serve to reinforce the message conveyed by research over a period of some thirty years, namely that children in public care are not well served by the education system (Colton and Jackson, 1993). Although the foster children performed no worse than the comparison group, the findings are nonetheless disappointing in that the foster children were a particularly favoured group of children in care, with the majority having had long-term settled placements with foster parents who showed every indication of providing an environment - emotional, social, cultural, and material - conducive to educational progress.

Moreover, the finding of low attainment among children in care cannot be explained away by the special difficulties of children in residential care or by frequent placement breakdowns because it applies to children in long-term foster care as well. Nor can it be explained away by the sense of impermanence affecting many foster homes. There was no difference in attainment or progress between children where the eventual outcome was adoption or custodianship and those who remained as foster children. Data collected on the children's behaviour were also consistent with previous research on children in care in that a high overall level of behavioural problems was observed among the foster children. However, whilst the link between educational attainment and behaviour was clearly discernable in the scores of the comparison group, it was not readily apparent in the results on the foster children. Overall, children in the comparison group who showed no evidence of disorder either at home or at school were attaining at levels on, or just above, the national average in reading and vocabulary. By contrast, the overall attainment scores of the foster children in reading, vocabulary and maths were consistently below the national average, regardless of whether there was evidence of behavioural problems.

One popular explanation for lack of educational progress has been the self-fulfilling prophecy of low teacher expectations. It is therefore worth noting at this juncture that we failed to find any evidence that the children of whom the teachers expected more made greater progress than those of whom they expected less. The teachers' judgements were consequences rather than causes of the pupils' performance (Heath et al., 1993).

However, evidence was collected which suggests that children's early histories before entry to care may have a profound effect on their educational attainment in middle childhood. Table 5.9 shows that there were marked differences between the foster children when they were categorised according to the primary reason for care.

Table 5.9: Primary reason for care

Scores on the reading test				
	1st round	2nd round	3rd round	N
Abuse/neglect	82 (16)	85 (11)	87 (11)	12
Other reasons	98 (12)	95 (10)	93 (9)	31
Scores on the vocabulary test				
	1st round	2nd round	3rd round	N
Abuse/neglect	90 (16)	86 (13)	85 (12)	12
Other reasons	96 (13)	98 (17)	96 (12)	30
Scores on the maths test				
	1st round	2nd round	3rd round	N
Abuse/neglect	79 (11)	-	81 (9)	11
Other reasons	94 (11)	-	92 (12)	25

* Figures in brackets give the standard deviations

On all three tests, and in all rounds of testing, the children who came into care for suspected child abuse or neglect scored significantly lower than did the other foster children. (The differences, using a t-test, were significant at the 0.01 level on the maths and reading tests and at the 0.05 level on the vocabulary test). There was some evidence on the reading test that these children caught up over the period of the study, but this pattern is not replicated on the other two tests and we should not place great reliance on it. The predominant impression is of continuing disadvantage.

This finding is sustained when we control for other aspects of the children's social work histories, such as the number of placements, length of time in care, and expectations about the duration of the placement. (See Aldgate et al., 1992 for further details.) In other words, even long-term and settled placements did not seem to have overcome the educational disadvantages of early child abuse or neglect. In the case of the remaining foster children who had come into care for other reasons, however, the picture was somewhat more encouraging. They were still below the national average in their scores, but clearly were not nearly so disadvantaged. Nonetheless, even these children failed to catch up educationally in the way we had expected over the course of the study.

Children's early histories also appear to have lasting effects on their behaviour. Table 5.10 divides our whole sample according to the reasons for care or social work involvement. As would be expected, the highest scores on both the parental and the first round of teachers' questionnaire are where the reasons for care or social work involvement are the child's behaviour or delinquency. Predictably, there is a degree of selection bias in our sample in that youngsters with severe behavioural difficulties are more likely than others to enter care or to receive social work help. This seems to be part of the explanation for the finding that overall levels of behavioural disturbance among our two groups exceeded those observed for the general population by Rutter and his colleagues.

Table 5.10: Reasons for care/social work involvement and current behaviour

	Mean Scores on the :	
	Parental Questionnaire	Teachers' Questionnaire
Reasons for Care/Social Work Involvement :-		
- Child's behaviour or delinquency	12.4 (13)	10.2 (9)
- Suspected child abuse or neglect	11.6 (24)	8.0 (23)
- Parental problems	8.4 (27)	5.0 (25)
- Multiple family problems	12.2 (26)	8.4 (24)

* Figures in brackets give the numbers of children in each category

It is also apparent that children who were suspected of being the victims of child abuse or neglect, or whose families had multiple problems, had significantly higher scores than children whose problems had primarily been parental. By contrast, neither the number of placements which the foster children had experienced, nor the length of time in their current placements correlated significantly with their scores on either the parents' or the teachers' questionnaires. Given that, in the majority of cases, the reasons for admission to care concerned situations which existed long before we embarked on our research, these results indicate that children's early histories may have lasting effects on their behaviour as well as on their educational attainment. This helps to account for the high levels of behavioural problems among our foster children. Equally, the reasons for social work involvement with the families of our comparison group also go a long way towards explaining the high level of behavioural problems observed among that group.

Nevertheless, as can be seen from Table 5.9, children who had come into care for reasons other than abuse or neglect were still somewhat below the national average in their attainment. Thus, something more than "normal" family life and "normal" parental interest may be required to compensate for earlier deprivation. The foster parents in the present study were in general an average group in terms of their social class and education. They were not themselves "high-fliers" educationally. Is it perhaps so surprising that, when "average" educational inputs are given to children with "above-average" educational needs, these children fail to make "greater-than-average" educational progress?

It is notable that the two foster children in our study who had the highest attainment scores had been with the same, highly-qualified foster families since an early age. Interestingly, this is consistent with the findings of Schiff et al. (1980 and 1981) on the educational consequences of adoption in France (Heath et al., 1993). The majority of our foster parents, however, were around the national average in their occupational and educational attainments, and they had not in general been fostering the children since birth. Whilst not wishing to imply that the answer to the educational problems of children in care is early placement into highly-qualified families, it is evident that something more than "normal" family life and "normal" parental interest may be required to compensate for earlier deprivation. Gains can be made, but they do not come easily or cheaply. Quite simply, average inputs are not enough for children with above-average educational needs. Our research indicates that much higher priority should be given to the educational needs of separated children. Thus, the emphasis given to the education of separated children by the "Looking After Children" project (Parker et al., 1991) represents an encouraging step forward for social work practice.

References

Aldgate, J, Colton, M., Ghate, D., & Heath, A.F. (1992), 'Educational attainment and stability in long-term foster care', *Children and Society*, vol. 6, 38-60.

Colton, M., Aldgate, J. & Heath, A.F. (1991), 'Behavioural problems of children in and out of care', *Social Work and Social Sciences Review*, vol. 2, 177- 191.

Colton, M. & Jackson, S. (1993), 'Against All Odds', *Community Care*, April, 1993.

Essen, J. Lambert, L. & Head, J. (1976), 'School attainment of children who have been in care', *Child Care, Health and Development*, vol. 2, 339-351.

Heath, A.F., Colton, M.J. & Aldgate, J. (1989), 'The education of children in and out of care', *British Journal of Social Work*, vol. 19, 447-460.

Heath, A.F., Colton, M.J. & Aldgate, J. (1993), 'Failure to Escape: A Longitudinal Study of Foster Children's Educational Attainment', *British Journal of Social Work* (accepted for publication, June 1993).

Jackson, S. (1988), 'The education of children in care', *Adoption and Fostering*, vol. 12, 6-10.

Parker, R., Ward., H., Jackson, S., Aldgate, J. & Wedge, P. (1991), *Looking After Children: Assessing Outcomes in Child Care,* London, HMSO.

St. Claire, L. & Osborn, A.F. (1987), 'The ability and behaviour of children who have been 'In-Care' or separated from their parents', *Early Child Development and Care* (special issue).

Schiff, M. (1980), 'L'echec scolaire n'est pas inscrit dans les chromosomes', *Psychologie*, vol. 181, 51-56.

Schiff, M. et al. (1981), 'Enfants de travailleurs manuels adoptes par des cadres: effet d'un changement de class sociale sur le cursus scolaire et les notes de QI', *Travaux et Documents*, vol. 93.

6 Short-term and long-term outcomes in extrafamilial care

Nicola MADGE

Introduction

In the early days of extrafamilial care, questions about outcomes were not asked. Children were admitted to institutions to rescue them from abandonment or to remove them from 'bad' families. With this simple aim in view, positive results were almost inevitable. Life in a residential home was a matter of containment and care. Little thought was given to the emotional needs of the children, family contacts were rarely maintained and were certainly not encouraged, and scant attention was paid to such issues as stigmatisation and normalisation. On the whole, institutions provided potentially long-term solutions to what were invariably seen as long-term problems.

As time has gone on, however, this simple model has been challenged, and both the reasons for separating children from their families and the requirements of the substitute care offered have become much less straightforward. The reason for placement may be emergency care, assessment, treatment, rehabilitation, or perhaps sometimes simply to provide a more suitable place than home. At the same time, there has been greater recognition of the fact that different children have different needs, accompanied by a trend towards decreasing numbers in children's homes and increasing numbers in foster placements. In general, we have come to realise that many forms of extrafamilial care are far from perfect and that services must be offered cautiously.

These developments have been accompanied by a growing concern to understand the outcomes - both good and bad - for children and young people who spend periods apart from their natural families. This paper examines some of the available evidence on the sequelae of extrafamilial care, mainly focusing on the outcomes of stays in "ordinary" children's homes.

Examining outcomes

Before turning to the empirical evidence, it is worth making two brief comments on the interpretation of findings.

The first comment concerns ways of measuring outcomes: that is, ways of assessing the results of care. When different forms of care are being compared, results are usually measured in terms of whether the placement broke down or how "successful" the placement was. Although "a successful placement" is hard to define, different forms of care can be adequately compared provided the same definition is used is every case. However, it is a lot more difficult to determine whether children who have returned to their families or to the community would have been better off if they had never been removed. Rough assessments can be made: similarities and differences before and after the care experience can be looked at; differences between children in various types of care can again be examined; and children who have been in care can be contrasted with general population groups or indeed with their own siblings who have stayed at home. All these kinds of assessment answer certain questions, but none addresses what is perhaps the central issue: what would the characteristics or circumstances of a child be had she or he remained in the natural family home? That question can never be properly answered.

The main message is that the absence of a suitable control group can make it very difficult to dissociate the effects of care from other influences. For instance, favourable outcomes might reflect the benefits of care, but they might also reflect spontaneous recovery, the effects of maturation, or later good fortune such as finding a rewarding job or making a happy marriage. Conversely, unfavourable outcomes might result from poor care, but they might also reflect characteristics of the child or family that are hard to change, or they might be due to other factors resulting from the care experience, such as separation from a best friend.

The second comment on the interpretation of findings concerns time frames. Longitudinal studies, conducted over years, often run into problems because the child care structure being examined does not remain constant for the duration of the study. Philosophies and organisations in the field of child care are forever changing, and there are probably few ways in which life in a children's home today resembles life in a residential setting one, two, or three decades ago. Studies from the past are more useful in documenting problems that *did* and *could* arise with respect to residential care than in pointing to problems which presently exist or are likely to occur. In other words, there are considerable difficulties in generalising from the past to the present.

Short-term outcomes

Assessment of short-term, and indeed longer-term, outcomes for children and young people who have been in care will usually include attention to the child's recent feelings and experiences. These experiences may well have involved adjustment problems and coping with stigma (Dartington Social Research Unit, 1992). In much more rare instances they may have included the endurance of serious malpractice by care staff. In Britain, there has been a spate of revelations of severe oppression, degrading treatment and sexual abuse (Levy and Kahan, 1991; Williams and Macreadie, 1992), but there is little documented evidence on the legacy of these experiences for the children concerned.

A comprehensive examination of the short-term consequences of child care would also seek to answer a series of other questions on which evidence is generally lacking. How well do children settle back into their families and communities? Do old problems become resolved or do they resurface once the novelty of the return home has worn off? What new problems are likely to develop if the child returns to a family with perhaps a new step-parent or a new brother or sister? There are probably as many answers as there are families, and quite clearly outcomes in this sense are not exactly outcomes of care. Nevertheless, these patterns are important because they affect the child's adjustment after care, and it may be argued that they should be considered in any assessment of the effects of care.

It is not surprising that, in the main, methodological constraints have led researchers to focus on somewhat simpler measures. Some studies which look at the success of placements, consumer views, and the situation and circumstances of children and young people once they have left care, are considered below.

Placement success

Many studies examining short-term outcomes of care have adopted criteria such as the "success" or "failure" of placements, or the continuity of care as judged by the number of placements the child has had.

One of the best studies in this tradition is that conducted by Rowe et al. (1989). The Child Care Placement Outcomes Project looked at over nine thousand placement endings and compared the outcomes of residential, foster and "home on trial" provision. Social workers were asked to indicate if placements had lasted as long as the children needed them. Overall, from the social workers' perspective, 62 per cent had lasted as long as needed, 22 per cent had not lasted this long, and 14 per cent had lasted longer. The younger the child, the more likely the placement was to have lasted as long as needed. Residential placements, followed by foster care, were found most likely to last as long as necessary, with "home on trial" most often breaking down before time.

Social workers were also asked to rate the success of placements aimed at temporary care, assessment and the achievement of treatment goals respectively. By far the most success was achieved when the aim was temporary care, aims being met either fully or in most respects in 86 per cent of cases. A comparable level of success was gained in 62 per cent of instances when the primary aim was assessment, and in 42 per cent of cases when the primary aim was achieving treatment goals. It is apparent that assessment, and particularly treatment, are tasks which it is extremely difficult to undertake successfully.

Rowe et al. (1989) decided that if a placement lasted as long as the child needed it, and if it met the primary aim in at least most respects, it could be regarded as "successful". Conversely, if it broke down before time and met its aim only partially or not at all, it was "unsuccessful". On the basis of these criteria, it was found that foster homes had the best outcomes (60 per cent of placements were successful, 15 per cent were unsuccessful and 25 per cent had mixed ratings), followed by residential establishments (46, 16 and 38 per cent respectively), and lastly by "home on trial" (36, 27 and 37 per cent).

Similar patterns have been found in other countries. Research in the Netherlands (Smit, 1991) has suggested that some 40 per cent of young people leaving residential care have unsuccessful outcomes in the sense that they run away, are transferred to a stricter environment, are discharged because the home cannot cope with them, or fail to achieve initial placement goals.

Consumer views

Studies of children's attitudes towards care experiences may present rather personal and idiosyncratic viewpoints, but they can also provide telling insights. Studies such as those conducted by Page and Clarke (1977) and Kahan (1979) have been able to explore in detail what it is actually like to spend time in care, documenting feelings of insecurity and stigma, relationships with staff, problems encountered when leaving care, and so forth. Investigations of parental attitudes to care have also been shown to be valuable (Aldgate, 1989).

Such studies aid the exploration of outcomes in a number of ways. First, they are important in demonstrating the enormous differences in the experience of care - from the largely positive to the largely negative - which result from the highly variable quality of placements. Second, they can help to illuminate the respective outcomes of different forms of care. Colton's (1988) study, which incorporated children's views into a comparison of residential and foster care, provides a good example. As Colton and Aldgate (1989) noted, it is impossible in a study of this kind to be quite sure that like is being compared with like, and so it is difficult to compare placement types directly. Nonetheless, the research did suggest that children living with foster families were generally more satisfied with their placements than children in residential homes. Foster children rated their caretakers as less strict and more supportive and the children they lived with as more friendly than did the "residential" children in the sample.

The recent Report of the Committee of Inquiry into the Selection, Development and Management of Staff in Children's Homes (1992) recognised the value of consumer views and stressed the need to listen more closely to the views of young people about the running of children's homes.

Circumstances after leaving care

A recent Department of Health report (1991) commented that "It is salutary to reflect that far from remedying existing deficiencies, research is showing that periods in public care have further impaired the life chances of some children and young people because of poor educational achievement, uncorrected health problems and maladjustment". It seems that care experiences do not cause these difficulties: rather, they do not do enough to deal with the problems the children bring with them. There is often insufficient appropriate medical attention, education is frequently a low priority for social workers, and too few efforts are made to counterbalance the disrupting effects of moving schools and other changes.

The Department of Health report expressed great concern at the circumstances of many young people who have left care for independence. It noted that young people seem to be leaving care and having to fend for themselves earlier than in the past - and certainly rather sooner than most young people who live with their own families. It also pointed out that many of these young adults lack educational qualifications or training and have limited employment and housing opportunities. Frequently, they are not on good terms with their natural families, and they tend to be offered little more than very limited after-care services. More than one in three return to their former placements for assistance.

This general picture is supported by a number of recent surveys (Stein and Carey, 1986; Bonnerjea, 1990; Biehal et al., 1992; Garnett, 1992). Compared to national averages, these young people are overrepresented among the homeless, the unemployed and those lacking qualifications. A large proportion of young women become pregnant either before leaving care or shortly after. A series of studies in the Netherlands has reported generally similar findings (Smit, 1991).

Outcomes in the longer-term

Most studies of long-term outcomes of extrafamilial care are rather old, and the conclusions of many are not generally applicable today. Nonetheless, these investigations have been extremely important in documenting the potential dangers of poor institutional care and, hence, in influencing change. They have shown fairly conclusively that many children in institutions in the past ran the risk of severe and lasting damage. One classic study demonstrated how gross deprivation commonly resulted in poor intellectual ability (Skeels and Dye, 1939). The causal nature of this link was confirmed by a follow-up study of the same children which showed that the IQ of those transferred to an institution where they received more personal care and a more varied range of experiences rose from the retarded range to average (Skeels, 1966).

Much early work in this area has pointed to the significance of mother-child relationships and to the impact that separation can have. Bowlby's work (1946; 1951) was especially influential in affecting practice. More recent studies, too, have tended to confirm possible long-term effects of the separation of young children and their mothers. Some researchers discovered that children with behaviour problems were particularly likely to have experienced earlier multiple separations (Douglas, 1970) and others found an association between repeated admissions to hospital and both disturbed behaviour and psychiatric conditions in a general population study of 10 year-old children (Quinton and Rutter, 1976). In all such studies, however, factors other than residential placements were almost certainly critically important. Children are extremely likely to have behavioural or psychiatric problems when admitted into care (Schaffer and Schaffer, 1968; Wolkind, 1991), and many of the children in these early studies had come from families displaying severe discord. The children may well have had unpleasant experiences while in care, but they also tended to come from home backgrounds characterised by considerable deprivation and disadvantage.

Some early researchers laid emphasis on the way children's personalities were affected by institutional experiences. A serious failure in early bonding was said to lead to what was termed "affectionless psychopathy" which prevented children and young people from developing and maintaining "good" relationships. On the surface, these young people seemed friendly, but the problem was that they were friendly with everyone and did not make any *special* friendships. Goldfarb (1943) was among those examining and documenting the effects of residential care on adolescent personalities. Often, it seemed that an institutional syndrome of some kind was being described. More recently, Tizard and Hodges (1978) have shown that early institutional care can result in "shallow" relationships at 8 years of age.

Dinnage and Pringle (1967) summarised a lot of the early work in this field, and suggested that two main aspects of institutional care stood out as having *potentially* unfavourable effects. The first was the environment in care which could be damaging if impoverished and unstimulating. The second was the child's position in the environment: the child would thrive only if able to develop a personal sense of identity with a past, a present, and a future. These authors concluded that a general effect of prolonged poor experiences in institutional care during early childhood was to leave young people particularly vulnerable to stress.

Later studies have built on this early work, confirming some of the general patterns but refining the analysis and interpretation. Among these, Rutter et al. (1983) conducted an interesting study which considered long-term outcomes of care on parenthood in two ways. On the one hand, the researchers looked at the early background of parents who currently had children in care and, on the other hand, they looked at the current parenting behaviour of children who had grown up in care. By looking backwards and forwards in this way, the researchers drew a very alarming picture of the sequelae of care. First, it was found that the children in care were especially likely to have parents who had had similar experiences. Second, the adults who had been admitted to residential homes in infancy and remained there throughout childhood turned out to be particularly poor parents. There were, however, complex patterns of causes and effects, and it seemed that conditions in adult life also had implications for behaviour. About one in four of the women in care as children showed good parenting skills, and it emerged that a very important mediating factor was a good marital relationship with a non-deviant husband.

A similar story was told by Wolkind (1977; Kruk and Wolkind, 1983). Among a large number of women attending ante-natal clinics for the birth of their first babies were six per cent who had previously been in care. These women were found to be particularly disadvantaged on a whole range of measures. They were younger, they were more likely to be single parents, and they portrayed much higher levels of disturbance than the others. These mothers and their children were followed up over the next six years, and their relatively deprived position was maintained. For example, they suffered more poverty than the other women and they appeared to have poorer relationships. Their difficulties seemed to be passed on to their children who, at six years, showed more behaviour problems at school than the other children in the study born at the same time.

Triseliotis and Russell (1984) followed up 40 young adults aged about 23 years who had spent an average of 11 years in residential care during childhood, as well as a group of young adults who had been adopted. Members of the residential care group were much less likely to report satisfaction with their early upbringing. The few who did value their experiences stressed the importance of feeling cared for, close relationships with staff, flexibility and a relaxed environment. Those who had remained with siblings were far more satisfied than those who had not. At the time of the study, material, social and personal circumstances were considerably worse for the residential than for the adopted group. They were more likely to be poor, unemployed, in poor housing, and to have poor relationships. Many people in this group seemed generally unhappy and half of those who already had children mentioned problems in parenting. It was true to say that this group had grown up from disadvantaged children into disadvantaged adults.

These studies emphasise the adverse sequelae of institutional care. They suggest that outcomes of care are reflected not only in the adult lives of the children concerned, but also in the lives of the next generation.

A rather more optimistic note is sounded by Corbillon et al. (1991) who reviewed follow-up studies of adults formerly in care. Among the studies cited is one reported by Salo (1956) from Finland which compared 742 adults who had been in care with their 437 brothers and sisters who had not. It appeared that the "in care" group were experiencing somewhat better social conditions than their siblings and that they showed no evidence of poorer relationships. The conclusion seemed to be that admission into care had been a better option than leaving the children in deprived homes. Corbillon et al. also mentioned a Dutch study which followed up children with earlier long residential placements into their thirties (Van der Waals, 1960). Again, no particularly negative outcomes could be detected, although "many" of those followed up did report that they felt "unlucky" or "unhappy".

Corbillon et al. (1991) concluded that there are no major differences in long-term outcome between those placed in care and others from the same social groupings. They believed that adaptation mechanisms may play an important role, and that we need not be as gloomy about the effects of care as we often are.

Some factors affecting outcomes

Research studies, including those already discussed, suggest that apparent outcomes of care depend on much more than just the care experience itself. Intake characteristics as well as a variety of other factors have been shown to make unfavourable outcomes either more or less likely. In general, policy development has been responsive to these findings, and it is largely for this reason that the characteristics of child care have changed so markedly in recent years.

Some of the most important factors - other than the quality of the care itself - affecting short-term and long-term outcomes of care are summarised briefly below. The list is by no means exhaustive.

Age of children

The views and findings of Bowlby and many others have consistently discouraged the placement of young children in residential care. As a result, the population of children in children's homes has become considerably older in recent years, both in the UK and in other European countries. Nonetheless, there is some evidence that residential placements are less successful for older than younger children (Rowe et al., 1989).

At the same time, studies have shown that foster placements also tend to be less successful for older than younger children (Parker, 1966; Trasler, 1976; Berridge and Cleaver, 1987). The chances of success are particularly low for young people with serious behaviour problems placed during adolescence (Parker, 1966; Berridge and Cleaver, 1987; Rowe et al., 1989). These findings have contributed to the development of specialised fostering schemes (Hazel, 1981).

Maintaining family links

Evidence is overwhelming in suggesting the benefits to children of maintaining family links wherever possible. Those who have regular contacts with their families have fewer problems with placements (Millham et al., 1986; Berridge and Cleaver, 1987) and show better social and behavioural adjustment (Lasson, 1978). There is also no doubt that child care placements are more likely to be successful if siblings are placed together (Trasler, 1976; Triseliotis, 1980; Berridge and Cleaver, 1987).

Residential care practice has taken these findings to heart, and the importance of retaining family ties is now enshrined in the Children Act 1989. In relation to foster care, there has been a noticeable shift in emphasis from foster parents as substitute parents to foster parents as friends and helpers who complement the child's own family.

Minimum lengths of time in care

Millham et al. (1986) were very influential in showing that children who stayed in care for more than six weeks were likely to stay for a considerably longer period still. Their research has contributed to the recent trend towards shorter placements than in the past.

A similar trend is discernible in foster care. Prior to the 1970s, much fostering was long-term and a large proportion of placements broke down (Parker, 1966; Trasler, 1976). By 1987, however, there were many short-term placements (Berridge and Cleaver, 1987).

Characteristics of children

Millham and Little (1991) observed that the population of children in care is exceedingly diverse. Some primarily show behavioural problems, some come from very deprived backgrounds, some have suffered from adverse family relationships and behaviour, and some are simply in need of a short-term placement until a family crisis is resolved. Research is hardly necessary to determine that the outcomes for these different groups are likely to be very different.

Recent attention has been directed at the amount and type of services offered to certain groups of children who may have special needs. For example, the case of children from ethnic minority groups has been highlighted by Utting (1991). There are no national statistics on the ethnic background of children in residential homes, although some areas do keep figures, and there is some concern that black children may be overrepresented among those in care. There is also concern that the background of children is not always sufficiently taken into account in the recruitment of staff, the development of staff training, and the preparation and support given to those leaving care. Clearly, policy and practice in these areas will affect the outcomes of care for the young people involved.

Children with disabilities are a second group to merit special concern. Following the Children Act 1989, many more children with disabilities have been received into the care of local authorities. The outcomes for such children will depend very much on the provisions made for their special vulnerabilities and dependence.

Realistic goals

Realistic goals will lead to better outcomes. Two examples can be given. The first is that there are limits to what can realistically be expected from residential care. Millham and Little (1991) have pointed out that it is possible to modify certain behaviours such as absconding, aggressive behaviour and poor social skills, but extremely difficult to reduce persistent delinquency. It is indeed widely believed (Parker, 1980; Utting, 1991) that residential care is best suited to fulfilling short-term functions, such as preparing young people for foster placements or for leaving care. As Rowe et al. (1989) have shown, activities of this kind seem to have more successful outcomes than more ambitious activities, such as treatment.

The second example concerns the fostering of children with difficult behaviour. As Berridge and Cleaver (1987) concluded, "The assumption that damaged children can be accommodated in an "ordinary" family environment ... is frequently over-optimistic, if not naive." This does not mean that difficult children cannot be fostered, but rather that success can only be achieved if suitable preparation and planning takes place.

Patterns of placement

If certain types of placement suit some children while other types suit others, the overall pattern of outcomes of care will to some extent depend upon the correspondence between children in care and the placements available for them.

This point is highlighted by Cliffe and Berridge (1992) who examined the effects of the decision of one county council in England to close all its children's homes in 1986. A clear result was that undue stress was put on the fostering services. Some children who might have been more suitably placed in traditional children's homes were fostered instead, and the increased demand for foster families - despite a small number of children being placed in residential homes in neighbouring counties -

meant that it was not possible to "match" all children and placements. One negative consequence was a greater than average turnover of foster placements, and hence less favourable outcomes for some children.

Care as a long-term process

Care is most successful when there is adequate preparation beforehand and suitable follow-up support afterwards.

The need for adequate preparation is particularly well illustrated by foster care. The breakdown of placements is often due to poor relationships, sometimes between natural and foster parents, and sometimes between natural and fostered children (Berridge and Cleaver, 1987). Such problems may well be minimised or avoided if there is adequate preparation and support of all family members. No doubt, good planning contributes to the success found in some specialised fostering schemes (Hazel, 1981).

Help and support after care also increase the chances of favourable outcomes. It has already been shown that young people leaving care for independence show high levels of disadvantage and, although it may not be possible to find them jobs or money, help with coping may be of great value. Even those who retain family links may not be in a position to derive support from families who are very likely to be overburdened themselves. This is illustrated very vividly by Bebbington and Miles (1989) who showed that a child in the age range five to nine was 700 times more likely to be admitted to care if she or he came from a disadvantaged than from a non-disadvantaged background. By "disadvantaged", the authors meant that the family received income support, was supported by a single adult, contained four or more children, was of mixed ethnic origin, and lived in privately rented accommodation with one or more persons per room. "Non-disadvantaged" children were characterised as coming from white, two-parent families, with three or fewer children, which were not on the poverty line and lived in an owner-occupied home with more rooms than people.

Training and experience of staff

Preparation includes the whole area of training and skills, and is as necessary for foster parents as for residential workers. The issues involved have recently been, or are currently being, considered by both the Howe Enquiry (1992) and the Warner Enquiry (1992).

What do we still need to know?

There is no such thing as a typical experience in care. Children come into care with different characteristics and different problems. They spend varying amounts of time in one of several forms of provision, they have differing levels of contact with other members of their families, and they are cared for by staff with contrasting levels of training and expertise. Not surprisingly, outcomes of care are not the same for all children and it is not possible to predict with any degree of certainty whose will be better and whose will be worse. Where do we go from here?

The impression gathered from existing research and comment is that the main gaps in our knowledge concern what goes on between the time a child is received into care and the time she or he is discharged. Our understanding in the area is very poor indeed. Cliffe and Berridge (1992) are among the many authors to comment on our patchy knowledge of the working and effects of child-care services. This state of affairs is unfortunate since better information would, of course, lead to better outcome predictions.

Needless to say, rectifying this omission is no easy task. Residential workers have different professional orientations, homes implement different policies and regimes and, in the final analysis, the child's experiences are likely to be determined in a critical way by the head of the home in which the child is in care (Berridge, 1985) or by the personalities and existing family of the foster parents. Why indeed should we expect children's homes and foster parents to be any more alike than "ordinary" homes and parents?

However, we still need to know about the process of care - about the factors contributing to short-term and long-term outcomes for many children and young people. As a step towards acquiring this knowledge, the Dartington Social Research Unit (1992) has suggested two areas of research to break new ground in the study of children. "The first suggestion is for an evaluation of outcomes based upon random allocation of children to different approaches, centres or regimes...The second study would be to consider the outcome of different combinations of intervention. For example, it should be possible to compare the effects of one residential placement with those produced by a combination of residential care, fostering and placements at home or with relatives."

Valuable though these suggestions are, they still may not address the *process* of care. In relation to the first suggestion, for example, it would be important to know what the "approaches, centres or regimes" stood for, and what their critical elements were. Ethical considerations with respect to the random allocation of children would also need to be taken into account, in line with the Dartington Unit's usual research procedures. Regarding the second suggestion, it would seem that we do not now need to know about the *effects* of categories of care experience so much as *exactly what goes on within these categories.*

Especially promising may be approaches adopting the package of assessment schedules recently developed by Parker et al. (1991). These schedules are suitable for use with children living away from home and were produced as part of a Department of Health initiative following the recent emphasis by the Children Act 1989 on the need for monitoring and assessment of residential services. The enormity of the task faced by Parker and colleagues is reflected in the fact that it took them four years to reach a point at which they could publish their findings, and throughout their report they described the difficulties they encountered. While recognising that there may be public, service, professional, family and child outcomes, they focused on the last of these possibilities. The measures they developed provide for the collection of factual details, observation and professional judgements. The sum of the information gathered is quantifiable, but yet is able to take account of different personal perspectives.

The essence of this approach is to look at children's development in relation to age across the seven dimensions of health, education, emotional and family difficulties, family and peer relations, self-care skills, identity, and social presentation. The development of these schedules is still at an early stage. However, it is hoped that they will prove valuable both in identifying areas of difficulty for individual children and in identifying possible "causes" by considering outcomes in these areas alongside "inputs" from both the family and the placement. In population terms, they may be able to help identify the value of different institutional policies and practices. Much of the success of the approach will depend on the quality of information on process that the schedules are able to elicit.

It seems that the best way forward is to combine research and practice skills so that we can act in the short-term while still learning more about process at both individual and population levels. Long, elaborate studies may provide valuable long-term results but more immediate results are required if we are to have any meaningful impact on outcomes for children in care in the near future.

Conclusions

Useful lessons have been learned from longitudinal studies of children in care and it is encouraging to see how far research findings have been used to guide policy and practice. Many of the horrific conditions and outcomes of even a generation or so ago have disappeared as service providers have become more conscious of the potential effects of taking children into care. Residential placements too may have their positive side since it seems they can "help with education and offer children stability in an otherwise disrupted life. Certain psychological gains can also be made and useful social skills acquired" (Dartington Social Research Unit, 1992).

Nevertheless, there is no room for complacency and every reason to believe that the short-term and longer-term outcomes of care are not good for many young people. Placements continue to break down, children become disturbed and disrupted, and many young people leave the problems of care for problems of independence. We can only guess at other less tangible outcomes.

As a consequence, we need more research: particularly, we need a greater understanding of what actually happens to children in care. We know something about them at the time of admission, and we know something about them at discharge, but we know very little about what happens in the "black box" in between. Research into practice in residential and foster homes is needed, but it should be research conducted with the aid of the practitioners themselves, practice-based research which can support as it surveys. This convergence of practice and research skills and experience is the essence of the 1990s.

References

Aldgate, J. (1989), 'Foster families and residential care for older children: some interpersonal dynamics', *Children & Society*, vol. 3, 19-36.

Bebbington, A. & Miles, J. (1989), 'The background of children who enter Local Authority care'. *British Journal of Social Work*, vol. 19, no. 5.

Berridge, D. (1985), *Children's Homes*, Basil Blackwell.

Berridge, D. & Cleaver, H. (1987), *Foster Home Breakdown*, Basil Blackwell.

Biehal, N., Clayden, J., Stein, M. & Wade, J. (1992), *Prepared for Living? A survey of young people leaving the care of three local authorities*, National Children's Bureau.

Bonnerjea, L. (1990), *Leaving Care in London*, London Boroughs Children's Regional Planning Committee.

Bowlby, J. (1946), *Forty-four Juvenile Thieves : their characters and home life*, Tindall and Cox.

Bowlby, J. (1951), *Maternal Care and Mental Health*, WHO.

Cliffe, D. & Berridge, D. (1992), *Closing Children's Homes. An end to residential childcare?* National Children's Bureau.

Colton, M.J. (1988), *Dimensions of Substitute Child Care*, Avebury.

Committee of inquiry into the selection, development and management of staff in children's homes (Warner Inquiry) (1992), *Choosing with Care,* HMSO.

Corbillon, M., Assailly, J. & Duyme, M. (1991), 'The effects of placement and the adult of formerly placed children', in W. Hellinckx, E. Broekaert, A. Vanden Berge & M. Colton (eds), *Innovations in Residential Care,* Acco.

Dartington Social Research Unit (1992), *A review of Research into Residential Care for Children.*

Department of Health (1991), *Patterns and Outcomes in Child Placement,* HMSO.

Dinnage, R. & Pringle, M. Kellmer (1967), *Residential Child Care : facts and fallacies*, Longman.

Douglas, J.W.B. (1970), 'Broken families and child behaviour', *Journal of the Royal College of Physicians London*, vol. 4, 203-210.

Garnett, L. (1992), *Leaving Care and After,* National Children's Bureau.

Goldfarb, W. (1943), 'The effects of early institutional care on adolescent personality', *Journal of Experimental Education*, vol. 12, 106-129.

Hazel, N. (1981), *A Bridge to Independence*, Basil Blackwell.

Howe Enquiry (1992), *The Quality of Care: Report of the Residential Staff's Enquiry*, Chaired by Lady Howe, Local Government Board.

Kahan, B. (1979), *Growing Up in Care*, Basil Blackwell.

Kruk, S. & Wolkind, S. (1983), 'A longitudinal study of single mothers and their children', in N. Madge (ed.), *Families At Risk*, Heinemann.

Lasson, I. (1978), *Where's My Mum,* Pepar.

Levy, A. & Kahan, B. (1991), *The Pindown Experience and the Protection of Children*, Staffordshire County Council.

Millham, S., Bullock, R., Hosie, K. & Haak, M. (1986), *Lost in Care*, Gower.

Millham, S. & Little, M. (1991), 'Specialised residential treatment for difficult adolescents. Some recent findings', in W. Hellinckx, E. Broekaert, A. Vanden Berge & M. Colton (eds), *Innovations in Residential Care*, Acco.

Page, R. & Clarke, G. (eds) (1977), *Who Cares? Young People In Care Speak Out*, National Children's Bureau.

Parker, R. (1966), *Decisions in Child Care*, Allen and Unwin.

Parker, R. (1980), *Caring for Separated Children*, Macmillan.

Parker, R., Ward, H., Jackson, S., Aldgate, J. & Wedge, P. (Eds) (1991), *Assessing Outcomes in Child Care,* HMSO.

Quinton, D. & Rutter, M. (1976), 'Early hospital admissions and later disturbances of behaviour: an attempted replication of Douglas' findings', *Developmental Medicine and Child Neurology*, vol. 18, 447-59.

Rowe, J., Hundleby, M. & Garnett, L. (1989), *Child care now,* British Agencies for Adoption and Fostering.

Rutter, M., Quinton, D. & Liddle, C. (1983), 'Parenting in two generations: looking backwards and looking forwards', in N. Madge (ed.), *Families At Risk*, Heinemann.

Salo, R. (1956), *Municipal child welfare work as promoter of social adjustment*, Lassa.

Schaffer, H.R. & Schaffer, E.B. (1968), *Child Care and the Family*, Bell.

Skeels, H.M. (1966), 'Adult status of children with contrasting early life experiences', *Monograph on Social Research in Child Development*, vol. 31, no. 3.

Skeels, H.M. & Dye, H.B. (1939), 'A study of the effects of differential stimulation on mentally retarded children', *Proceedings and Addresses of the American Association on Mental Deficiency*, vol. 44, 114-36.

Smit, M. (1991), 'Leaving residential care. A stressful experience', in W. Hellinckx, E. Broekaert, A. Vanden Berge & M. Colton (eds), *Innovations in Residential Care*, Acco.

Stein, M. & Carey, C. (1986), *Leaving Care*, Blackwell.

Tizard, B. & Hodges, J. (1978), 'The effect of early institutional rearing on the development of eight-year-old children', *Journal of Child Psychology and Psychiatry*, vol. 19, 99-118.

Trasler, G. (1976), *In Place of Parents : a study of foster care,* Routledge & Kegan Paul.

Triseliotis, J. (1980), *New Developments in Foster Care and Adoption*, Routledge & Kegan Paul.

Triseliotis, J. & Russell, J. (1984), *Hard to Place*, Heinemann.

Utting, Sir William (1991), *Children in the Public Care: a review of residential child care*, HMSO.

Van der Waals, P. (1960), 'Former foster children reflect on their childhood', *Children*, vol. 7.

Williams, G. & MacReadie, J. (1992), *Ty Mawr Community Home Inquiry*, Gwent County Council.

Wolkind, S. (1977), 'Women who have been in care', *Journal of Child Psychology and Psychiatry*, vol. 18.

Wolkind, S. (1991), 'The psychological effects of residential care, what we know and what we need to know', in W. Hellinckx, E. Broekaert, A. Vanden Berge & M. Colton (eds), *Innovations in Residential Care*, Acco.

7 Longitudinal studies on the effectiveness of care services for juveniles

Evert SCHOLTE

Introduction

In West European countries, three major trends can be distinguished with regard to care services for juveniles at risk of emotional and behavioural disorders (Colton, Hellinckx, Bullock and van den Bruel, 1991).

First, centres for residential care are increasingly becoming specialised treatment options in a continuum of care. Juvenile welfare policy in most West European countries nowadays is guided by the idea that care services for juveniles "at risk" must be as light, as short term and as appropriate as possible. Also, juveniles' families must be involved to the greatest possible extent. Because of this policy, the care process is increasingly being organised as a continuum. Care begins with relatively light community services, such as preventative action directed at at-risk families, and then moves up towards the more specialised areas of day care services or short term ambulant treatments. It is only when all these "lighter" facilities have proved unsuccessful that the juveniles are sent to residential institutions. As a result, the residential centres will increasingly becoming populated with problematic youngsters. As van der Ploeg and Scholte (1988; 1989) have shown in their population studies of residential care in the Netherlands, in the last decade there was indeed an increasing number of juveniles admitted to residential care showing more severe psychosocial problems than before. This trend indicates that residential care centres in the future will have to improve the diagnostic skills of their staff in order to enable them to correctly assess the exact nature of the problems of the juveniles admitted. In addition, centres will have to equip their professionals with the skills to select and adminster appropriate treatments; and they will have to set up systems to monitor the effectiveness of care.

The second trend with respect to care services is that there is a growing awareness of the complexity of the problems of at-risk juveniles. Nowadays, the behavioural and emotional disorders of children are no longer seen just as part of the child's personality, but are also considered to be related to past, present and future risk factors in the child's social environment: that is, to the family, to school or work, and to the peer group (Scholte, 1992). This implies that the care process must not only be directed at the behavioural and emotional problems initially presented by the child: it must also consider past and present social environmental influences and must account for the dynamics of future development. In other words, treatment strategies designed to help the child cope in the outside world must focus not only on the child but on the whole environment in which the child is supposed to function.

The third trend has to do with an increasing demand for process and outcome evaluation: that is, evaluation of the specific methods used in care and treatment, and the results which these methods achieve. Not only do the authorities providing the funding want to know if their money has been well spent: consumers also want to know about the benefits of care. Nowadays, parents and children even have a legal right to be informed of what is going on in care and how it will affect their lives.

These three tendencies - the growth of services towards a continuum of care, the awareness of the complexity of the problems of at-risk children, and the demand for evaluation - are forcing mental health professionals to approach the care process in a more methodical way than before (Knorth, 1987). This chapter shows how longitudinal studies can be helpful in formulating this more methodical approach.

The need for a methodical approach

The purpose of care services is to resolve problems. When at-risk juveniles are provided with community services, treatment programmes, or foster or residential care, the purpose is clearly to resolve the psychosocial problems of the juveniles in question. If the goal of care is to diminish problems, then its effectiveness can be evaluated in terms of the degree to which the problems have been diminished. It is exactly this concept that can give the caring process the methodical shape so badly needed (Van der Ploeg, 1986; Knorth and Smit, 1990; Scholte, 1991).

Figure 7.1 below illustrates the care process as a rational, goal-oriented activity striving for maximum effectiveness. The figure shows that when a juvenile "at risk" for emotional and behavioural disorders is reported to the care-system, the first thing the social worker has to do is to get a clear picture of the child's problems. This is called the diagnostic intake phase. On the basis of the diagnosis, the social worker formulates the care goals: that is, he identifies the problematic aspects of the child's situation which need to be improved. The second thing the social worker has to do is to find the most appropriate service to cope with the identified problems. The most appropriate service can be defined as that service which offers the maximum chance of diminishing the problems within a reasonable period of time - say, within six months. The third thing the social worker has to do is to provide the appropriate service; and the fourth thing, of course, is to determine whether the care goals were reached. If the goals were reached, the care process can be terminated and the intervention can be said to have been successful. If not, the whole process of defining the problem, identifying the appropriate service, and providing and evaluating the service has to be gone through again.

Figure 7.1 shows the entire care process as a methodical, goal-oriented activity. However, the individual parts of the process can also be viewed as goal-oriented activities, interlinked to form the whole. At intake, for example, the goal is to identify the most appropriate service, based on an analysis of the child's situation and the formulation of care goals. If a major care goal is to improve the child's delinquent behaviour, where on the continuum of care can this best be achieved? At home, or somewhere else on a chain of increasingly more restrictive placements? At the treatment level, there is also a goal: to identify and implement the particular set of treatment strategies which will be most effective in accomplishing the care goals. Will it be best to work with the parents, teaching parenting skills, or to provide the child with one of a number of different therapies, or to address the family system as a whole, or some combination of these?

Often, social workers and other mental health professionals, such as psychologists, have no definitive answers about what type of placement would be best and what treatment strategies would be most effective. They will not be able to provide such answers until, to paraphrase Wilson and Lyman (1983:1084), "they know what kinds of settings with what kinds of interventions produce what kind of developmental outcomes on what kind of problem-children and their families".

It is precisely here that longitudinal outcome research on the development of at-risk children comes into play because this type of study can, in principle, provide this information. To begin with, such studies

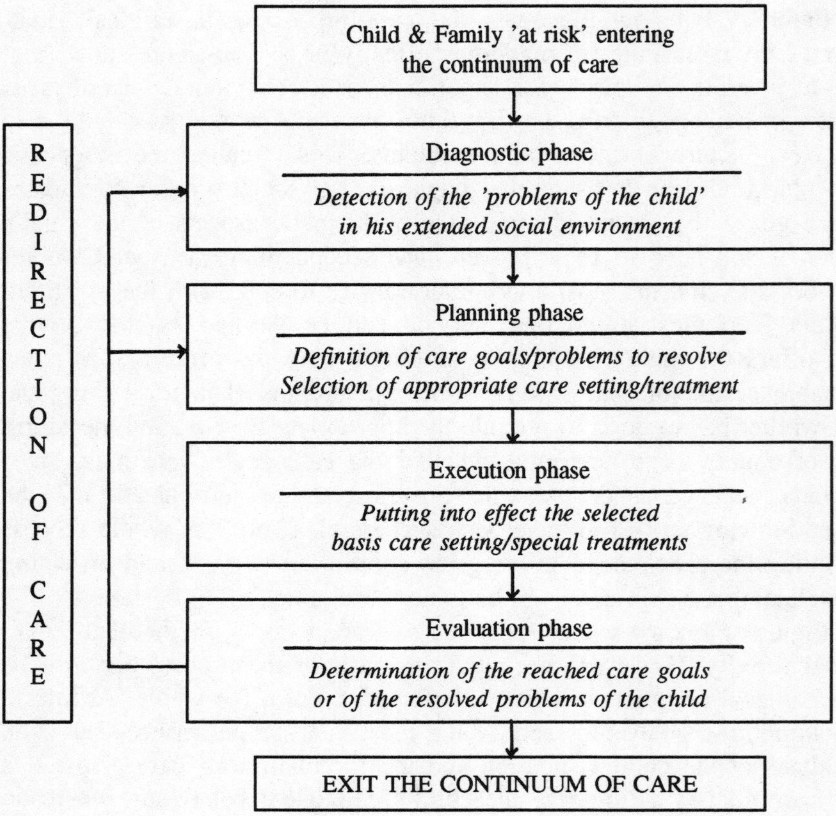

Figure 7.1: Goal effectiveness oriented approach to care

yield data about the psychosocial factors which are related to problematic child development. These factors can be used by intake mental health professionals as a checklist when they want to diagnose *the exact nature of the psychosocial problems of the child at risk.* Further, longitudinal studies which explore the developmental outcomes of at-risk children in various areas of the care system provide information about *which kinds of settings and interventions are most effective with which types of juveniles.* For example, if longitudinal studies show that the proportion of "adjusted" juveniles discharged from setting A was twice as high as the proportion of "adjusted" juvenile of the same type discharged from setting B, then of course juveniles of this type should be sent to the more effective setting A in future. Let us consider these two points in a little more detail.

Defining the problems of the child

The idea of the care process as a rational, goal-oriented set of activities is more easily described in theory then applied in practice. For example, in an analysis of the intake files of three institutions for residential treatment in the Netherlands, van den Bergh (1992) found that basic information about the problem situation for most of the admitted children was lacking. Needless to say, goal-oriented treatment plans existed in hardly any of the admitted cases. According to Colton et al. (1991), the same seems to be true in Flanders and Britain. With respect to Britain, Milham and Little (1991:237) state that it is "the availability of a bed [that] is the overwhelming criterion to allocate children in residential care".

However, it is not really surprising that care workers in practice often fail to shape the care process in a methodical way. The problems of at-risk children are very varied and complex and have numerous, interlinking causes. Problems can vary from depression, anxiety or aggression to a number of anti-social behaviours: such problems may stem from poor parenting skills but may also result from a wrong choice of school, physical or sexual abuse, family poverty, or indeed an emotional or personality disorder in the child. Naturally enough, different professional groups tend to focus on those problems relevant to their own areas of expertise (Milham and Little, 1991), with the result that the problem situation is rarely described in its entirety.

In theory, the confusion arising from the different perspectives of various professionals with respect to defining children's problems can be easily addressed. What is needed is a model summarising all the major empirical risk factors which - according to longitudinal outcome studies on at-risk children - influence problematic behavioural and emotional development. Such a model could then be used by mental health professionals as a standard conceptual framework to make an overall diagnosis of the psychosocial situation of any child encountering difficulties. The socio-ecological model proposed by van der Ploeg and Scholte (1990) and empirically tested and applied by Scholte (1991; 1992a; 1992b) can serve this purpose very well.

The socio-ecological model

The socio-ecological model has been developed on the basis of the findings of longitudinal studies on the development of children at risk of emotional and behavioural disorders, and has also been empirically tested (Scholte, 1991; 1992a; 1992b). In the model, the behaviour problems of children at risk are classified into two main syndromes (Achenbach and Edelbrock, 1986). The first comprises those types of behaviour which are strongly oriented towards the outside world, such as hyperactivity, aggression, and anti-social behaviours like truancy and stealing. Behaviours like these are termed *externalising*. The second sydrome comprises types of behaviour which are strongly oriented towards the self, like loneliness and depression, anxiety and social withdrawal. These types of behavioural problems are termed *internalising*. Both internalising and externalising behaviours are viewed as the outcomes of an interaction between risk factors in the personality of the child and risk factors in the child's environment (Sameroff and Chandler, 1975; Rutter, 1985).

According to Van der Ploeg and Scholte, 1990, and Scholte, 1991; 1992a; 1992b, the principle risk factors in *the primary care environment* are: (1) severe family conflicts; (2) insecure attachment and poor family communication; (3) poor supervision; and (4) non-responsive, non-democratic and permissive child-rearing practices. The main risk factors *at school* include: (1) poor school motivation and academic performance; (2) conflict with teachers; (3) a poor school culture with low standards of achievement; and (4) undemocratic teaching styles. Important risk factors in the *peer group* are: (1) anti-social behaviour in friends, (2) risky behaviour in leisure time, like hanging around the streets, combined with alcohol and drug abuse; and (3) relationship problems with peers.

There are also a number of personality traits of the child which heighten the risk of emotional and behavioural disorders developing. Most of these traits have to do with defects in cognitive-emotional skills (Block and Block, 1980), such as poor ego-control, low self-esteem, external locus of control, and ineffective coping skills.

With regard to the mechanism of development, the model relies on cognitive social learning theory (Bandura, 1987). According to this theory, human behaviour is shaped by processes of negative and positive reinforcement in such a way that positively reinforced behaviour has a greater likelihood of becoming a behaviour pattern than negatively or non-reinforced behaviour. The shaping of behaviour is externally controlled by punishments and rewards from the environment (environmental controls), and internally controlled by the expectations of reward the child has formed in his mind (ego controls). From this perspective, risk factors in the family, at school and in the peer group are seen as external impulses which heighten the risk that the child will develop emotional or behavioural problems. Similarly, risk factors related to the child himself express the internal impulses which heighten the risk that the child's development will turn out to be problematical.

Figure 7.2 summarises the model, including all the relevant risk factors.

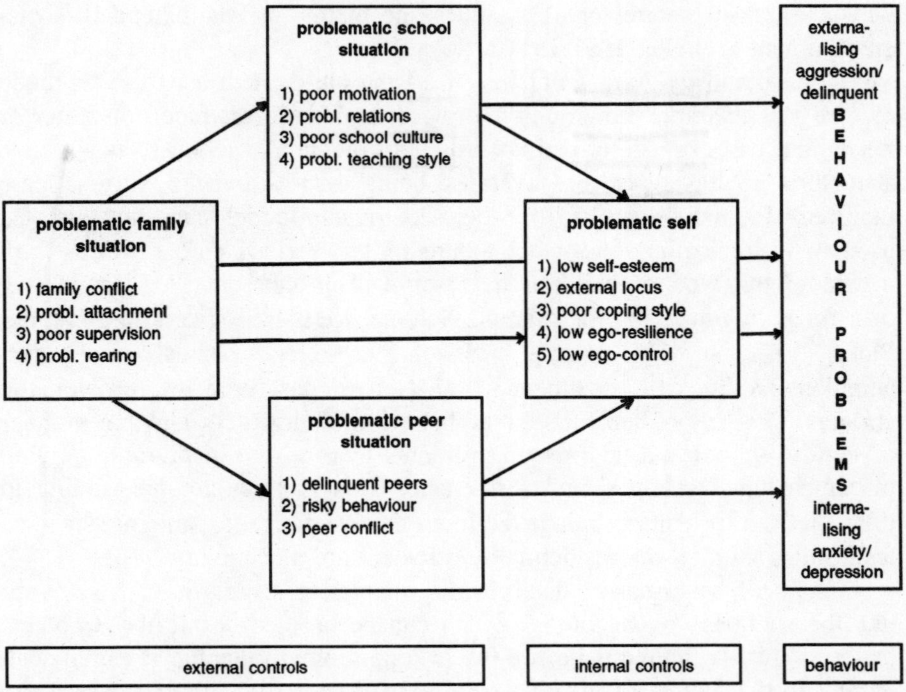

Figure 7.2: The socio-ecological model

The model can be interpreted as follows: When problematic personality traits in the child are accompanied by problematic conditions in the family, in the peer group or at school, there is a heightened risk that the child will develop emotional and behavioural difficulties in the near future.

Frameworks like the socio-ecological model can be used by social workers and other mental health professionals to diagnose the psychosocial problem situation of the child in a systematic and methodical way (Scholte, 1991; 1992b). When a child is being considered for care, the intake mental health professional can use the model to express clear opinions about the child's behaviour patterns and about the personal and environmental risk factors in operation. With respect to the child's behaviour patterns, is the child internalising - showing depression and anxiety - or externalising - showing aggressive or anti-social behaviours? With respect to personal risk factors, is the child deficient in ego-control or possessed of low self-esteem? With respect to environmental factors, are there severe conflicts in the family, does the school curriculum fits the needs of the child, is the child influenced by deviant peers, and so forth. These are all questions which need to be asked anyway, but the model allows them to be asked *systematically*, encouraging the care worker to make explicit in a logical way the exact nature of the child's problems in his extended social environment (Scholte, 1991:151).

Furthermore, if the problems of all the children in a particular mode of care (for example, community services, ambulant treatment, or foster or residential care) are described according to the same model, then we have a picture of the types of juveniles being served by the various care facilities. Frameworks like the socio-ecological model can thus also be used to make explicit the exact nature of the various care facilities with regard to the type of children they serve. This can provide illuminating data for policy makers. For example Scholte, Messing, Nijkerk and van der Ploeg (1991) showed, on the basis of the socio-ecological model, that ambulant facilities for treatment in the Netherlands serve less problematic children in terms of the number of behavioural disorders and the number of family, school and peer-group problems than do the institutions guiding placements in residential and foster care. This is a remarkable finding in light of the fact that ambulant facilities receive far more funding than the institutions guiding the residential and foster care placements.

As will be discussed later in the chapter, a standardised framework like the socio-ecological model which can be used to define the problems of the child is a prerequisite for future longitudinal outcome research with respect to the effects of juvenile care. However, we will first take a closer look at the second issue to be addressed through longitudinal studies: the question of what kind of placement and treatment works best for what kind of at-risk child.

Defining optimum care

As already mentioned, the first step in rationalising the care process is to introduce a standard diagnostic model to enable the problems of the child to be clearly and uniformly defined. The next step is to identify the most appropriate placement and treatment: that is, to decide what kind of care/treatment facilities offer the best chance of resolving the psychosocial problems previously defined. For example, suppose we know that the behavioural problems of a particular child are anti-social in nature and that they are correlated with a low level of self-esteem, severe conflicts in the family and uncertainties with regard to vocational choice. We also know that a substantially greater number of such children reduce their anti-social behaviour when they are placed in a structured residential setting with an institutional educational-vocational programme and a parent-guidance facility than when they are placed in an unstructured setting with an outside educational programme and without parental guidance. It would obviously be sensible for an intake mental health professional to place this particular child and all children with the same problem syndrome in the structured setting since, in this care setting, there is a maximum chance that the child's problems will diminish.

However, such a sensible solution will not be possible if we do not know what kind of care and/or treatment situations can best resolve what kind of problem situations experienced by at-risk children. There are a number of longitudinal research studies which have explored the effects of different placements and treatment interventions on the development of children at risk. It is worth taking a closer look at the findings of these studies.

Number of children improved

The first question some researchers have tried to answer is how many children show adaptive development after they have left the juvenile care system. For example, in his summary of the early reviews of Beskind (1968), Curry (1991) notes that about 50 per cent of the adolescents treated in psychiatric hospitals were reported as having improved at discharge and follow-up. Hartman, Glaser, Greenblatt, Solomon and Levinson (1968) found that 44 per cent of a sample of 55 adolescents who had been treated in adult inpatient units at a mental health centre received a diagnosis of schizophrenia at discharge. At follow-up, ten years later, only 42 per cent were rated as having good or fair adjustment. Gosset, Lewis and Barnhart (1983) reported on 68 boys and 52 girls, 12-19 years old, who had been in a private residential facility. In an eight-year follow-up, they rated the overall outcome as fair to good for 71 per cent of the sample. The Bellefaire study followed 50 boys who had been in residential treatment for at least six months (Allerhand, Weber and Haig, 1966). The study's major findings were that most boys' adaptation improved during the residential treatment, and 71 per cent were functioning adequately at a short term follow-up. However, adaptive functioning at long term follow-up was strongly related to the stress level of the post-discharge environment. A study by Lewis, Lewis, Shanok, Klatskin and Osborne (1980) on the development of 51 boys and girls who were treated in residential centres with milieu therapy, intensive psychotherapy, special education, and parent therapy found favourable outcomes in only 33 per cent of the cases. All these authors note that most of the subjects improved during treatment, but that this improvement was not related to improvement during follow-up. In the Netherlands, Smit (1992) reviewed the findings of 12 longitudinal outcome studies in the area of residential care and treatment with regard to various dimensions of psychosocial functioning (for example, emotional and behavioural development, personal relationships, adaptation to society) and concludes that "somewhere between half and 90 per cent of the juveniles" have adapted satisfactorily, according to the standards used by the various researchers.

When we look at the above findings, we must conclude that our knowledge about the number of children improving after juvenile residential care, is only very rough and hardly informative. The results range from a very low positive outcome (33 per cent) - implying that hardly anyone benefitted from the care - up to a very high positive outcome (90 per cent) - implying that practically everyone benefitted very much. It is unfortunately not possible to be more specific than this about outcome figures on the basis of the available research evidence. The main reason for this is that most of the programmes reviewed to date are not comparable. They are all directed at different populations in different settings at different periods of time, with no specific information about the populations served or the treatments given. In addition, a variety of research designs have been employed, using different follow-up periods and varying criteria for measuring success.

Limitations in research design are the major problem in outcome research with respect to juvenile care (Tramontana, 1980; Quay, 1986; Quay and Werry, 1987; Kazdin, 1987; 1988; Pfeiffer, 1989; Pfeiffer and Strzelecki, 1990). According to Wilson and Lyman (1983; 1985) "the investigation of residential care has not been such that there is anything approaching a science or a clear model of what works". Curry (1991) notes that the recurring problems are: sketchy and non-validated data on diagnostic criteria about the problems of the child; lack of control groups; ample use of pretest-posttest designs; inadequate descriptions of the care settings, the active treatment ingredients and the integrity of the applied treatment; sparse outcome data; unclear and non-validated outcome measures to define the developmental success, adjustment or adaptation of the child; and a non-standardised approach to collecting data. These shortcomings prohibit firm conclusions about what types of settings and interventions work with what types of children at risk.

However, doubts about the results of longitudinal research programs in juvenile care does not mean that we know nothing at all, and it is worth exploring the points on which there seems to be some agreement. To limit the scope of the subject, we will focus our attention mainly upon the areas of in- and outpatient residential treatment and care.

The narrative and meta-analytic approaches

The fact that the various longitudinal studies all use a different kind of methodology to establish treatment effects seems to call for a qualitative review describing the various studies in their own right. However, as Smith, Glass and Miller (1980) have pointed out, reviewing studies in a qualitative or "narrative" way leads to the striking phenomenon that varied conclusions can be drawn about the same literature. When the objective is to generalise the findings of various research programmes studying the same subjects but using different outcome measures and methodologies, a meta-analytic approach is more suitable than a narrative approach. The key of meta-analysis is to compute effect-sizes, where the term *effect size* refers to statistics which portray the strength of association between variables. Effect size statistics reflect the strength of association found in any study, no matter what outcome measure is used, in terms that are comparable across studies. Thus, they enable us to compare the effects of different treatment interventions across studies using different types of outcome measures. Effect size can be calculated as the difference between the means of an experimental group and a control group, divided by the standard deviation of the control group: or sometimes the standard deviation used in the calculation is the pooled standard deviation of the two groups combined or an estimate of the standard deviation of the population to which the study is attempting to generalise. This produces a metric interval scale, to be used in a parametric statistical analysis (Kazdin, 1988:33). Effect-size can also simply be coded as yes or no, leading to a nominal effect measure, to be used in non-parametric statistical analysis (Pfeiffer, 1990).

The existing meta-analyses, however, do not cover the whole area of juvenile residential care. Studies to date primarily focus upon the areas of: 1) residential psychiatric care (Pfeiffer and Strzelecki, 1991); 2) residential and institutional treatment of delinquency (Garret, 1985; Davidson, Redner, Amdur and Mitchell, 1990); and 3) psychotherapy with children and adolescents (Casey and Berman, 1985). As Wilson and Lyman (1983) have shown, residential treatment centres are quite distinct in several dimensions from inpatient psychiatric hospitals and from institutions treating adjudicated delinquents[1]. However, outcome studies in residential care are mostly only reviewed in a narrative way. Because of their superior external validity, we will rely primarily upon the findings of the meta-analytic reviews. When relevant, however, we will also quote the findings of some of the narrative studies.

Pfeiffer and Strzelecki (1991) meta-analysed 34 outcome studies on children and adolescents treated in residential psychiatric facilities. The studies included six investigations of children aged between 3 and 12 years, 17 investigations of adolescents aged 12 to 21 years, and 11 combined studies with an age range of 3 to 21 years. Eleven studies were designed as post-discharge (follow-up) studies, whereas the remaining 11 studies evaluated outcome status at the time of discharge. Because only a few studies reported both means and standard deviations on the outcome variables, an effect measure was rated by independent observers with an inter-rater agreement of .91, using a code of one for a positive effect, a code of zero for a non-significant effect and a code of minus one for a negative effect (vote counting method). Effect size was corrected for the size of the sample, giving more weight to the studies with larger samples. The observers explored the effect size of ten predictor variables: intelligence, organicity, psychiatric diagnosis, symptom pattern, age at admission, sex, family functioning/involvement, treatment, length of stay, and aftercare/post-discharge environment. Table 7.1 shows the results of their analysis.

When we look at the outcome studies on children and adolescents in residential psychiatric care, there is evidence for a weak relationship between outcome and gender of the child, and between outcome and age of admission. The relationship between outcome and intelligence (IQ) seems to be moderately strong, with a higher IQ implying a better chance that the child will leave with a positive status. The relationship between length of stay and outcome is also moderately strong, implying that longer hospitalisation is associated with more positive development. This may be due to the fact that treatment goals can be more fully realised over a longer treatment duration.

Rather highly predictive for positive outcome is the absence of a diagnosis of severe psychiatric disorder at the time of admission. The absence of bizarre, anti-social and primitive symptoms is also associated with a more positive outcome, as is less severe problems in the sphere of organicity (for example, malfunctioning of the central nervous system). Family functioning and family involvement in treatment is also rather strongly related to positive development, supporting the well-known fact that the degree of marital conflict and the frequency of both parent-child conflict and separations during early childhood is highly related to maladjusted child development (Rutter and Giller, 1983). However, the factor most predictive for positive post-discharge status is whether children do indeed receive or complete their planned treatment, and whether they receive adequate after-care. This suggests that both treatment and an adequate after-care environment (for example, outpatient therapy, the availability of a foster home, or a supportive post-discharge environment with a low level of stress (Koret, 1980)), contribute greatly to a positive outcome in residential psychiatric care[2].

Table 7.1: Outcome predictors of children and adolescents in residential psychiatric treatment* (N=34)

Variable	Weighted Predictive Value	Number of Studies
Intelligence	0.30	7
Organicity	-0.80	4
Diagnosis	-0.67	10
Symptom pattern	-0.75	13
Age of admission	0.19	12
Sex	0.15	6
Family functioning/involvement	0.70	9
Treatment	1.00	4
Length of stay	0.48	7
Aftercare/postdischarge environment	1.00	4

* 1975-1988.

From: Pfeifer, S.I. and S.C. Strezelecki (1990), 'Inpatient Psychiatric Treatment of Children and Adolescents: A review of Outcome Studies', *Journal of the American Academic Child and Adolescent Psychiatry*, Vol.29, no. 6, 850.

Effects of residential treatment on anti-social behaviour

More is known about the effects of residential and institutional treatment on delinquent juveniles than about the effects of residential psychiatric care. Here, two meta-analytic studies are available.

The first analysis was performed by Garret (1985) who analysed 111 studies subsequent to 1960 in order to assess the amount of change associated with various treatments of adjudicated delinquents. The majority of the studies (52 per cent) employed research designs which are generally considered to be good experimental designs (for example, random, matched, pretest equivalency assignment procedures), while the other studies (48 per cent) had a less rigorous design (non-random, pretest-posttest/no control). The subjects in the studies had an average age of 15.8 years, and the sample comprised 85 studies on males, 16 on females and

12 on both males and females. The subjects were white Caucasians in 8 studies, from minority groups in 11 and of mixed ethnic origin in 57. About 20 per cent of the treatments took place in a community residential setting, so most treatment was in an institutional residential setting.

Effect sizes were calculated as the mean posttest difference between the experimental and the control conditions divided by the standard deviation of both. Effect sizes were calculated on recidivism, institutional adjustment, psychological adjustment, community adjustment, academic improvement, vocational adjustment and overall adjustment. The inter-coder agreement was .95. The treatments analysed were psychodynamic therapy, behavioural therapy and basic life skills training. Table 7.2 summarises the findings of this meta-analysis.

Table 7.2: Effect-outcome by treatment category

Type of Adjustment	Average Treatment	Psychodynamic Treatment	Behavioural Treatment	Life Skills Treatment
Average	.37	.17	.63	.31
Recidivism	.13	-.01	.18	.28
Institutional	.41	.25	.63	-.08
Psychological	.52	.43	.72	.42
Community	.63	.62	.63	.38
Academic	.78	.22	1.19	.36
Vocational	.00	.08	-.23	-.09

From: Garret, C.J. (1985), 'Effects of Residential Treatment on Adjudicated Delinquents: a Meta Analysis', *Journal of Research in Crime and Delinquency*, Vol. 22, no. 4, 229.

As the first column shows, the mere fact that delinquent youths are being treated by any one of the three types of treatments already produces a positive average adjustment outcome effect of .37. Looking at the separate adjustment types, we see that adjustment is absent or rather low with regard to vocational performance and recidivism, is substantial with regard to institutional and psychological adjustment, and is high with regard to academic and community adjustment. Our first conclusion must therefore be that adjudicated delinquents in institutions who receive treatment are better off then their counterparts who do not receive treatment, whatever the nature of this treatment.

Table 7.2 also tells us what kind of therapies produce what effect sizes. For children in institutional or residential care coping with the externalising problem behaviour syndrome of delinquency, a psychodynamic approach is clearly less beneficial. This kind of therapy produces only an average adjustment effect size of .17, although the effects are quite substantial for community adjustment (ES=.62), and moderate for psychological growth (ES=.43).

Table 7.2 clearly shows that behavioural therapy is most effective, producing an average effect size of .63, with high effect rankings on institutional adjustment (ES=.62), community (ES=.63) and psychological adjustment (ES=.72), and a very high ranking on academic performance (ES=1.19). The information that behavioural therapy works best with anti-social children is still rather general because various kinds of therapies and techniques fall into this category. However, the Garret meta-analysis also provides information about what kinds of specific therapies produce what kinds of effects. These are summarised in Table 7.3.

With respect to psychodynamic therapy, Table 7.3 shows that the individual and group-centred approaches produce hardly any meaningful overall effects. However, the group-centred approach produces a few specific effects, particularly improvement in adjustment to the community (ES=1.02) and enhancement of academic performance (ES=.89). Furthermore, the family-centred psychodynamic approach produces rather substantial effects (ES=.81), especially on institutional (ES=.75), community (ES=.83) and psychological adjustment (ES=2.07). This confirms the beneficial power of family involvement in the treatment of juveniles in residential care, also found in the study presented previously.

In the area of behavioural therapy, the techniques of contingency management and behaviour contracting produce slightly better overall results (ES=.86) then the cognitive behavioural techniques (ES=.58). More specifically, the cognitive techniques produce optimum results in the area of academic performance (ES=1.77), while contingency management techniques with behaviour contracting produce optimum results with regard to psychological (ES=1.14) and institutional adjustment (ES=1.19), as well as with regard to academic performance (ES=1.25). Guided group interaction/positive peer influence (ES=.24) and milieu therapy (ES=.31) produce rather moderate overall effects. However, in the behavioural area, guided group interaction in a positive peer culture of mixed pro-social and anti-social youths can contribute substantially to the psychological adjustment of the anti-social (delinquent) youths.

Table 7.3: Treatment by average and specific outcome

Specific Type of Treatment	Overall Effect	Effects on the various areas of adjustment Institutional	Psychological	Community	Academic
Psychodynamic	.17				
1 Individual	.14	.20	.20	-.09	-.21
2 Group-centred	.17	.32	.48	1.02	.89
3 Family-centred	.81	.75	2.07	.83	-.-
Behavioural	.63				
4 Contingency	.86	1.19	1.14	.63	1.25
5 Cognitive	.58	.55	.62	-.-	1.77
6 Guided Group	.24	.37	1.04	-.-	.28
Life Skills	.31				
7 Drugs&Alcohol	.28	.22	-.-	.67	-.-
8 Academic	.39	-.13	.51	-.-	.42
9 Vocational	.05	-.-	.27	-.13	.16
10 Outward Bound	.38	.49	.05	-.-	-.-

From: Garret, C.J. (1985), 'Effects of Residential Treatment on Adjudicated Delinquents: a Meta Analysis', *Journal of Research in Crime and Delinquency*, Vol. 22, no. 4, 301.

In the area of life skills interventions, we only see very moderate results. Treatment for alcohol and drug abuse seems to improve adjustment to society. Academic training leads to an improvement in psychological adjustment, and - not really surprisingly - to a better academic performance. Outward bound can result in a better institutional adjustment of anti-social youths.

A second meta-analysis in the field of delinquency was performed by Davidson et al. (1990). In this review, 91 studies were analysed, using means and standard deviations as an effect size, as well as the vote counting method described above by Pfeiffer and Strzelecki (1991). The overall effectiveness rating used was a combination of recidivism, self-reported delinquency, programme, vocational, academic and other social behaviour, as well as school/work attendance and the self concept of the juveniles.

The analysis group comprised institutional treatments for delinquent juveniles (34 per cent), as well as community residential (14 per cent) and community non-residential settings (47 per cent). The average percentage of males was 79 and the average age was 14.9 years. Further, 77 per cent of the studies in the analysis group were on adjudicated delinquent youths. The mean duration of treatment was 22.89 weeks. Table 7.4 gives the results of the various treatment approaches on the overall effectiveness rating of this meta-analysis.

Table 7.4: Treatment by overall effect/outcome

Type of treatment	Rated Positive Adjustment	Number of studies
Behavioural therapy	73%	30
Educational-Vocational	57%	7
Individual therapy	40%	5
Group psychotherapy	66%	15
Case work/Probation	33%	9
Other nonspecific	52%	25

From: Davidson, W.S., R. Redner, R.L. Amdur and C.M. Mitchell (1990), *Alternative Treatments for Troubled Youth*, New-York, Plenum Press, p. 31.

As Table 7.4 shows, the results of this second meta-analysis on the treatment of anti-social juveniles also demonstrate the superiority of the behavioural approach, showing positive outcome results in 73 per cent of the studies reviewed. Group psychotherapy and educational-vocational training also show positive results in quite a number of studies, indicating that they can be promising approaches in the treatment of delinquent youths.

Individual psychodynamic therapy and case-work/probation, however, are far less convincing, with only 40 and 33 per cent of studies respectively showing positive treatment effects. On the basis of these figures, they can hardly be considered as serious treatment approaches for juveniles with anti-social, delinquent behaviour syndrome, at least with regard to the treatment of the anti-social behaviour itself. However, the figure for these two approaches may be misrepresented by the fact that they were calculated on the basis of relatively few studies.

Davidson et al. (1990) also analysed the influence of other moderators than treatment on the effect size, such as gender, age and setting. They conclude that there are no effect differences between boys and girls, nor between different age groups, nor between the various care settings analysed (institutional, community non-residential and community other). The duration of the treatment did not show any impact on the size of the effect either. However, the intensity of the treatment was negatively related with rated effectiveness, indicating that the less voluntary and more stressful treatments were associated with less positive results.

Psychotherapy with children and adolescents

Casey and Berman (1985) completed a meta-analysis of research in child psychotherapy, mainly in non-residential settings. Their review included 75 studies, covering a wide range of traditional therapies (for example, psychodynamic, client-centred) and behavioural therapies (for example, behaviour therapy, cognitive-behavioural treatments). The studies involved children with an age range of 3 to 15, and an average age of about 8.9 years, 60 per cent of whom were boys. The mean duration of treatment was 9.5 weeks. The clinical problems investigated were of a varying nature. About 40 per cent of the studies dealt with aggressive and withdrawn behaviours, 13 per cent investigated the hyperactive or impulsive behaviour syndrome, and 12 per cent were directed at phobias. For the analysis, effect sizes were constructed by calculating standardised mean differences between experimental and control conditions. Table 7.5 presents the results of the Casey and Berman meta-analysis.

Table 7.5 shows that all types of therapies grouped together have a positive effect size (ES) of .71 standard deviation above the non-treatment condition. Next, behavioural therapies (ES=.91) appear to have substantially larger effects than non-behavioural therapies (ES=.40). With respect to behavioural therapy, the techniques which tackle problem behaviour directly (for example, contingency management, behaviour contracting) show slightly better results then the techniques which tackle problem behaviours more indirectly (for example, cognitive behavioural training). In the non-behavioural area, the client-centred techniques are shown to be more effective than the psychodynamic-oriented techniques.

Casey and Berman also analysed the influence of moderators, such as sex, type of problem treated and type of therapy setting. Here, the findings were as follows: therapies with female subjects produced slightly better results than therapies with male subjects for both the behavioural and non-behavioural approaches. Effect sizes varied substantially for the type of problems treated. Children with problems related to fear, anxiety, impulsive and hyperactive behaviour, phobia, somatic complaints and cognitive skills deficits seem to benefit more from treatment than children with problems in the area of social adjustment.

Table 7.5: Effects of psychotherapy with children

Treatment	Number of studies	Effect Size Mean	Effect Size SD
All therapies	64	0.71*	0.73
Behavioural therapies	37	0.91*	0.77
Behavioural	26	0.96*	0.79
Cognitive behavioural	14	0.81*	0.84
Nonbehavioural therapies	29	0.40*	0.37
Client-centred	20	0.49*	0.65
Dynamic	5	0.21	0.22

* The mean effect size differs reliably from zero ($p<.05$).

From: Casey, R.J. and Berman, J.S. (1985), 'The outcome of psychotherapy with children', *Psychological Bulletin*, 98, 388-400.

However, both this finding, and the finding of the greater effectiveness of the behavioural approaches, could be due to the fact that relatively few of the non-behavioural studies reviewed were addressing the former types of problems. The "overflow" of behavioural studies reviewed in the meta-analysis all reported large effect sizes for the treatment of fear, anxiety, hyperactivity, phobia and deficits in cognitive skills. Although this does not prove that the non-behavioural approaches are totally ineffective, the mere fact that behavioural approaches are applied so often with great success does suggest that they can be more effectively used with externalising behavioural disorders than the psychodynamic approaches.

With regard to type of therapy setting, there were no significant differences in effect size between individual therapy, group therapy and play therapy. Nor did the effect sizes of the schoolchildren treated, of the inpatient and outpatient children, and of the children enrolled in special projects differ reliably. This suggests that choices amongst the features in treatment setting could be made on criteria other than effectiveness, such as the personal preference and expertise of the therapist, or the specific professional resources a residential institute has at its disposal.

As Casey and Berman state, the findings do not permit firm conclusions about what form of treatment is more effective for what kind of specific problem. However, their findings emphasise the major conclusions of the meta-studies presented before. When we are dealing with children at risk for emotional and behavioural disorders, treatment seems to be better than no treatment, regardless of whether the children are in an inpatient or an outpatient setting. Furthermore, treatment differences tend to favour behavioural rather than non-behavioural techniques, at least when we have to deal with behavioural problems of the externalising syndrome type.

The findings of the three meta-analytic reviews presented above echo, to a large extent, the major findings of some of the more qualitative, narrative reviews. For example, Gossett, Lewis and Barnhart (1983) found that less severe psychopathology at admission (or a less severe DSMIII-admission diagnosis), a reactive onset of disturbance, an average to above average intelligence, an internal locus of control and a length of stay greater than three months were consistently indicative of a more favourable outcome at follow-up. Participation during hospitalisation in an adolescent treatment programme which included an educational component, completion of the goals of hospitalisation and continuing therapy after discharge also contributed to a more favourable status at follow-up. Furthermore, the results suggested that supportive peer relationships during hospitalisation, and staff who were supportive of family relationships both during hospitalisation and during discharge, were important for a successful course of treatment.

The importance of a stress-buffering environment during hospitalisation, as well as during the post-discharge period, is also emphasised by the older outcome studies in residential care. In the Children's Village study, it was noted that participation by child and parents (attendance at school during treatment, child or staff contacts with parents during treatment) were associated with adaptation after discharge (Tayler and Alpert, 1973). In the Bellefaire study it was found that follow-up status was not directly related to adaptation within the residential care program, but to the stress level of the post-discharge environment (Allerhand, Weber and Haug, 1966). Lewis, Lewis, Shanok, Klatskin and Osborne (1980) note that subjects with a favourable outcome at follow-up were somewhat younger at admission, with less psychotic symptomatology and less parental psychopathology. These authors also noted that most subjects improved during treatment, but that adjustment at follow-up was not related to improvement during treatment.

Several reviewers (for example, Durkin and Durkin, 1975; Quay, 1979; Wilson and Lyman, 1983; Whittaker and Pecora, 1984; Curry, 1991) have derived implications from these findings for the shaping of the process of residential care, namely:

1) the need to work with the child and his family for an extensive period of time, both during treatment and after care;
2) the need to include in treatment programmes as many as possible opportunities for learning which can be generalised to the outside world; and
3) the need for adequate after-care treatment, or at least guidance.

These "directives" reflect what seems to be a major issue in modern residential care, namely that admission to residential care represents a disruptive event within the usual adaptive process between the child and his environment. Admission to residential care may well be justified when the adaptive process has been impaired, and valuable development may take place in the residential centre. However, in order for the placement to work out well, residential care must equip the child with the skills to adapt optimally to his future environment. This implies in the first place that the treatment and care setting should be the least restrictive possible relative to the child's environment, and that the child's primary environment should be a major treatment concern, not only during admission, but also before admission (so that admission can possibly be prevented) and after discharge (so that re-admission can possibly be prevented). Second, residential treatment must provide a maximum amount of the type of learning that can be generalised to the environment outside the programme. It should focus, for example, on adaptive skills for relating to peers, parents and authorities, and for adaptive functioning at school and at work. Programmes should therefore expose youngsters to realistic community demands during treatment. Finally, society must offer the "rehabilitated" child opportunities to adapt optimally to society: in other words, society must offer discharged children chances to engage in meaningful school, work and leisuretime activities.

Conclusions

On the basis of the materials presented above, we can reach certain conclusions.

The first point to note is that the various longitudinal outcome studies produce a variety of positive outcome figures. The number of juveniles showing a positive outcome at discharge or at follow-up varies from only a few (33 per cent adapted) to nearly all (90 per cent adapted). This variation is mainly due to the conceptual differences in the various studies and the different methodologies used. For example, if one study defines adaptive behavioural development as no police record during a certain period, and another study defines it as no reported delinquent acts during the same period, than the second study will find many more poorly adapted youngsters than the first study, with repect to the same population. The difference will be due to the fact that the self-report method produces a more complete picture of delinquency than the method of inspecting police records (Hindelang, Hirschi and Weis, 1981).

The major conceptual and methodological problems cited in the reviews of longitudinal outcome studies in residential care were:

1) no or inadequate descriptions of diagnostic criteria to define the psychosocial problems of the admitted children;
2) no or inadequate descriptions of the conditions of the basic care settings;
3) no or inadequate descriptions of the specific ingredients of the special treatment provided;
4) no or inadequate descriptions of the integrity of the basic care conditions and of the applied special treatment;
5) use of different measures for developmental outcome or success;
6) lack of validated research instruments and standardised procedures to measure the variables in these five areas;
7) lack of rigorous research design (research designs with an adequate internal validity), for example, ample use of pretest-posttest designs, and ample use of treatment-alternative treatment-control contrasts.

It is hardly necessary to point out that future longitudinal research, which aims to study the impact of residential juvenile care on the development of juveniles "at risk" of emotional and behavioural disorders, must resolve these issues first before it can further contribute to the scientific debate on the effectiveness of residential juvenile treatment and care.

The second point to note is that, despite the methodological shortcomings cited above, some evidence about what works and what does not has in fact been obtained. The meta-analytic approach can overcome at least the problem of having to deal with different outcome measures, and when we consider results from this perspective, we can be fairly certain about the following points:

1) treating problem children is more effective than not treating them, no matter what the nature of the child's problems and the care/treatment given;
2) continuing the care/treatment towards the desired end contributes more to a healthy behavioural, emotional and societal adjustment than does a premature ending of the care/treatment process (for example, not reaching the care/treatment goals, being expelled from the institution, or running away);
3) involving and treating family-members contributes to a more favourable outcome for the child; and
4) creating an adequate after-care environment (for example, a half-way home, outpatient therapy) is a prerequisite if we want the child to generalise his achieved developmental adjustments to the outside world after the care.

However, when we consider the findings from the perspective of our original question - "What works with what kind of problem children?" - than we must conclude that there is still too little empirical evidence to answer this question in any detail. In the first place, there is hardly any evidence from outcome research with regard to what conditions of basic care (for example, restrictive versus non-restrictive primary group environments) produce what kind of effects on the development of what kind of at-risk children. Secondly, there is only limited specific knowledge about what kind of special treatment works best with what kind of problem children. Although we know that the behavioural approaches in general are much more effective than the psychodynamic approaches, the specific evidence in this area comes mainly from the treatment of children demonstrating externalising problem behaviour, in particular delinquency.

With respect to the treatment of internalising problem behaviour (for example, depression, anxiety and social withdrawal), and with respect to the mixed syndrome of both internalising and externalising problem behaviour, there are only a few outcome studies available. The evidence here seems to indicate that behavioural and psychodynamic approaches are equally effective.

With regard to the issue of involving the family in the treatment of juveniles in residential care, there is meta-analytic evidence that a therapeutic involvement of the family can substantially improve the child's adjustment within the residential centre, as well as in the outside world. Behaviour structuring approaches such as parent management training (Patterson, 1982) and functional family therapy (Kazdin, 1988) seem to produce rather satisfactory results. However, here too, most of the evidence is limited to the treatment of families with anti-social youths.

Directives for future research

The most striking fact to emerge from our discussion is that our knowledge of what works and what does not work in juvenile care is very limited. We know only a few things for sure, and the few things we do know are too general in nature to serve the purpose of adequate directives on what kind of basic care and/or what kind of specific treatment can best be given to what kind of problem children. This conclusion is not only true for the residential care sector, but will also hold for all the other sectors in the continuum of care, since we simply do not know as yet what types of community services, specific ambulant treatments, day-care facilities, foster-family placement situations or residential care settings produce optimum developmental outcomes with what kind of at-risk children.

This lack of knowledge is partly due to the fact that the longitudinal studies looking at the development of at-risk children in the various sectors of the juvenile care system in the past were not explicitly designed to systematically answer the question of "what works best with what kind of juvenile". As the implementation of the continuum of care progresses, the need for a clear answer to this question will grow.

In the first place, there will be a need for clear answers at the organisational level of the care continuum. Here, mental health professionals will increasingly become case managers, responsible for planning the care process. In order to do this effectively, they will need valid procedures to assess the problems of the child and directives about what works best with what kind of problem children. They will also need valid procedures to monitor the progress of care since, from the perspective of goal-effectiveness, the care process will need to be redirected when care goals are not met within the specified timeframe.

Second, a need for clear answers arises at the level where the care and treatment is actually provided. Here too, there will be an increased need for valid diagnosis of problems and for accurate selection of appropriate basic care and additional special treatments. Accurate monitoring of the progress of care will also be needed since care providers will increasingly be required to account for the progress of care to others: for example, to case managers and funding bodies.

As a result of these demands, more longitudinal outcome research on at-risk children in juvenile care is needed. With respect to the continuum of care, future longitudinal studies need to find out more about what kind of ambulant, day-care, foster and residential services produce what kind of developmental outcomes with what kind of at-risk children. At the level of the care itself, future studies must become specific about what conditions produce what kind of developmental effects.

Shaping these future programmes on longitudinal outcome research requires the elimination of the major shortcomings which have thus far beleagured most research programs in juvenile care. In other words, future research studies must preferably be designed according to rigorous (internally valid) research standards. This implies that valid pre, intermediate, post and follow-up measurements must be made with regard to the development of the children, preferably at standardised intervals, and that, during the care process, valid measurements must be made to ensure the integrity of the care provided. At the same time, an identical set of measurements must be made with comparable children who are not experiencing care or who are experiencing alternative care conditions. Comparing the developmental outcomes of children in various care conditions can, in theory, answer the question of what works, what does not work, and what works better with what kinds of problem children in juvenile care. However, internally valid research designs alone are not enough to resolve the problem of geographically scattered research findings in juvenile care. If we wish to compare research findings across care settings within nations, or across care settings in different nations, research studies must also be externally valid. Therefore, future longitudinal research programmes must at least use a uniform conceptual model to adequately describe the psychosocial problem situation of at-risk children. In addition, they must use a uniform conceptual model to describe the nature and integrity of the care provided in the primary group (for example, restrictive versus non-restrictive), as well as a uniform model to describe the ingredients and integrity of the applied special treatments (for example, behavioural therapy, social skills training, educational-vocational training, psychodynamic therapy). On the basis of these uniform models, a set of valid and reliable research instruments must be designed so that future research programmes can measure all these various factors in a standardised way.

With regard to the first conceptual issue - the need for a conceptual model to describe the problems of at-risk children in a uniform way - the socio-ecological model can provide a guide. This model not only identifies the core dimensions of problem behaviour (for example, aggression, hyperactivity and anti-social behaviour) and the main facets of problematic emotional functioning (for example, depression, anger, social withdrawal) but also relates these internalising and externalising problems affecting at-risk children both to the personality development of the child (ego-control, self-esteem, locus of control and coping style), and to the relevant risk factors in the social environment (risk conditions in the family, at school/work and in the peer group/leisure time). The model can thus be used to screen the whole complex psychosocial situation of a child in order to identify the specific elements which contribute to risk (Scholte, 1991). Comparing the "risk-profiles" of children in care at the time of admission, during the care process, at discharge and at follow-up can give a clear overall view of the childrens' psychosocial development. As we have shown in our study on early interventions with children at risk of delinquency, this overall picture can easily be used to analyse the various effects of intervention programmes (Scholte, 1992a).

With regard to the second conceptual issue, - the need for a uniform model to identify the relevant dimensions of basic care and to make explicit the ingredients and integrity of the treatments - more work is needed because this area is still very much in the process of development. With regard to the conceptualisation of basic care, the proposals of Mesman Schultz (1986) and the findings of Van der Ploeg and Scholte

(1988; 1989; 1991) on the methods of basic care in residential treatment centres in the Netherlands are useful as a starting point. With respect to the conceptualisation of specific treatment, the reviews of Kazdin (1987; 1988), Casey and Berman (1985) and Hoghughi (1988) are helpful.

Finally, something must be said about the end-product of future studies. As the continuum of care becomes more and more a reality, the demand for an approach to the care process which is goal-oriented and effectiveness-oriented will also increase. This demand can be translated as a request from mental health practitioners to provide them with both valid, reliable measuring instruments to accurately diagnose the problems of children at risk, and with a valid, reliable way to monitor the progress of care. For the social scientist, the implication is that it is not enough to report on what works and what does not in juvenile care: the research findings must also be translated into a set of applicable tools, which can be used to structure the processes of care according to the principles of goal-effectiveness. Because these tools will have to be used by mental health practitioners, future longitudinal research in juvenile care can best be conducted in close co-operation with these professionals. In other words, research will be most effective when it is aimed directly at "the caring heart" of the care process itself.

Notes

1. Residential centres can be characterised by a heterogeneity of children's presenting problems and length of stay, and have a varying physical location and census size. They are less disease-, diagnosis- and treatment-oriented, and are less regimented and restrictive than inpatient or psychiatric hospitals, but are more restrictive than foster homes and group homes.
2. This finding, however, must be interpreted with care, because of the relatively low number of studies used in the meta-analysis to reach this conclusion (N=4) (Blotsky and Dimperio, 1991).

References

Allerhand, M., Weber, R. & Haug, M. (1966), *Adaption and Adaptability*, New York, Child Welfare League.

Bandura, A. (1987), *Social Foundations of Thought and Action*, Prentice Hall, Englewood Cliffs.

Berg, P.M. (1991), *Beslist geinformeerd*, Garant, Apeldoorn/Leuven.

Beskind, H. (1962), 'Psychiatric inpatient treatment of adolescents', *Comprehensive Psychiatry*, no. 3, 354-369.

Block, J.A. & Block, J. (1980), 'The Role of Ego-control and Ego-resilience in the organization of behavior', in W.A. Collins (ed.), *Development of Cognition, Affect and Social relations*, Erlbaum, Hillsdale.

Blotsky, M.J. & Dimperio, T.L. (1991), 'Outcome of Inpatient Treatment' *Journal of the American Academy of Child and Adolescent Psychiatry*, vol. 30, no. 3.

Casey, R.J. & J.S. Berman (1985), 'The outcome of psychotherapy with children', *Psychological Bulletin*, no. 98, 388-400.

Colton, M, W. Hellinckx, R. Bullock & B. van den Bruel (1991), 'Caring for troubled children in Flanders, The Netherlands and the United Kingdom', *British Journal of Social Work*, no. 21.

Curry, J.F. (1991), 'Outcome research on residential treatment: Implications and suggested directions', *American Journal of Orthopsychiatry*, vol. 61, no. 3,

Davidson, W.S., R. Redner, R.L. Amdur & C.M. Mitchell (1990), *Alternative Treatments for Troubled Youth*, Plenumm Press, New York.

Davidson, W.S., R. Redner, R.L. Amdur & C.M. Mitchell (1990), 'Empirical History of Treatment Efficacy', in *Alternative Treatment for Troubled Youth*, Plenum Press, New York.

Garret, C.J. (1985), 'Effects of Residential Treatment on Adjudicated Delinquents: a Meta Analysis', *Journal of Research in Crime and Delinquency*, vol. 22, no. 4.

Gosset, J., J. Lewis & F. Barnhart (1983), *To find a way: The outcome of hospital treatment of disturbed adolescents*, Brunner, New York.

Hartman, E., B. Glasser, M. Greenblatt, M. Solomon & D. Levenson (1968), *Adolescents in a mental health center*, Grune and Stratton, New York.

Hindelang, M., T. Hirschi & J.G. Weis (1981), *Measuring Delinquency*, Sage, Beverley Hills.

Hoghughi, M. (1988), *Treating Problem Children*, Sage, London.

Kazdin, A. (1987), 'Treatment of Anti-social Behavior in Children: Current Status and Future Directions', *Psychological Bulletin*, no. 102, 187-203.

Kazdin, A. (1988), *Child Psychotherapy. Developing and Identifying Effective Treatments*, Pergamon Press, New York.

Knorth, E.J. (1987), *Opname of maat*, ACCO, Amersfoort/Leuven.

Knorth, E.J. & M. Smit (1990), *Residentiele Jeugdhulpverlening. Mogelijkheden voor planmatig werken*, Garant, Apeldoorn/Leuven.

Koret, S. (1980), 'Follow-up study on residential treatment of children ages six through twelve', *Journal of the National Association of Private Psychiatric Hospitals*, no. 11, 43-47.

Lewis, M., D.O. Weis, S.S. Shanock, E. Klatskin & J.R. Osborne (1980), 'The Undoing of Residential Treatment: A Follow-up Study of 51 Adolescents', *Journal of the Academy of American Child Psychiatry*, no. 19, 160-171.

Mesman Schultz, K. (1986), *Evaluatie van gedifferentieerde residentiele hulpverlening aan jeugdigen*, LISBON, Leiden.

Miham, S. & M. Little (1991), 'Specialized Residential Treatment for difficult Adolescents. Some recent findings', in W. Hellinckx, E. Broekaert, A. VandenBerge & M. Colton (eds.), *Innovations in residential care*, ACCO, Amersfoort/Leuven.

Pfeiffer, S.I. (1989), 'Follow-up studies of children and adolescents treated in psychiatric facilities: a methodological review', *Psychiatric Hospital*, vol. 20, no. 1.

Pfeifer, S.I. & S.C. Strezelecki (1990), 'Inpatient Psychiatric Treatment of Children and Adolescents: A review of Outcome Studies', *Journal of the American Academic Child and Adolescent Psychiatry*, vol. 29, no. 6.

Rutter, M. & H. Giller (1983), *Juvenile delinquency*, Penguin, London.

Patterson, G.R. (1982), *Coercive Family Process*, Castalia Publishers, Eugene.

Ploeg, J.D. van der (1986), 'Is kwaliteit in de residentiele hulpverlening een meetbaar begrip?' in W. Hellinckx (ed.), *Kwaliteit in de Hulpverlening m.b.t. kinderen met psychosociale problemen*, ACCO, Amersfoort/Leuven.

Ploeg, J.D. van der & E.M. Scholte (1988), *Tehuizen in beeld*, COJ, Leiden.

Ploeg, J.D. van der & E.M. Scholte (1989), *BJ centra in beeld*, COJ, Leiden.

Ploeg, J.D. van der & E.M. Scholte (1990), *Lastposten of slachtoffers van de samenleving*, Lemniscaat, Rotterdam.

Ploeg, J.D. van der & E.M. Scholte (1991), *BJ centra in beeld 2*, NIPPO, Amsterdam.

Quay, H. (1987), Institutional Treatment. *Handbook of Juvenile Delinquency*, John Wiley, New York.

Quay, H. (1986), 'Residential treatment', in Quay & Werry (eds.), *Psychopathological disorders of childhood.*

Rutter, M. (1985), 'Family and School Influences on Behavioral Development', *Journal of Child Psychology and Psychiatry*, vol. 26, no. 3.

Samaroff, A.J. & M. Chandler (1975), 'Reproductive Risk and the Continuum of Care Taker Casualty', in Horowitz (ed.), *Review of child development*, University of Chicago Press, Chicago.

Scholte, E.M. (1991), 'The socio-ecological approach to problem behavior: a perspective on integrated treatment', in W. Hellinckx, E. Broekaert, A. VandenBerge & M. Colton (eds), *Innovations in residential care*, ACCO, Amersfoort/Leuven.

Scholte, E.M. (1992a), 'Identification of Children ar Risk at the Police Station and the Prevention of Delinquency', *Psychiatry*, vol. 55.

Scholte, E.M. (1992b), 'Prevention and Treatment of Juvenile Problem Behavior: A Proposal for a Socio-Ecological Approach', *Journal of the Abnormal Child Psychology*, vol. 20, no. 3.

Scholte, E.M., C.T.H.M. Messing, J. Nijkerk & J.D. van der Ploeg (1991), *Probleemgedrag en Interventie*, DSWO-Press, Leiden.

Smit, M. (1991), 'De situatie van jongeren na een tehuisverblijf. Resultaten uit een literatuur onderzoek', *Tijdschrift voor Orthopedagogiek*, vol. 30, 476-492.

Smith, M.L., G.V. Glass & T.I. Miller (1980), *The benefits of psychotherapy*, John Hopkins University Press, Baltimore.

Taylor, D. & S. Alpert (1973), *Continuity and support following residential treatment*, Child Welfare League, New York.

Tramontana, M.G. (1980), 'Critical Review of Research on Psychotherapy Outcome with Adolescents', *Psychological Bulletin*, vol. 88, no. 2.

8 Evaluating quality in residential care

Walter HELLINCKX
Benedikte VAN DEN BRUEL

The need to reflect on and investigate the quality of care for children and youth with psychosocial problems is strongly felt in the entire welfare sector. Practitioners have expressed an interest in the quality theme, and policy makers stress the need for evaluation of quality as a means towards improvement. This interest in quality is not new. In the seventies and eighties, quality was the focus of many symposiums and conferences, some of them involving care workers (Colton and Hellinckx, 1993; Knorth and Smit, 1990). In addition, journals have been published, especially in America (e.g. Evaluation Review; Evaluation Quarterly; Evaluation and Program Planning) and manuals have been made available (Durkin and Durkin, 1975; Streuning and Guttentagh, 1975) which are entirely dedicated to this theme.

A point of interest in the literature is the wide variety of the terms used to refer to "quality" and the many different meanings associated with it. We do not yet seem to have arrived at any precise definition of quality, particularly not one that can be operationalised. As Van der Ploeg (1986) remarks, so long as "quality" is elusive and has not been defined with more precision, we run the risk that it will remain subjective and its measurement will be ambiguous. However, the different definitions in the literature do seem to agree that the evaluation of quality has to do with the extent to which the quality of care or some of its aspects meet certain specific criteria. Quality evaluation, then, means the process of comparing the care which is actually provided to the care which is theoretically desired. The literature cites numerous methods, models, techniques and instruments which have been used to evaluate quality.

In this chapter, we shall focus on quality evaluation in *residential care*: that is, short-term or long-term substitute care in which children and youngsters reside separately from their families. It is in the area of residential care that the need for quality evaluation has been most strongly felt, partly because the greater amount of government subsidies for supporting children and youth with psychosocial problems is spent on residential care in most European countries. It is in this area too that funding cuts are felt to be most problematic (Colton and Hellinckx, 1993; Oud and Janssens, 1988).

Nowadays, however, the need for quality evaluation is also felt outside the area of residential care because of the recent development of alternative, community-based forms of care, such as foster care, day-care centres, supervised independent living arrangements, and family centres. These different care alternatives give rise to the need to evaluate residential care not just separately but in comparison and in combination with other forms of care (Colton and Hellinckx, 1993).

This chapter is limited to residential care for children and youths with psychosocial difficulties, who have been placed as a result of adverse family circumstances, or because of their own emotional or behavioural problems, or some combination of both. Facilities for children and youths with mental handicaps, or psychiatric or other problems are not discussed, although in these areas, too, the trend towards quality evaluation is growing (Motmans and Steen, 1993; Masure, 1987; Smeets, 1986). In this chapter, we focus first on the reasons for the growing interest in the subject of quality. Next, we define the term "quality" and discuss different ways of measuring it, referring to the work of Harinck and Smit (Chapter 9) for an summary of what already has been done in the field of quality evaluation. In conclusion, we give an outline of likely future developments.

Reasons for evaluating quality in residential care

Different reasons can be given for the growing interest in the theme of quality (Hellinckx and Van den Bruel, 1993; Twijnstra, 1991; Van der Ploeg, 1990; 1986; Smeets, 1986; Johnson et al., 1976). In residential care, three of the most important reasons have to do with: (1) concern about the benefits of residential care; (2) a growing demand for criteria and norms; and (3) economic recession.

Concern about the benefits of residential care

Since the 1960s, we have increasingly come to realise that care is not by definition a quality product. The literature contains many criticisms of residential care, citing a diversity of factors relating to process as well as impact, and leading to serious questions about the benefits of this type of care. After the second world war, studies were undertaken with regard to the effect of residential care on the emotional and intellectual development of young children. Findings suggested that the absence of the mother-child bond is a severe threat to the development of the personalities of children in residential care.

Goffman has described residential care as a "total institution", characterised by the fact that it is shut off from the wider context of the outside world. Goffman's concept of totality was used as a source of inspiration for numerous research projects. King, Raynes and Tizard (1971), among others, studied the ways in which workers deal with children in residential care. This type of research established a link between residents' behaviour and certain structural elements of residential care, such as the facility's size and the ratio of workers to children. In addition to drawing attention to other factors, it emphasised the importance of small-scale services and the presence of a sufficient number of qualified personnel.

Polsky (1962) has also advocated a reorganisation of residential care, but from a different viewpoint. Studying the group culture of delinquent boys in residential care, he observed strong similarities with the culture of so-called "gangs" outside residential care. Violence and manipulation are the primary means by which the informal leaders of gangs and their helpers control the rest of the group. Polsky showed that care workers were aware of a similar subculture in residential homes and even nurtured it by, for example, attempting to influence the informal leaders. His research demonstrated the importance of the social system in residential care in influencing the behaviour of the children. According to Polsky, effecting a change in delinquent behaviour requires a conscious effort to influence and guide the whole social system of the group, especially the informal structure, with respect to roles, relations and norms.

Subsequent to 1968, in the wake of movements critical of the social structure, and especially in German-speaking countries (for example, "emanzipatorische Pädagogik"), residential care was criticized in a far more fundamental way. This criticism was aimed at the entire concept of residential care, which was considered to be an instrument of the ruling class, designed to preserve the existing social inequality. Workers in the care facilities themselves joined in the condemnation, publicly drawing attention to their difficult working conditions. In several European countries, personnel demanded an increase in wages, more adequate staffing, and a diminution of the number and difficulty of the tasks with which they were charged (Colton and Hellinckx, 1993).

Later, at the end of the seventies and eighties, there was widespread criticism with respect to policy in residential care. Criticism in Anglo-Saxon literature focused on the programmes: they were not methodical enough, they were too categorical, too specialized, too fragmented, too expensive and too inefficient. At the macro-level, critics pointed to the lack of differentiation in services offered to different target groups. At the meso-level, the criticism was that the care-process itself was often vague. Van der Ploeg used the term "black box" to describe the vagueness of care in residential institutions. At the micro-level, there were complaints that the residential care process contributed to the depersonalization and dependence of children and youngsters. In addition to this, it was held that the link between scientific research and residential practice was still too weak (Smeets, 1986; Van der Meulen, 1978; Johnson et al., 1976).

Growing demand for criteria and norms

The second reason for the interest in the theme of quality is the growing demand in child care for criteria and norms which will be generally accepted and which careworkers themselves will consider to be relevant (Shyne, 1976). The need of child-care professionals for information became increasingly stronger in the latter half of the 1970s (Colton and Hellinckx, 1993; Smeets, 1986). Clients too were claiming more quality, becoming aware of their right to quality care and requiring more information (Colton and Hellinckx, 1993; Colton et al., 1991; Masure, 1987). This emphasis on consumer involvement is part of a general social trend towards giving the client a wider choice and limiting the power of professionals (Colton et al., 1991).

Economic recession

The third reason for interest in quality is that child care, in common with other domains, has been subject to financial cuts during the economic recession of the last decade. Since the resources available have been insufficient to cope with the increasing demand for service, it has become necessary to account not only for the amount of money being spent but also for the way in which the money is being used.

In the United States, there is a tradition of accountability, whereby facilities which are publicly funded have an obligation to account for their activities and a certain proportion of their budget must be spent on research evaluation. This explains the upsurge in evaluative acitivities in America in the latter half of the seventies (Smeets, 1986). As previously noted, a vast evaluation literature arose and many conferences were organised around the quality theme.

Another consequence of the recession was that care professionals, along with professionals in other areas, were forced to seek alternative ways of working which did not affect quality. Expensive residential care, for example, had to make way for less expensive forms of care, such as foster care, day care, supervised independent living and home-based treatment (Colton and Hellinckx, 1993). The use of qualitative as well as quantitative criteria and data were found to be necessary to implement this reorganisation (Hellinckx and De Munter, 1990; Van der Ploeg and Scholte, 1988; Smeets, 1986).

Defining "quality evaluation"

Since the mid-1970s, the meaning of the terms "quality" and "evaluation" in care has been the subject of much debate. In the seventies and eighties, publications in the Anglo-Saxon literature around this topic were abundant (e.g., Mordock, 1979; Menninger, 1977; Shyne, 1976; Durkin and Durkin, 1975; Struening and Guttentagh, 1975). Most publications were not restricted to the topic of residential care but discussed social programmes of which residential care was a part. The term "programme" in this context was used by some authors to indicate a specific treatment method and by others to refer to a care organisation as a whole (Harinck, 1990; Donker, 1987; Smeets, 1986). For example, a residential service for children with psychosocial problems might be called a "programme" and so might any specific treatment given to the children while they were in residence.

A whole range of terms is currently used to describe the process of reaching conclusions about quality, sometimes with different meanings being ascribed to one and the same term. Anglo-Saxons commonly refer to "programme evaluation", a term which was already being used in the late 1960s. The original meaning of "programme evaluation" was an evaluation of a programme's products or outcomes, usually by means of an experimental or quasi- experimental research design. Later, the term took on a wider meaning and was used to refer to any applied research activities designed to gather information about a particular programme. (Harinck and Smit, Chapter 9; Harinck, 1990). A variety of programme characteristics might be assessed: needs, feasibility, process, outcomes, cost-effectiveness, programme "logic" pertaining to links between resources, process and outcomes, and a number of other qualities. All these are embraced by the general concept of programme evaluation and they involve many different research activities and methodologies.

When the focus is on the effects of care, the terms "evaluation of effectiveness", "effectiveness evaluation" or "outcome evaluation" are often used. Depending on the purpose of the evaluation, the term "evaluation of effectiveness" may have one of two meanings. On the one hand, it may refer to research whose purpose is to contribute to the development of theory on a certain type of care. Here, quasi-experimental research designs are mostly used. On the other hand, it may refer to research whose purpose is to enhance quality in care (Munson and Blincoe, 1984; Mordock, 1979; Shyne 1976; Durkin and Durkin, 1975).

The term "evaluation research" has mostly been used in connection with practice-oriented evaluation research. In the 1970s, the term pertained to research on the effects of measures and programmes for solving social problems of various kinds and was considered to be relevant to all the social sciences (Struening and Guttentagh, 1975).

In contrast, the term "quality assurance" was originally associated solely with physical care, and utilised standards, set by physicians themselves, which all members of the medical profession were expected to meet (Smeets, 1986). Whenever the care provided failed to reach these standards, the case was submitted for review to a committee of peers: the so-called peer-review or quality review method. Outside the medical world, little use was made of the quality-assurance procedure.

The word "quality" occurs again in the term "quality evaluation" which, in the context of residential care, has a very wide and usually vague application, encompassing every aspect of the process and effects of different residential systems. In order to dispel this vagueness, the first question that needs to be answered is: What exactly do we mean by "quality"?

Quality itself is a relative term, referring to the degree of excellence to be found in an object or process: we may talk about "quality" child care, for example, meaning that the care reaches a high standard of excellence. However, if we do not know what particular process we mean when we refer vaguely to child care, and if we do not know what particular standards we are trying to reach, then the term "quality child care" is essentially meaningless. It will only make sense in the context of a specific child care programme, aimed at reaching specific goals.

In the literature pertaining to quality evaluation, the emphasis tends to be on the degree to which children and youths have changed, hopefully for the better, as a result of their stay in residential care. In other words, as Harinck and Smit remark in Chapter 9, much evaluation is focused only on effects. However, in order to shed light on those care elements which cause the effects being measured, it is also necessary to pay attention to the care facility's processes and components. Only then will it be possible to obtain a complete picture of a facility's quality through research results which have utility for improving the quality of practice (Masure, 1987).

Suchman's definition of quality evaluation is useful in this regard because it is not restricted to the domain of effects. It differentiates between five domains of evaluation and essentially constitutes a framework in which the other definitions can be placed. The five domains are:

1. effort: this is the energy put into care, including the resources expended. Indicators of effort may include, for example, the number of clients, the nature of their problems and the number of staff, among many others
2. performance: this is the result or effect of care
3. adequacy: tuning the supply of care to the demands of those in need of care
4. efficiency: the ratio of performance to effort
5. the care process: the specific activities which use the effort in order to bring about the results.

These five domains of quality evaluation are relevant at the micro-, the meso- and the macro-levels of care, as defined below.

- the micro-level, bearing on the client, the care worker and their relationship
- the meso-level, bearing on the facility's organisation
- the macro-level, relating to regional, provincial and national policy.

In the literature, different aspects are stressed, depending on how the concept of quality has been applied by the particular author in a particular context. According to De Ruyter (1986), the quality of residential care is related to the ratio of clients' progress to the total investment made by clients and care workers. Here, quality is understood in terms of efficiency and the criterion employed is the best that can be achieved, taking into account the actual state of affairs. This is a very workable notion in care for it makes clear to clients as well as care workers what they have to do in order to achieve the best possible results. In this sense, the interpretation of quality in terms of efficiency is feasible and realistic for clients as well as care workers.

De Ruyter's definition of quality is based on the work of Williamson and Kazdin. Williamson defines the quality of care as the degree to which the client profits from care with a minimum needless use of resources. For

Kazdin, quality is related to the achievement of the desired change at the lowest possible cost, where cost is measured in terms of time, money, effort and emotional stress.

From De Ruyter's point of view, quality evaluation - the assessment of quality - consists partly of effect evaluation and partly of process evaluation. Like Stufflebaum (see Oud and Janssens, 1988), De Ruyter differentiates between quality evaluation and effect evaluation. Effect evaluation alone might establish that clients have not changed even though they and the care workers have invested a lot. Quality evaluation should take this investment into account since lack of improvement and high quality can go hand in hand (De Ruyter, 1986).

In contrast to De Ruyter, Van der Ploeg gives a more general definition of quality. With respect to residential care, he maintains that it is necessary first to define the objectives, second to identify the group for whom they are intended, third to identify the methods used to achieve them, and fourth to ensure that there are adequate links between the target group, the objectives and the methods used (Van der Ploeg, 1986). These four aspects constitute the "identity" of a residential facility and provide a picture of the way that care should ideally be given (Van der Ploeg, 1990). Once an ideal exists, it is possible to make a comparison between the ideal and the care which is given in reality. According to Van der Ploeg, the degree of discrepancy between the real and the ideal allows us to make statements about quality. The larger the discrepancy, the lower the quality, and the smaller the discrepancy, the higher the quality.

We might argue here that, the lower the ideal, the greater is the chance of reaching the ideal and the higher will be the quality. However the ideal will always be formulated on the basis of the consent of the several parties concerned, who are unlikely to allow irresponsibly high or low estimates of the kind of care expected. This in itself is a guarantee that a realistic ideal will be set (Van der Ploeg, 1990).

Van der Ploeg's general definition leaves room for quality evaluation relating to all possible aspects of care on the micro-, meso- and macro-levels. Depending on the level at which quality is being assessed, some aspects will be stressed more than others. Van der Ploeg's definition is reminiscent of Menninger (1977), who defines quality as "... the goodness of fit between the problem requiring therapeutic attention, the desired outcome (the goal of treatment) and the treatment used".

When defining "quality" in care, it is inevitable that there will be a subjective dimension depending on who is doing the defining: clients, funding authorities, care workers or researchers. Care workers will be interested in effects since they hope that their interventions will be successful in resolving problems. Funders, on the other hand, will set great store by the cost-effect ratio. Independent researchers will point to continuity in care, the internal cohesion of facilities and tuning care to needs.

However, despite these differences in emphasis, it appears from most definitions that quality evaluation is practice-oriented. The aim of quality evaluation is to improve practice on the level of structure and policy. In this sense, quality evaluation is different from theoretical evaluation research, whose primary purpose is to increase knowledge of a particular intervention (Harinck, 1993; 1990; Smeets, 1986). However, such a distinction is somewhat artificial since the results of theoretical research may indirectly contribute to an improvement in practice (Harinck, 1993; 1990; Shelly, 1982).

In sum, quality evaluation in the field of residential care means making a comparison between the actual care provided and the care desired. It is a continuous, practice-oriented and cyclical process which provides prompt feedback as a means towards improvement. Ideal or desired care can be operationalised in concrete terms by establishing criteria to act as indicators of quality. These same criteria or indicators can then be used to measure the quality of the actual care provided.

An important requirement of quality evaluation is that it is undertaken in a planned and systematic way, using scientific methods (Masure, 1987). This requirement may be difficult to meet in a practice setting where the rigours of research methodology have to be balanced with ethical considerations related to the needs of children and staff. In addition, researchers must take into account the informational needs of potential research users. (Shelly, 1982). Since practitioners will be the main consumers of practice-oriented research, attention should be paid to developing a co-operative relationship between researchers and practitioners in order to increase the relevancy of the research findings to the actual practice of care.

Methods of quality evaluation in residential care

When evaluating quality in residential care, two main domains might be considered. First there is the domain of the care process itself, where evaluation may focus on determining the degree to which goals are being achieved or on discrepancies between the ideal and real identities of the care situation. The second domain is the domain of bordering conditions: that is, the physical and psychosocial environment in which the care process takes place. Bordering conditions include such things as accommodation, the number of care workers and their qualifications, the structure of the organization, group dynamics, and so forth (Van der Ploeg and Scholte, 1989). In this chapter, we will consider first the measurement of effects and, second, the measurement of process, including the measurement of the bordering conditions or psychosocial environment.

Measurement of effects

In order to measure the effectiveness of care for any particular child, two related questions must be answered: Has the child improved during his or her stay? and Was the improvement due to the stay? (Harinck, 1990) The focus here is the child not the care; but it may be argued that the effectiveness of care as a whole is no more than the aggregation of its effectiveness for a number of individual children. The measurement of effectiveness in this sense is mostly approached through outcome and follow-up studies.

However, the measurement of effect gives rise to certain problems which have been noted by Harinck (1990), Van der Ploeg (1986) and Harinck and Smit in Chapter 9, among others. These problems are summarised briefly below:

- Who decides whether the goals have been reached - the researcher, the young person who is receiving help, or the care workers? Of obvious relevance here is the subjective dimension of quality which we previously discussed. Research shows us, for example, that care workers tend to have a different opinion of the effectiveness of treatment than do their clients (Wouda, Van der Ploeg and Smit, 1987). One reason for this may be that the clients and care workers are aiming for different goals. When a client's behaviour has improved, this does not necessarily mean that the client feels better or vice versa (Eyer, 1975). If the client's goal is feeling better and the care worker' goal is the client's improved behaviour, it is not surprising if they disagree on the matter of goal achievement. It follows that careful specification of goals is extremely important in effect evaluation (Mordock, 1979).
- It is not clear whether the effect (assuming we are able to measure it) is due to residential care or to extraneous causes. A child may fail to make a satisfactory improvement even though the care worker has done a good job because of factors which have nothing to do with the care provided. Conversely, a child may improve despite a faulty care process merely because of increased maturity or a positive friendship, or some other factor.
- It is often difficult to decide whether a measured lack of improvement is due to a faulty intervention or to the faulty

implementation of a perfectly adequate intervention. This question can only be resolved through a combined process/outcome evaluation which measures what was actually done as well as the result.

- Good effect evaluation often depends upon methodological rigour which is difficult to achieve in a practice setting. For example, the sample sizes which can be practically obtained may be too small to draw valid conclusions. Similarly, the measuring instruments which can be practically used may be less valid and reliable than would be wished.
- Effect evaluations are often summative: that is, they are designed to aid decisions about accepting or rejecting a programme or care strategy, rather than making suggestions for improvement. The question of effect may not therefore be the most relevant question for practice, particularly not at earlier stages of programme development.

In sum, effect evaluation tends to be highly subjective, particularly with respect to the goals of care, which may be different for different actors. In addition, the effects being assessed will never be solely due to the care provided since there are so many extraneous factors which cannot be identified, let alone controlled for or measured (Van der Ploeg, 1986).

Because the effects of the care process itself are so nebulous, it is particularly important to provide aftercare so that young people leaving a residential facility can receive further support and their progress can be monitored. From the young person's perspective, aftercare means that gains made during the care process are more likely to be maintained. From the research perspective, longitudinal data may enable staff to gauge the durability of the gains: that is, to determine how long the positive effects of care will last when subjected to the stresses of the outside world. Naturally, the longer the effects last, the more reason there is to deem the care successful.

When the young person's problems were severe to begin with, both the gains themselves and their durability may be fairly minimal. However, it may be argued that "success" does not lie solely in the resolution of problems: a diminution of the problem level or an increased ability to cope with still-existing problems may also indicate success. This is particularly important in light of the fact that the young people entering residential care today tend to have more severe problems than used to be the case. It is unrealistic to expect that these young people will function at the same level as other youngsters after leaving care; and it therefore unreasonable to suggest that care has "failed" because a young person who was severely damaged at entry does not leave care completely healed (Van der Ploeg, 1986).

Measurement of process

The second element of care to be considered is the care process itself. This involves an understanding of the psychosocial environment in which the care takes place, including such things as the relationship between the care workers and child, and organisational aspects such housing, the number of care workers and their qualifications, the structure of the organization, and so forth.

The evaluation of process addresses an important limitation which is inherent in measuring effect. It is not possible, on the basis of effect evaluation, to give concrete and practical feed-back concerning the different aspects of the pedagogical functioning of residential services. Process evaluation makes this possible (Durkin and Durkin, 1975).

Within the larger field of process evaluation, there is room for many specific evaluation types (Van der Ploeg, 1986). Since Harinck and Smit explore a number of these in Chapter 9, the discussion in this chapter is restricted to four types of process evaluation: describing the care process, checking quality criteria, measuring the pyschosocial environment, and measuring client satisfaction.

Describing the care process. Since any residential programme has a large number of components, all contributing in different ways to the overall result, the first difficulty in describing the care process is to select the particular component or components which are most worthy of attention. A focus on just a few components will require a selection process which is difficult and time-consuming in itself. An alternative is to provide a global description of the distinct parts of a residential program: for example, the living unit, school facilities, leisure time facilities, and individual or group therapy provisions. This type of component evaluation can be helpful in aiding placement decisions for individual youngsters, provided that the precise nature of the services offered by any residential facility is specified so that the people making the placement decision can know which facility will best meet the needs of the young person being placed. As Harinck and Smit remark in Chapter 9, a knowledge of what particular of service is offered by which facility can also be helpful when organising overall service provision in a geographical area.

Process in any one facility can also be described by means of monitoring evaluation: that is, through the routine and ongoing collection and collation of data concerning such things as staff and client characteristics and programme activities. Some of these data will be available in the institution's records: others can be collected by observing interactions and activities.

Checking quality criteria. In Chapter 9, Harinck and Smit state that process elements should have quality in themselves, quite apart from their contribution to outcome. The quality, or degree of excellence possessed by an element can be measured by determining the degree to which the element meets certain criteria of quality previously developed by researchers. The difficulty here of course is developing the criteria in the first place. Criteria may be based on systematic research but they are also very often based on personal opinions.

Sometimes, they are the result of consultation. Well known in this respect is the "quality review" or "peer review" process in which professionals consult with one another to develop quality criteria for the care-process, and then monitor among themselves the degree to which each individual's work meets the established criteria. The Delphi method is another well-known technique, which explicitly uses the practical and theoretical expertise of practitioners to establish criteria for quality evaluation. Swaans-Joha (1989) looks upon Delphi research as an interactive research technique designed to facilitate feed-back and information exchange between researchers and key informants. The basis of the technique lies in the belief that the best and most useful research will result from an alliance between researchers, who can contribute expertise about research methods, and practitioners, who are more intimately acquainted with the institution or care strategy being studied. A number of group discussions are organised in which practitioners, in the presence of the researcher, regularly confront each other with differing opinions as to the goals, methods and philosphies of care. The object of the discussion is to reach concensus about goals or processes which may then be further explored through research.

The Delphi technique has come into favour in recent years because it allows the recommendations which researchers give to policy makers to be practice-based. Such recommendations are liable to be more valid and realistic than recommendations made by either researchers or practitioners alone and are thus more likely to be followed.

Describing the psychosocial environment. The "psychosocial environment" means here the non-material aspects of a living situation which both influence and are influenced by an individual or group. The group environment is very important to children in residential care and has a marked influence on their behaviour. The psychosocial environment thus constitutes an important aspect of care which needs to be evaluated (Masure, 1987).

Moos (1979) has tried to find a method for measuring and evaluating the psychosocial environment. On the basis of comprehensive research, he came to the conclusion that, in a residential setting, the following three basic characteristics are always to be found:

1. a relational dimension, describing the nature and intensity of personal relations in the group and encompassing:
   - mutual concern
   - mutual support
   - openness and spontaneity
2. a personal dimension, describing the direction of personal growth and development towards:
   - independence
   - social independence
   - norms and values
3. an organisational dimension, describing the degree to which the environment is organised, regulated and arranged, including:
   - order
   - clarity
   - control

These basic dimensions are characteristic of facilities for children and youngsters with psychosocial problems and may differ from facility to facility. In addition, there are three other aspects which may influence the group's environment: its size, its composition and the characteristics of its care workers (Masure, 1987).

A number of scales have been developed by Moos, and much research has been conducted on the basis of Moos's insight (Van der Ploeg, 1986). The living group environment scales comprise a number of instruments which enable care workers and young people to evaluate the group environment. These scales provide a way of gathering systematic information on a number of aspects of the psychosocial environment from the perspectives of young people and care workers. At the same time, they enable discrepancies between the real and ideal care environments to be examined.

Measuring client satisfaction. Interest in the degree of satisfaction felt by the recipients of care has grown in recent years. In one sense, the evaluation of satisfaction is an effect evaluation, based on the idea that the more sucesssful a treatment is, the more satisfied are its clients (Van der Ploeg, 1986). However, satisfaction is also important from a process point of view as it allows insights into the strengths and weaknesses of care as perceived by those who are experiencing it.

Such an approach is still practically unknown in residential care, and there is a distinct lack of studies analysing the clients' perspective with regard to all aspects of the care experience (Colton and Hellinckx, 1993). The assessment of satisfaction is almost impossible with young children but is not nearly so difficult with older children or families. As Van der Ploeg (1986, p. 44) remarks, research findings on satisfaction can constitute a part of real care work.

Conclusions and final remarks

The material in this chapter may lead us to the conclusion that the evaluation of quality is a largely subjective affair which is difficult to address by means of objective criteria. This then raises the question of whether or not quality evaluation deserves the label "scientific".

Together with Veerman (1988), the present authors believe that quality evaluation does not necessarily need to have a quantitative experimental character in order to be labelled scientific. The development of quality criteria and the making of measurements can both be undertaken in a scientific way. For example, goals for the care process can be established by means of objective choices based in part on research findings. Also, quality can be measured in an intersubjective way on the basis of a mutually-developed framework of concepts and norms (Twijnstra, 1991; Van der Ploeg, 1988). Staff in residential service can themselves undertake quality evaluation by carefully describing the goals of the care process, the target groups and the care methods used. This kind of systematic data collection can then be used as a legitimate foundation for scientific activity (Harinck, 1993; Smeets, 1986).

An important question is the degree to which quality evaluation has already been integrated into the daily practice of residential care. Although, in recent years, many data-collection systems have been initiated, quality evaluation seems to be restricted to informal discussions in many cases. The majority of residential services have no written criteria for success or failure, nor do they systematically research the effect they have on their clients. Evaluative assessments are made too often on the basis of feelings and individual observations and are frequently restricted to global judgments (Masure, 1987). Some of the reasons for the lack of systematic and planned evaluation, are summarised below:

- lack of funding and staff time in residential services
- problems concerning the content of evaluation
- lack of appropriate methods for quality measurement
- resistance on the part of residential services towards unwanted information and changes

In addition, practitioners who are interested in knowing how to help individual clients usually judge their own knowledge and experience to be more relevant than evaluation results (Harinck and Smit, Chapter 9). They often perceive any introduction to quality evaluation as threatening or as an attack on their professional autonomy (Masure, 1987).

However, quality evaluation of residential care would seem to be a necessity in the context of the recent tendency towards a more methodical approach adopted by residential practitioners. This approach includes planning the care process, implenting the process by working as planned, and finally *evaluating* the care process (Knorth and Smit, 1990). Evaluation of existing services in also constantly required on the macro-level, with respect to organising services and ensuring that target groups in each region have a full range of services available to them.

In recent years, emphasis has been placed on the role of government inspectors in relation to quality evaluation. Although it has been stressed that quality control is primarily the responsibility of the residential services themselves, the government which subsidises the services also supports the evaluative effort by sending an external inspection team. In addition to controlling the quality of the services, the inspectors encourage service providers to check quality for themselves and to make quality a subject for discussion. In this way, the inspection takes on the character of a "dialogue" through which the inspectors are enabled to report to the government and develop proposals for improvement (Tilanus, 1992).

There is presently a demand for more quality inspection concerning the pedagogical functioning of services. When the pedagogical concept and/or the therapeutic model of residential services is taken into account, it is apparent that clear criteria for quality evaluation must be formulated. Criteria need to be developed specific to every target group on the basis of discussion between theoreticians and practitioners (Casaert, 1992; Hellinckx and De Munter, 1990).

In this connection, the authors have recently begun a research project in Flanders with the aim of developing a valid and reliable instrument concerning the pedagogical functioning of residential services.

A crucial step in planning an evaluation project is drawing up a list of quality aspects or criteria with which to compare the reality (Sketchley-Kneppelhout, 1981). Such criteria of quality need to be both unambiguous and measureable and, from time to time, they will need to be reviewed (De Vries, 1992; Masure, 1987). If they are to be used by government inspectors, they will also need to take into account meso-level concerns, bearing on the organisation of the residential facility.

During the development of the instrument some quality aspects will be transformed into pedagogical criteria which, at a later stage, will be operationalised. On the basis of these criteria, inspectors can check to determine whether certain quality criteria are being realised in a particular residential service. In addition to the evaluation of an individual service, this instrument also makes it possible to gather information concerning many services, quickly and in a standardised manner. Thus, it provides an opportunity to gather information which will allow the government to perceive possible tensions between policy and practice (Hellinckx and De Munter, 1990).

Quality evaluation is not restricted to residential services. We mentioned earlier that, in recent years, child-care policy and practice appear to be converging towards family and community-oriented services (Colton and Hellinckx, 1993; Colton et al., 1991). Quality evaluation of these services is becoming more and more of a necessity in order to discover whether these new types of care actually do help the children and families for whom they are meant, so that their function is complementary with respect to that of residential services.

References

Attkisson, C.C & Brokowski, A. (1978), 'Evaluation and the emerging human service concept', in C.C. Attkisson, W.A. Hargreaves, M.J., Horowitz & J.E. Sorenson (eds), *Evaluation of human services programs* (pp. 3-26), New York, Academic Press.

Attkisson, C.C., Hargreaves, W.A., Horowitz, M.J & Sorenson, J.E. (eds) (1978), *Evaluation of human services programs,* New York, Academic Press.

Bartak, L. & Rutter, M. (1975), 'The measurement of staff-child interaction in three units for autistic children', in J. Tizard, I. Sinclair & R. Clarke (eds), *Varieties of Residential Experience* (pp. 171-202).

Bell, R.A., Nguyen, T.D., Warheit, G.J., Buhl, J.M. (1978), 'Service Utilization, social indicator and citizen survey approaches to human service need assessment', in C.C. Attkisson, W.A. Hargreaves, M.J., Horowitz & J.E. Sorenson (eds), *Evaluation of human services programs*, New York, Academic Press.

Bennett, E.M. & Trute, B. (1983), *Mental Health Information Systems: Problems and Prospects*, Lewiston, NY, Edwin Mellen.

Berger, M.A. & Jagers, J.D. (1986), 'Voorbeeld van follow-up onderzoek bij jongeren. Follow-up van ex-bewoners van een rijksinrichting', *Tijdschrift voor Orthopedagogiek,* vol. 25, 326-337.

Bowlby, J. (1951), *Maternal care and mental health*, Geneva, WHO.

Brosch, P. (1971), *Fürsorgeerziehung. Heimterror und Gegenwehr*, Frankfurt a.M., Fischer.

Bullock, R., Little, M. & Millham, S. (1993), *Residential Care for Children. A Review of the Research*, London, HMSO.

Casaert, J. (1992), *Reorganisatie van de administratieve en pedagogische inspectie van het bestuur bijzondere jeugdbijstand*, Brussel, Administratie Gezin en Maatschappelijk Welzijn, Bestuur bijzondere Jeugdbijstand (niet-gepubliceerd).

Claus-Stuy, N. (1978), *Evaluatie, waarom niet? Een exploratief onderzoek naar factoren die evaluatie in de weg staan*, Leiden, Rijksuniversiteit, Vakgroep klinische en orthopedagogiek (doctoraalscriptie).

Clifton, D.S. & Fyffe, D.E. (1977), *Project Feasibility Analysis*, New York, John Wiley.

Colla-Müller, H. (1993), 'Germany', in M. Colton, & W. Hellinckx (eds), *Child Care in the EC. A country-specific guide to foster and residential care* (pp. 71-95), Aldershot, Arena.

Colton, M. & Hellinckx, W. (eds) (1993), *Child Care in the EC. A country-specific guide to foster and residential care*, Aldershot, Arena.

Colton, M., Hellinckx, W., Bullock, R. & Van den Bruel, B. (1991), 'Caring for Troubled Children in Flanders, The Netherlands, and the United Kingdom', *British Journal for Social Work*, vol. 21, 381-392.

Coursey, R.D. (Ed.) (1977), *Program Evaluation in Mental Health. Methods, strategies and participants*, New York, Grune & Stratton.

De Ruyter, P.A. (1979), 'Hoe komen wij tot de beoordeling van de kwaliteit van de hulpverlening?' in *Lezingencyclus winter 78/79* (pp. 12-22), Amsterdam, Wijn.

De Ruyter, P.A. (1986), 'Op zoek naar de kwaliteit van de residentiële hulpverlening', in W. Hellinckx (ed.) *Kwaliteit in de hulpverlening m.b.t. kinderen met psycho-sociale problemen* (pp. 11-31), Leuven/Amersfoort, Acco.

De Vries, D. (1992), 'Kwaliteit moet je meten en telkens water geven: interne auditing in BJ centra, *BJ- Bulletin*, vol. 14, 2-4.

Donker, M.C.H. (1987), *De toets der goede bedoelingen*, Utrecht, NcGv-reeks 100.

Durkin, R. & Durkin, R. (1975), 'Evaluation Residential treatment programs for disturbed children', in E.L. Struening & M. Guttentagh (ed.), *Handbook of evaluation research* (pp. 275-339), London, Sage.

Eckensberger, D. (1971), *Sozialisationsbedingungen der öffentlichen Erziehung*, Frankfurt a.M., Suhrkamp.

Eyer, M. (1975), *Winst en verlies: Resultaten van residentiële behandeling bij emotioneel gestoorde, delinquente adolescenten*, Naarden, Los.

Frankel, M. & Sinclair, C. (1982), 'Quality assurance: an approach to accountability in a Mental Health Center', *Professional Psychology*, vol. 13, no. 1, 79-84.

Goffman, E. (1961), *Asylums. Essays on the social situation of mental patients and other inmates*, Harmondsworth, Penguin.

Goodman, L.J. & Love, R.N. (1980), *Project Planning and Management*, New York, Pergamon.

Guttentag, M. & Streuning, E.L. (eds) (1975), *Handbook of evaluation research*, Volume 2. Beverly Hills/London, Sage.

Harinck, F.J.H. (1990), 'Programma-evaluatie in tehuizen', in E.J. Knorth & M. Smit (eds), *Residentiële jeugdhulpverlening. Mogelijkheden voor planmatig werken* (pp. 157-170), Leuven/Apeldoorn, Garant.

Hebborn-Brass, U. (1991), *Verhaltensgestörte Kinder im Heim: eine empirische Längsschnittuntersuchung zu Indikation und Erfolg*, Freiburg im Breisgau, Lambertus.

Hellinckx, W. (1986) (Ed.), *Kwaliteit in de hulpverlening m.b.t. kinderen met psycho-sociale problemen*, Leuven/Amersfoort, Acco.

Hellinckx, W., Broekaert, E., Vanden Berge, A. & Colton, M. (1991) (eds), *Innovations in Residential Care*, Leuven/Amersfoort, Acco.

Hellinckx, W., & De Munter, A. (1990), *Voorzieningen voor jongeren met psychosociale problemen. Onderzoek naar residentiële voorzieningen, diensten voor begeleid zelfstandig wonen en dagcentra*, Leuven/Amersfoort, Acco.

Hellinckx, W. & Van den Bruel, B. (1993), 'Recente ontwikkelingen in de tehuishulp voor kinderen en jongeren in problematische opvoedingssituaties in Vlaanderen', *Onze Alma Mater. Leuvense Perspectieven* (publikatie in voorbereiding).

Holroyd, J. & Goldenberg, I. (1978), 'The use of goal attainment scaling to evaluate a ward treatment program for disturbed children', *Journal of Clinical Psychology*, vol. 34, no. 3, 732-739.

Jesness, C.F. (1972), 'Comparative effectiveness of two institutional treatment programs for delinquents', *Child Care Quarterly*, vol. 1, no. 2, 119-130.

Johnson, H.L. et al. (1976), 'Program evaluation in residential treatment: some practical issues', *Child Welfare*, vol. 55, no. 4, 279-287.

Kazdin, A.E. & Wilson, G.F. (1978), *Evaluation of Behavior Therapy*, Cambridge Massachusetts, Ballinger.

King, R., Raynes, N. & Tizard, J. (1971), *Patterns of Residential Care. A comparative study of units, including some children's homes, for children with handicaps*, Routledge & Kegan Paul.

Knorth, E.J. & Smit, M. (1990) (eds), *Residentiële jeugdhulpverlening. Mogelijkheden voor planmatig werken*, Leuven/Apeldoorn, Garant.

Masure, D. (1987), *Literatuurstudie met betrekking tot het evalueren van residentiële hulpverlening voor kinderen en jongeren met psychosociale problemen*, Leuven, K.U.Leuven, Faculteit der Psychologie en Pedagogische Wetenschappen (Licentiaatsverhandeling).

Meinhof, U. (1971), *Bambule, Fürsorge Sorge für wen?* Berlin, Verlag Klaus Wagenbach.

Menninger, R.W. (1977), 'What is quality care? A clinican's view', *American Journal of Orthopsychiatrie*, vol. 47, no. 3, 476-483.

Mesman Schultz, K. (1984), *Het Driehuizen-project*, Effecten van zeer intensieve behandeling. Amsterdam, SISWO.

Miedema, S. (1986), ''Relevantie en precisie' over de relatie tussen kwalitatieve en kwantitatificerende methoden van empirisch-pedagogisch onderzoek', *Pedagogische verhandelingen*, vol. 9, 3-30.

Millman, H.L. & Schaefer, C.E. (1975), 'Behavioral change: program evaluation and staff feedback', *Child Welfare*, vol. 54, no. 10, 692-702.

Mollenhauer (1973), *Erziehung und Emanzipation*, München, Juventa Verlag.

Moos, R.H. (1979), *Evaluating Educational Environments*, San Francisco.

Mordock, J.B. (1979), 'Evaluation in residential treatment: the conceptual dilemma's', *Child Welfare*, 58, 5, 293-302.

Motmans, K. & Steen, V. (1993), *Onderzoek naar de kwaliteit van de hulpverlening bij mentaal gehandicapte personen in residentiële voorzieningen. Analyse van het taalgebruik van personeelsleden ten aanzien van de bewoners*, Leuven, K.U.Leuven, Faculteit der Psychologie en Pedagogische Wetenschappen (Licentiaatsverhandeling).

Munson, R.F. & Blincoe, M. (1984), 'Evaluation of a residential treatment center for emotionally disturbed adolescents', *Adolescence*, vol. 19, no. 74, 253-261.

Neuber, K.A. (1980), *Needs Assessment: A model for Community Planning*, Beverly Hills, CA, Sage.

Nierman, G. (1979), *De leefgroepklimaatschaal (LKS)*, Amsterdam, Vrije Universiteit, orthopedagogiek en methodologie.

Oud, J. & Janssens, J. (1988), 'Kwaliteitsevaluatie in de orthopedagogiek', *Tijdschrift voor Orthopedagogiek*, vol. 27, 3-22.

Pancer, S.M. & Westhues, A. (1989), 'A developmental stage approach to program planning and evaluation', *Evaluation Review*, vol. 13, no. 1, 56-77.

Patton, M.Q. (1986), *Utilization-Focused Evaluation*. Beverly Hills, CA, Sage.

Polsky, H. (1962), *Cottage Six. An investigation of the social systems created by delinquent boys in residential treatment*, Sage foundation.

Posavac, E.J. & Carey, R.G. (1985), *Program Evaluation: Methods and Case Studies*, Englewood Cliffs, New York, Prentice-Hall.

Pringle, M.L & Bossio, V. (1960), 'Early prolonged separations and emotional adjustment', *Child Psychology and Psychiatry*, vol. 1, 37-48.

Roth, J. (1973), *Heimkinder. Ein Untersuchungsbericht über Säuglings und Kinderheime in der Bundesrepublik*, Köln/Berlin, Kiepenhauer & Witsch.

Rutman, L. (Ed.) (1977), *Evaluation research methods: a basic guide*, London, Sage.

Rutman, L. (1980), *Planning Useful Evaluations: Evaluability Assessment*, Beverly Hills, CA, Sage.

Scotch, C.B. & Haskett, U.B. (1978), 'Preparing social workers for an age of accountability: understanding cost analysis', *Journal of Education for Social Work*, vol. 14, 107-113.

Shelly, M.H. (1982), 'The role of evaluation in child care research', *Child care quarterly*, vol. 11, no. 1, 22-43.

Shyne, A. (1976), 'Evaluation in child welfare', *Child Welfare*, vol. 55, no. 1, 5-18.

Sijben, N. (1984), 'Programma-evaluatie ... wat is dat?' in G.M. Schippers, et al. (eds) *Programma-evaluatie in de geestelijke gezondheidszorg. Conferentieverslag* (pp. 11-27), Lisse, Swets & Zeitlinger.

Sinclair, C. & Frankel, M. (1984), 'The effect of quality assurance activities on the quality of mental health services', *Journal of Quality Assurance*, vol. 8, 7-15.

Sketchley-Kneppelhout, M. (1981), *Een speurtocht in de literatuur naar kwaliteitscriteria voor het inrichtingswerk*, Amsterdam, Vrije universiteit, Vakgroep Ontwikkelingspsychologie, Pedologie en Speciale Pedagogiek (Doctoraalscriptie).

Smeets, K. (1986), *Kwaliteitsevaluatie van de residentiële hulpverlening voor kinderen en jongeren met psycho-sociale problemen. Een literatuurstudie*, Leuven, K.U.Leuven, Faculteit der Psychologie en Pedagogische Wetenschappen (Licentiaatsverhandeling).

Stevens, R.E. & Sherwood, D.K. (1982), *How to Prepare a Feasibility Study*, Englewood Cliffs, NY, Prentice-Hall.

Stockey, E. & Zeckhauser, R. (1978), *A Primer for Policy Analysis*, New York, Norton.

Struening, E.L. & Guttentagh, M. (1975), *Handbook of evaluation research*, London, Sage.

Stufflebeam, D.L. (1971), *Educational evaluation and decision making*, Ithaca.

Suchman, E. (1967), *Evaluative Research: Principles and Practice in Public Service and Social Action Programs*, New York, Russell Sage.

Swaans-Joha, B.C. (1989), *Praktijkgericht onderzoek*, Leuven/Amersfoort, Acco.

Tilanus, C. (1992), *Jeugdhulpverlening en de overheid*, Utrecht, SWP.

Tizard, B. (1975), 'Varieties of nursery experience', in J. Tizard, I. Sinclair & R. Clarke (eds), *Varieties of Residential Experience* (pp. 102-121).

Twijnstra, M. (1991), 'Kwaliteit als mentaliteitsvraagstuk', *Tijdschrift voor Jeugdhulpverlening en Jeugdwerk*, vol. 3, no. 11, 6-10.

Van der Laan, P.H. (1985), *Residentiële hulpverlening aan Surinaamse, Turkse en Marokkaanse jongeren*, 's Gravenhage, CWOK.

Van der Meulen, J.H. (1978), 'Onderzoek en organisatie-ontwikkeling binnen de residentiële hulpverlening', in K. Helsinga et al. (eds), *Residentiële hulpverlening in de praktijk*, Groningen, Wolters-Noordhoff.
Van der Meulen, J.H. & Van Uhm, C. (1981), 'Twee follow-up onderzoeken', in J.D. Van der Ploeg (ed.), *Jeugd (z)onder dak* (pp. 265-279), Alphen aan den Rijn, Samsom.
Van der Ploeg, J.D. (1980a), 'Kwaliteit valt te meten', *Tijdschrift voor jeugdhulpverlening*, vol. 8, no. 2, 46-49.
Van der Ploeg, J.D. (1980b), 'Kwaliteitsmeting moet een dynamisch proces zijn', *Tijdschrift voor jeugdhulpverlening*, vol. 8, no. 9, 68-73.
Van der Ploeg, J. (1985), 'Plaats en functie van het kinderbeschermingstehuis in de toekomst', in J.F.W. Kok & M. Klomp (eds), *Ambulante en residentiële hulp?* (pp. 77-100), Leuven/Amersfoort, Acco.
Van der Ploeg, J. (1986), 'Is kwaliteit in de residentiële hulpverlening een meetbaar begrip?' in W. Hellinckx (ed.) *Kwaliteit in de hulpverlening m.b.t. kinderen met psycho-sociale problemen* (pp. 33-56), Leuven/Amersfoort, Acco.
Van der Ploeg, J. (1990), 'Residentiële hulpverlening: jeugdigen, doelstellingen, methoden en kwaliteit', in E.J. Knorth & M. Smit (eds), *Residentiële jeugdhulpverlening. Mogelijkheden voor planmatig werken* (pp. 29-39), Leuven/Apeldoorn, Garant.
Van der Ploeg, J. & Scholte, E. (1988), *Tehuizen in beeld*, Leiden, Rijksuniversiteit Leiden, Vakgroep Orthopedagogiek, Centrum Inderzoek Jeugdhulpverlening.
Van der Ploeg, J. & Scholte, E. (1989), *BJ-centra in beeld: verkorte versie*, Leiden, Rijksuniversiteit Leiden, Vakgroep Orthopedagogiek, Centrum Inderzoek Jeugdhulpverlening.
Van Yzerdoorn, M. & Miedema, S. (1986), 'De kwaliteit van kwalitatief onderzoek', *Pedagogische Studiën*, vol. 63, 498-505.
Veerman, J. (1985), 'Evaluatie van behandelingseffecten: mag het ook anders?' in F.X. Plooij & M.G.M. Van den Dungen (eds), *Hulpverleningspraktijk en dienstverlenend onderzoek. Handelingsplannen en directe observatie van opvoeder-kind interactie* (pp. 13-25), Lisse, Swets & Zeitlinger.
Verheij, F. (1993), *Behandelingsplanning in de jeugdhulpverlening, jeugd-GGZ en het speciaal onderwijs*, Utrecht, SWP.
Wholey, J.S. (1979), *Evaluation: Promise and Performance*. Washington, DC, Urban Institute.
Wholey, J.S., Scanclon, J.W., Duffy, H.G., Fukumoto, J.S, Vogt, L.M. (1970), *Federal Evaluation Policy: Analyzing the Effects of Public Programs*, Washington DC, Urban Institute.
Williamson, J.M. (1967), cited in Verstegen, M.C.G. (1977), 'Toetsing van kwaliteit', in *Kwaliteitsevaluatie en -promotie*, Brussel.
Wortman, P. (1975), 'Evaluation research. A psychological perspective', *American Psychologist*, vol. 30, 562-575.
Wouda, P., Van der Ploeg, J. & Smit, M. (1987), *Jongeren tussen wal en schip? I*, Leiden, Rijksuniversiteit, WOJ/Vakgroep Orthopedagogiek.
Woy, J.R., Lund, D.A & Attkisson, C.C. (1978), 'Quality assurance in human service programs', in C.C. Attkisson, W.A. Hargreaves, M.J. Horowitz & J.E. Sorenson (eds), *Evaluation of human services programs* (pp. 411-444), New York, Academic Press.
Yates, B.T. (1985), 'Cost-effectiveness analysis and cost-benefit analysis: an introduction', *Behaviour Assessment*, vol. 2, no. 3, 271-282.
Young, D.W. & Allen, B. (1977), 'Benefit-cost analysis in the social services: the example of adoption reimbursement', *Social Service Review*, vol. 51, 249-264.

9 Process evaluation in residential care

Frits HARINCK
Monika SMIT

Introduction

Evaluation researchers in the field of youth care are often urged to conduct outcome studies[1]. The high cost of residential treatment and the growing demand for accountability have given priority to questions of outcome and efficiency. Service providers are required to demonstrate that their programmes are accomplishing the goals intended. It is especially on the basis of summative evaluation that financial support will ultimately depend (Curry, 1991).

Important as outcome studies may be, the question of effect is often a treacherous one for several reasons, and there are serious pitfalls to overcome. However, interesting alternatives are available. Over the last few years, evaluation has increasingly come to be seen not merely as an instrument of accountability, but also as a tool for helping programmes to work better. Consequently, evaluation research has come to encompass a broader range of research activities which are used to assess outcome as well as formative, programme-related characteristics.

In the following paragraphs we will point out the disadvantages and limitations of effect evaluation. Then we will discuss those evaluation questions which - according to practitioners - are relevant in residential care practice. Next we will elaborate on the different types of process evaluation, presenting and discussing several examples.

Disadvantages and limitations of outcome studies

In spite of the high status of outcome evaluation, outcome studies are not always called for. All programs, including residential treatment programs, go through consecutive stages of development. Recently, some finely-grained models of the programme development process have been presented. An example is Pancer and Westhues' eight-stage model of programme development (Pancer and Westhues, 1989). Since, within the scope of this chapter, it is the principle that matters rather than the stages themselves, we shall distinguish no more than five successive, quite broad stages: determination of social needs; determination of programme goals; design and selection of programme alternatives; programme implementation and operation; and, finally, programme evaluation.

At different stages of a programme, different questions are important. Thus, in order to help answer these questions, an evaluation must be suited to a programme's stage of development. In each programme phase, except for the last, effect evaluation is premature and other evaluations are called for. As Rutman (1977, p. 19) states: "The premature testing of programmes which are not evaluable is likely to produce irrelevant studies which are of little use for programme planning, management, or as a basis of accountability". Table 9.1 offers an overview of relevant questions and suitable types of evaluation for each programme stage.

Table 9.1: Stages of programme development, relevant questions and suitable types of evaluation

Stage of Programme Development	Relevant Questions	Suitable Evaluations
Determination of social needs	To what extent are the standards our society is striving to meet, being met?	Needs assessment
Determination of goals	What needs to be done in order to meet those standards?	Goal analysis
Design and selection of programme alternatives	What programme alternatives are available and which one(s) should be selected?	Logic analysis of programs, feasibility study

Programme implementation and operation	How should the programme be implemented and does it operate as planned?	Implementation assessment and process evaluation
Programme evaluation	Is the programme having the desired effects at the desired costs? Should we continue or terminate the program?	Outcome evaluation

Even when outcome evaluation would be appropriate as far as the developmental stage of the programme is concerned, there are quite a few pitfalls to be considered, both in conducting outcome studies and in interpreting the results. Some of these pitfalls will be discussed briefly.

First, many effect studies lack methodological rigour because of small numbers of respondents, unreliable instruments, weak research designs, poor experimental conditions, restricted measurement points and/or limited measures of success (Durkin and Durkin, 1975; Whittaker, Overstreet, Grasso, Tripodi and Boylan, 1988; Harinck, 1991, 1992; Wilson and Lyman, 1983). This is a problem because nonsignificant results are often interpreted as failure of the treatment. If there is no proof of outcome, funders will tend to blame the institution and not the research (Lipsey, Crosse, Dunkle, Pollard and Stobart, 1987).

Another problem often mentioned is insufficient specification of client or programme goals and insufficient specification of treatment. This makes it difficult to choose justifiable outcome measures and it prevents greater insight into the so-called black-box of residential treatment. Furthermore, in order to decrease error variance and increase the chance of obtaining relevant results, outcome research requires sufficient standardisation and standardisability of the treatment. However, programmes tend not to be implemented precisely according to plan and are not always carried out in a standard manner (Finney and Moos, 1984).

Moreover, outcome depends on both the specific elements of the treatment and the characteristics of the young person and his environment. Therefore, there is no such thing as the effect of residential treatment in general, and it is pointless to focus *exclusively* on outcome variables.

Finally, although it is important to gain insight into the effects of residential care, information on the effect of treatment does not help practitioners who are striving for improvement in the quality of care. Outcome results usually lack guidelines for adjustments and improvement. If one agrees with Stufflebeam and Shinkfield (1985) that the most important purpose of evaluation is not to prove, but to improve, then utilisation-focused evaluation is called for. A prerequisite for utility and either direct or indirect utilisation of evaluation results is that the evaluation should help users answer questions that are relevant to them (Rothman, 1980; Patton, 1986). As will be argued in the next paragraph, it is doubtful whether the question of impact is the most important one for users.

Relevant evaluation questions

An interesting question is: what types of questions do evaluators usually tackle? Shadish and Epstein (1987) surveyed the practice of programme evaluators[2]. More than half (60 per cent) of the sample consisted of psychologists and educators. The respondents were asked to what extent their most recently completed programme evaluation included any out of a list of nine purposes. Table 9.2 shows the two purposes having the highest mean scores[3].

Table 9.2: Purpose of the evaluation

Purpose of the Evaluation	Mean
To measure programme effects	4.5
To improve programme performance	4.4

Table 9.2 suggests that both summative evaluation and formative evaluation are important. Shadish and Epstein also found that stakeholder information needs played a significant role in helping evaluators decide which questions to ask in their most recent programme evaluation. Central issues on which data were gathered in those evaluations concerned process variables as well as effect. Table 9.3 gives an overview of the two issues with the highest mean scores.

Table 9.3: Central issues on which data were gathered

Central Issues on which Data were Gathered	Mean
Manner in which programme is implemented	4.4
Changes in clients brought about by the programme	3.9

Here issues related to implementation score even higher than issues related to outcome[4].

Another point of interest is: what kind of questions would practitioners ask? In order to find out, we asked participants in a postgraduate course on residential care (almost all staff working in residential care homes) to list important questions they and their colleagues need to have answered during their work. After consulting their colleagues - welfare workers, group workers, unit co-ordinators, staff and managing directors in their institution - they produced 35 different questions.

Most questions stem from ignorance concerning how to act and reflect the need for assistance in implementing certain approaches and solving problems (for example: how do we motivate our residents to go to school?). Some questions reflect lack of information (for example: how many sessions do group workers have with the parents of their pupils?), and some are normative (for example: should group workers and parents equally share the responsibility for the care of the young people concerned?). Many questions call for answers in terms of supervision, staff communication, professional training, and more explicit mutual agreements. Only a few questions reflect a need for the kind of information that would entail evaluation research. Only one question is outcome-oriented, therefore requiring outcome evaluation.

Evaluation research: for whom and why?

Possible users of evaluation results, the so-called stakeholders, do not form one homogenous group. Different categories of stakeholders, with different decisional responsibilities and with different needs as far as evaluation is concerned, can be distinguished (Majchrzak, 1986; Patton, 1986). As Weiss (1984) points out, policy makers who have to decide on funding a programme will be interested in programme outcomes, programme managers who strive for improvement of a programme will be interested in differential outcomes for different types of clients according to the service received, whereas practitioners who are interested in how to help individual clients will usually consider their own knowledge and experience to be more relevant (Leviton and Hughes, 1981). These differences in information needs are closely related to the positions the stakeholders hold in the residential organisation, on a micro, a meso or a macro level (Payne, 1981). We will discuss these levels below.

At the *micro level* the focus is on the individual client and/or on small groups of clients (for example, living units or participants in group psychotherapy). The information needs are related to planning and providing help for the individual client or groups of clients within one institution: for example, a living unit.

At the *meso level* the focus is on the larger institution as a whole. The information needs concern the planning and organisation of individual residential settings and their components, including the co-ordination of all these components with one another.

At the *macro level* the focus is on the relationship between a number of different institutions. At this level, questions concern executive decision-making and strategy: for example, an estimate may be needed of how many residential services, and of what kinds, are needed in the country.

In sum, on the micro level the main question is how to work with the clients: on the meso level the question is how to work with the organisation: and, on the macro level, the question is how to organise residential care in a certain geographical area. On the micro level there is interest in detail and qualitative information, while on the macro level there is more of a need for quantitative and aggregated data. On the meso level there is interest in both kinds of data.

What is process evaluation?

The concept "process evaluation" has different meanings. Here, process evaluation refers to the general activity of gathering data on a treatment - process: that is, on a programme in practice. Examples of relevant evaluation questions are: what happens within the programme, what kind of clients enter the programme, what are the underlying assumptions, and which programme elements should be improved? Within the broad concept of process evaluation, more specific types of evaluation have been proposed. In this chapter, six types will be distinguished: component analysis, monitoring, underlying process evaluation, implementation evaluation, clarifying practitioners' concepts, and formative evaluation. Often two or more of these types are used in combination. In the following pages, we will discuss these types and give examples from research in the field of residential care. The main focus in the examples will be on the method, not on the results.

Component analysis

Component analysis focuses on a formal description of the distinct parts of a residential programme: for example, the living unit, school facilities, leisure time facilities, and individual or group therapy. The description is global and details are omitted. The components can also be presented as a number of sequential stages through which the client has to pass. Figure 9.1 gives an example of the results of a component analysis.

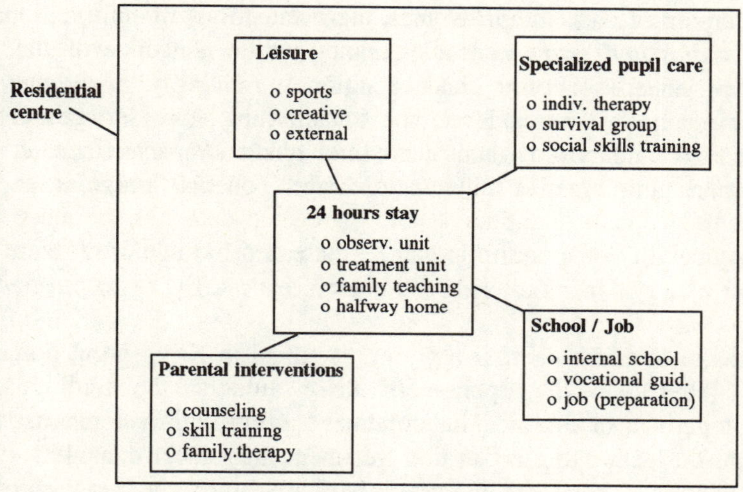

Figure 9.1: Results of a component analysis

Component analysis is a relatively simple kind of evaluation. For someone who is well acquainted with the institution, a component analysis can possibly be carried out in under one or two days. Nevertheless, component analysis gives a convenient and valuable overview of the services available. This is important both in placement decisions concerning individual clients and in the planning of new centres in a certain area.

Component analysis is of growing interest, since such analyses are urged upon youth care centres by funders and national government. Moreover, there is a great need for component analysis because of the diversification of residential treatment, which has increased in the last decades. Residential care has become a highly individualised affair, with many possible paths through the service system.

Monitoring evaluation

If component analysis is insufficient because the actual content of the services provided remains unspecified, monitoring evaluation may be a solution. This type of evaluation is essential if one is interested in what actually happens within a programme. Through monitoring evaluation, we can learn, for example, about the number of sessions held with parents, about the topics discussed in these sessions, or about the way staff members interact with parents. Generally, monitoring is limited to simple variables: data which are tangible, observable and can easily be counted or registered. Monitoring data comprise three main categories of information: *staff characteristics and staff mix* (for example, number and type of staff, years of experience, schooling and additional training); *programme activities* (for example, type and number of activities, how services are provided, intensity and cost of activities); and *client characteristics* (for example, number and type of clients, coverage[5], clients' progress and dropout rate).

The practicability of monitoring can be increased by regular measurements, so that changes in monitoring parameters can easily be discovered and responded to.

An example of *client monitoring*, may be found in Klingsporn, Force and Burdsal (1990). In the opinion of these authors, the traditional evaluative comparison of a residential treatment group with a comparison group does not do justice to the fact that treatment may differ considerably for different pupils. They are interested particularly in the amount of treatment completion and in the circumstances of treatment termination. In two residential treatment centres for boys (12 -17 years old), they studied the ways in which treatment termination occurred for 592 boys. Details about the boys and the treatment programme may be found in Klingsporn et. al. The focus in this chapter is on the way that treatment completion was conceptualised. Ten possible reasons for treatment termination were formulated. Among these were:

- treatment goals have been met (regular termination);
- (severe) acute misbehaviour;
- chronic misbehaviour;
- negative leadership (bad influence on others);
- being expelled from school;
- withdrawal by parents;
- incarceration;
- running away.

For a large majority of the boys (67 per cent) the reason for discharge was regular termination. Next came chronic misbehaviour (10 per cent) and (severe) acute misbehaviour (9 per cent). For reasons of institutional policy, the frequencies for these categories are interesting in themselves. In this study, follow-up data were also gathered at least two years after discharge, and the study thus combined process variables with outcome variables. The follow-up data included several domains of functioning. These were combined in one single coping measure and this measure was correlated with reason for termination. It turned out that regular terminators and pupils withdrawn by their parents showed the most positive results as far as coping after discharge was concerned.

Another example of *monitoring evaluation* is provided by van der Ploeg and Scholte (1988). In their evaluation project, a broad range of process data was studied[6]. They investigated different types of residential institutions, 59 in all. Several data-collection procedures were used, including questionnaires, interviews and analysis of documents. For each residential centre, among other things, data were gathered on: *pupil parameters* (for example, demographic data, family characteristics, reason for placement and referring institution); *institutional parameters* (for example, capacity, number and type of workers, length of stay, material resources and physical environment); and *treatment parameters* (for example, intake procedure, type and amount of group worker activities, intensity of contact with client and with parents, type of family involvement, daily routine procedures, rules in the living unit, and the use of sanctions).

Van der Ploeg and Scholte did not study the effectiveness of process parameters. They did use some interesting alternatives, including:

a) *relating client characteristics to method parameters.* For example, negative family circumstances proved to be associated with low parental involvement during residential care;
b) *testing for relations between treatment parameters.* They compared, for example, the way parents were involved in different kinds of treatment the pupils received;
c) *comparing the different types of institutions in their sample with regard to a number of treatment variables.* Thus, empirical differences between different categories were found and could be compared with institutional policy. An additional advantage of this approach is that reference data become available. Individual institutions might use these data to determine how closely they resemble the average institution of their type;
d) *comparing contemporary client characteristics with similar data gathered about a decade earlier.* The 1988 population turned out to be much more problematic in terms of social relations, behavioural problems, family circumstances and number of earlier experiences

with residential care.

The van der Ploeg and Scholte study is particularly useful for institutional management and government policy. The results make the institutions more conscious of their identity (mirror function) and provide the government with feedback on the correlation between its residential policy and the actual situation in residential institutions. Apart from this, in our opinion, many of the results of the study could be of interest to internal staff and group workers (meso level), if broken down for each individual institution. Unfortunately, the authors devote little attention to this possibility.

In a recently completed study by Klomp (1992), we find an example of the *monitoring of interaction patterns*. Klomp studied guidance activities of counselors in halfway houses using, among other things, written reports of counseling sessions. From these reports, he gathered counseling events: fragments where a youngster introduced a problem or where a counselor demonstrated guidance activities. Then, inductively, he derived a taxonomy for youngsters' problems and for guidance acts. Thus, he could determine simple frequencies for specific youngsters' problems and specific guidance acts (base rates). These data were analysed for interactional sequences. All "if-then" statements - statements in which a specific problem is followed by a specific guidance act - were gathered. For each type of problem he calculated the probability with which specific counseling acts would follow (conditional probability). These probabilities were compared with the corresponding base rates. Counseling activities which occur more frequently as a reaction to a specific problem are called typical responses. Figure 9.2 gives an example.

Problem description
Pupil wants to hit his girlfriend because she has got another (boy)friend

Typical responses
a) showing acceptance of feelings of anger
b) offering alternative reaction patterns

Figure 9.2: Example of typical problem - response patterns

The Klomp study summarises possible counseling acts and thus focuses on the micro level. For this reason and because of the inductive approach, the results will be of interest and recognisable to practitioners, such as counselors, trainers and supervisors.

Evaluation of underlying processes

While monitoring evaluation is restricted to tangible and easily observable characteristics, *evaluation of underlying processes* focuses on the identification and measurement of the theoretical concepts underlying a programme (Patton, 1986). Generally, these concepts are based on scientific theory and do not stem from practitioner concepts. Social climate is a well known and - in the field of residential care - highly relevant example of such a concept (Moos, 1975). An example of this kind of evaluation is provided by Theunissen (1986) who studied the social climate in four different types of residential treatment centres in the Netherlands. Theunissen started with a conceptual clarification of social climate, based on scientific theory and available research instruments. Next he constructed a voluminous questionnaire, partly representing the concept "educational style" and partly based on Polsky's concept of "functional imperatives". This questionnaire and other instruments were administered to a group of 355 pupils and 186 child care workers in 39 living units in 21 residential institutions. Factor analysis procedures were used to explore underlying dimensions of the social climate in his sample. The situation is complicated because the unit of analysis can be the individual child, the individual worker, or the living unit. However, 12 major factors appear, 6 of them team related, the other 6 pupil related. The factors reflect a broad distinction in educational style and functional imperatives, but the specific factors do not exactly match with the *a priori* theoretical structure.

The 12 climate factors are complemented with structural indices for social networks, derived from sociometric data. The climate factors and the network data form the basis for Theunissen's subsequent analysis. First, Theunissen aggregated data on climate for the individual living units and institutions, thus providing feedback to staff and internal managers (meso level). This is important because of the staff training necessary and internal decisions concerning placement in specific living units. Moreover, it enables the individual institution to compare the data with institutional policy.

Theunissen also aggregated his climate measures for the four different types of institutions. Thus he was able to study climate differences between types of institutions. Moreover, he related his climate indicators to a large number of other factors: for example, sex and age of pupils, large or small scale institution, size of team and sex of team workers.

One of the major values of this study is that it clarifies "social climate" in a residential setting and provides appropriate (if not simple) instruments. Thus, an empirical description of a living unit's climate becomes possible. However, as no outcome data were available, it is uncertain what climate characteristics will produce favourable outcome. Moreover, the highly abstract nature of the concepts used may interfere with practical application.

Implementation evaluation

In Frank Herbert's well known book "Dune", there is a statement: "The success of a plan depends as much upon concept as upon execution". This statement wonderfully reflects the essence of *implementation evaluation*: comparison of programme performance with a specified standard, usually the treatment concept. The purpose of such a comparison is to see if treatment performance is sufficiently close to the concept. The concept can be manifested in the form of a treatment manual but there are other standards with which to compare (Finney and Moos, 1984; Pietrzak, Ramler, Renner, Ford and Gilbert, 1990). Three alternative standards are:

- empirical reference data (norms derived from similar institutions);
- best practice standards (according to experts);
- a prescriptive theoretical model.

Smit (1993) offers an example of *implementation evaluation* using a *theoretical standard of comparison*. She carried out a study on the discharge of adolescents (12-21 years of age) from residential care. Among other things, information was collected about the way in which decisions concerning the discharge of 149 residents were made. The results were compared to standards for decision-making derived from a model of vigilant decision-making concerning admission, developed by Knorth (1987). The characteristic feature of a vigilant decision-making pattern is that four decisional phases are passed through systematically. Applied to discharge, these phases are: (1) assessing the desirability of discharge; (2) surveying alternative places of residence after discharge as well as the possibility of continuing the stay in the child care home; (3) weighing the alternatives; and (4) anticipating the consequences of the choice made, together with preparation for discharge, including limiting the inevitable negative effects. Smit investigated whether and how phases 2 and 4 were passed through systematically. She found that, according to the respondents, in almost half of all discharge decisions, the two conditions for vigilant decision making were met. The focus of this study is on the meso level. Co-ordinators and staff will be the most relevant stakeholders.

Clarifying practitioners' theory of action and cognitive processes

In this kind of evaluation, the focus is on clarification of the concepts and mental processes of field workers and decision makers. Often such concepts and processes are vague or implicit. The evaluator's task is to structure these concepts and make them more explicit. Three types of clarification can be distinguished, namely:

(a) goal clarification. In goal clarification the purpose is to clarify institutional or treatment goals. A popular approach is the Delphi technique. In this approach, a panel of practitioners is questioned about their goal conceptions. The evaluator analyses the answers, consults relevant literature and returns the results to the panel. The process is repeated until the goals are explicit and sufficient consensus on the goals has been reached;

(b) constructing impact models, also referred to as the *theory of action evaluation.* Here, the focus is on revealing the conceptual model, or the underlying dynamics of the program. The point is to determine how and why programme representatives think their activities will lead to specified goals. Ideally, an impact model contains underlying practitioners' assumptions and causal statements which link the diagnosed problems, the interventions used and the intended goals. In practice, such complete models are rare;

(c) clarifying decision processing. Here the focus is on the way practitioners make decisions. The evaluator tries to determine the steps and concepts involved and the rules that guide decision-making.

For an example of clarifying decision processing, we turn to a study by Ashford and Winston LeCroy (1988). They investigated the process by which intake decisions were made with respect to juvenile offenders who needed continued residential care after detention. The way placement decisions were made was not explicit and many factors seemed to be involved. In order to clarify intake decision-making, Ashford et. al. used structured interviewing techniques and group discussion with the workers involved. A central theme in placement decisions turned out to be the amount of structure (restrictiveness) required by an adolescent. Using the data obtained, Ashford et. al. identified the major variables involved and ordered them in a decision tree, part of which is presented in Figure 9.3.

Of course, clarifying practitioners' concepts does not mean that such concepts are valid and it does not guarantee better placement decisions. However, if these concepts are made more explicit, they will be more

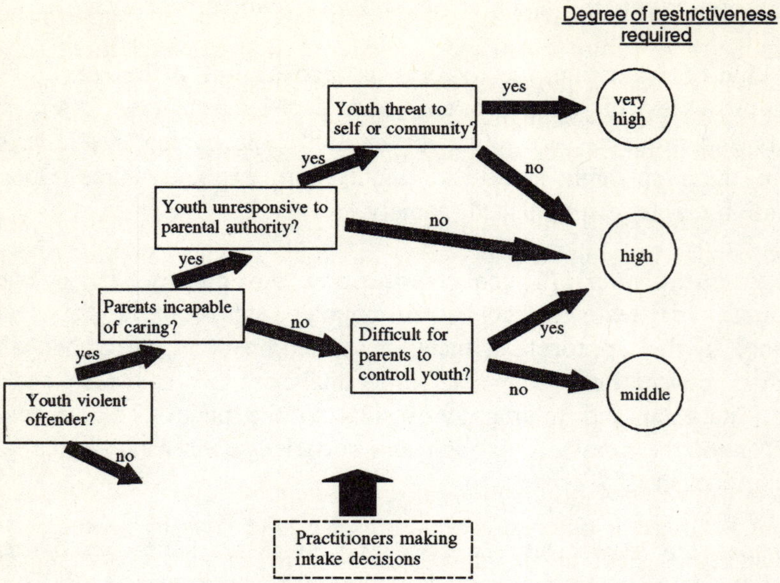

Figure 9.3: Part of a decision tree for placement decisions (adapted from Ashford et. al.)

accessible for research and for discussions with colleagues. Moreover, explicit decision models permit more efficient and more consistent placement decisions.

Formative evaluation

In a *formative evaluation*, the focus is on revealing the strengths and weaknesses of programme performance for the purpose of programme improvement. This kind of evaluation is usually based on clients' or staff's opinions, and the evaluator will often use structured questionnaires or interviews in which clients (or staff) judge the quality of specific treatment elements. In addition, the client is given ample space for critical remarks and suggestions.

An example of formative evaluation is provided by Slot (1988). With his associates he conducted several studies on the functioning of the so-called 'Kursushuizen'[7]. These studies covered both outcome and process questions. As the Kursushuis was a relatively new type of intervention, Slot included formative evaluation aimed at uncovering strengths and weaknesses in the programme. The pupils in the Kursushuis periodically completed a form about their stay in the Kursushuis, making judgements on such matters as "clarity of rules", "climate", and the "significance of discussing their future". An open-ended question allowed them to write down positive and negative remarks. As an illustration, the following are examples of *positive* evaluative remarks which were encountered on these forms: good atmosphere, external school, and good food. Examples of *negative remarks* are: little privacy, and strict rules.

The reader will understand that programme representatives do not always change programmes according to clients' wishes. If critical remarks concern vital parameters of the programme, usually the programme concept will prevail.

Process evaluation reconsidered

When we mentioned problems related to outcome evaluation, our intention was not to discredit outcome evaluation. We have no wish to return to the past when the effect of an intervention was not requested so long as the intervention was inspired by charitable motives and the efforts were undertaken in what the actors thought to be the best interests of deprived youth. Rather, we have indicated that outcome evaluation is not always required and that process measures can considerably improve the value of outcome results. From such a perspective, the aim of measuring process is, for example, to clarify the nature of the independent variables, to describe treatment elements and to isolate effective treatment parameters in order to increase the significance of outcome results. Thus, process evaluation provides a conceptual framework for outcome studies and helps us to understand certain outcomes.

However, supporting outcome studies is not the sole value of process evaluation. In this chapter we have identified several other options. One of these is the mirror function - that is, clarifying treatment content - which enables programme representatives to become more aware of the identity of their programme. The importance of this type of analysis has been stressed by some of the articles in the new Dutch law on youth care concerning the quality of that care[8]. This law obliges most institutions for youth care - which includes the majority of the residential institutions - to make general working plans for the institution. These plans should include among other things: a description of general policy in relation to the type of problems manifested by residents; treatment specification; and a list of central topics in client registration.

Another autonomous function of process evaluation is to analyse treatment elements to see if they meet quality standards. In our opinion, this is a very important function. Treatment elements should be of high quality, quite apart from their contribution to outcome. Preparation for discharge, for example, should be planned with care, even if careless planning does not necessarily lead to maladjustment in later life. Furthermore, process evaluation can help to identify relationships between subsequent process elements. It can show us what kind of treatment ingredients facilitate subsequent functioning in the programme. For example, it may be the case that negligent intake preparation results in a youth having a more difficult start in the living unit. This function is closely related to the hierarchical chain evaluation described by Patton (1986) which calls for the identification of chains of intermediate goals rather than a focus on final goals. The major advantage of this approach is that process elements can be linked to closer, more realistic goals. This may be more fruitful than the present practice of relating process measures to distant outcome measures. The weak correlations that are found with the latter approach may be indicative of the weak indirect link between process and final outcome.

Finally, we advocate a broad conceptualisation of "being successful", which is more comprehensive than "producing high client change at low cost" (see also Whittaker et al., 1988). From our point of view, success can mean getting the right clients into the institution and keeping the wrong ones out. We think success has been achieved if both the waiting list and the average treatment period are not any longer than necessary. Success may mean that few clients drop out and, if they do drop out, it is because there is better treatment for them somewhere else. In addition, the programme may be successful if the clients receive appropriate and adequate services and undergo a regular discharge. Success can mean that staff and workers have positive job satisfaction and are encouraged to be creative: or it can mean that former clients are satisfied with their stay and are afterwards better able to shape their own lives. Success may mean that clients' symptoms have been reduced or at least that the clients are better able to cope with their symptoms. Above all, success should mean the blending of these components into a balanced whole, bearing in mind the clients' needs as well as the potential of the staff and the institution.

Notes

1. Studies concerned with treatment outcome or treatment effectiveness may be designated in this chapter as outcome evaluation, effect evaluation or summative evaluation studies, using these concepts as synonyms.
2. Data were collected from 604 randomly sampled members of the Evaluation Network and the Evaluation Research Society. Complete data were obtained from slightly more than 200 respondents.
3. A Likert scale response format was used. The scale ranges from 1 (strongly disagree)

to 5 (strongly agree).

4. Interesting additional information is that 89 per cent of the respondents stated that the most recently completed evaluation was representative of the way they usually conduct evaluations, and only 18 per cent were of the opinion that these evaluations were *not* representative of the way programme evaluations *should* be conducted.
5. Correspondence between potential and actual clients.
6. Actually, this study includes several types of process evaluation. Here, the focus is on the monitoring part of the study.
7. A "Kursushuis" is a kind of family teaching project. In a Kursushuis, two teaching parents live together with six boys. Much attention is paid to teaching social skills, using behavioural techniques.
8. Besluit kwaliteitsregels jeugdhulpverlening, Stb. 1990, 503, art. 2.

References

Ashford, J.B. & Winston LeCroy, C. (1988), 'Placing juvenile offenders in residential treatment: a decision making model', *Residential Treatment for Children and Youth*, vol. 5(4), 33-41.

Curry, J.F. (1991), 'Outcome research on residential treatment: implications and suggested directions', *American Journal of Orthopsychiatry*, vol. 61, 348-357.

Durkin, R.P. & Durkin, A.B. (1975), 'Evaluating residential treatment programs for disturbed children', in M. Guttentag & E.L. Struening (eds), *Handbook of evaluation research, vol.2* (pp. 275-339), London, Sage Publications.

Finney, J.W. & Moos, R.H. (1984), 'Environmental assessment and evaluation research: examples from mental health and substance abuse programs', *Evaluation and program planning*, vol. 7, 151-167.

Harinck, F.J.H. (1991), 'Evaluatie in de instelling: wat kun je er mee doen? *Kind & Adolescent*, vol. 12, 215-226.

Harinck, F.J.H. (1992), 'Evaluatie van doelgerichte interventies', *Tijdschrift v. Opvoeding Vorming en Onderwijs*, vol. 8, 91-100.

Klingsporn, M.J., Force, R.C. & Burdsal, C. (1990), 'The effectiveness of various degrees and circumstances of program completion of young male offenders in a residential treatment center', *Journal of Clinical Psychology*, vol. 46, 491-499.

Klomp, M. (1992), *Hulpverlening aan adolescenten*, Nieuwegein, (dissertation).

Knorth, E.J. (1987), *Opname op maat,* Leuven/Amersfoort, ACCO (dissertation).

Leviton, L.C. & Hughes, E.F.X. (1981), 'Research on the utilization of evaluations; a review and synthesis', *Evaluation review,* vol. 5, 525-548.

Lipsey, M.W., Crosse, S., Dunkle, J., Pollard, J. & Stobart, G. (1987), 'Evaluation: the state of the art and the sorry state of the science', *Evaluation Studies Review Annual*, vol. 11, 153-174.

Majchrzak, A. (1986), 'Information focus and data sources, when will they lead to use? *Evaluation Review*, vol. 10, 193-215.

Moos, R. (1975), *Evaluating correctional and community settings*, New York, Wiley & Sons.

Pancer, S.M. & Westhues, A. (1989), 'A developmental stage approach to program planning and evaluation', *Evaluation Review, 13*, 56-77.

Patton, M.Q. (1986), *Utilization focused evaluation,* London, Sage publications.

Payne, C., (1981), Research and evaluation in group care', in F. Ainsworth & L.C. Fulcher (eds), *Group care for children,* London, Tavistock Publications.

Pietrzak, J., Ramler, M., Renner, T., Ford, L. & Gilbert, N., (1990), *Practical program evaluation,* London, Sage Publications.

Ploeg, J.D. van der & Scholte, E.M. (1988), *Tehuizen in beeld,* Leiden, Centrum Onderzoek Jeugdhulpverlening.

Rossi, P.H. & Freeman, H.E. (1989), *Evaluation; a systematic approach,* London, Sage Publications.

Rothman, J. (1980), *Using research in organizations,* London, Sage Publications.

Rutman, L. (1977), 'Planning an evaluation study', in L. Rutman (ed), *Evaluation research methods; a basic guide,* (pp. 13-38) London, Sage Publications.

Shadish, W.R. & Epstein (1987), 'Patterns of program evaluation practice', *Evaluation Review,* vol. 11, 555-589.

Slot, N.W. (1988), *Residentiële hulp voor jongeren met antisociaal gedrag,* Amsterdam/Lisse, Swets & Zeitlinger (dissertation).

Smit, M. (1993), *Aan alles komt een eind,* Leiden (dissertation).

Stufflebeam, D.L. & Shinkfield (1985), *Systematic evaluation,* Boston/Den Haag, Kluwer-Nijhoff.

Theunissen, H.L.A. (1986), *Het sociaal klimaat van de leefgroep,* Meppel, Krips Repro (dissertation).

Weiss, C.H. (1984), 'Toward the future of stakeholder approaches in evaluation', *Evaluation Studies; Review Annual,* vol. 9, 255-268.

Whittaker, J.K., Overstreet, E.J., Grasso, A., Tripodi, T. & Boylan, F. (1988), 'Multiple indicators of success in residential youth care and treatment', *American Journal of Orthopsychiatry,* vol. 58, 143-147.

Wilson, D.R. & Lyman, R.D. (1983), 'Residential treatment of emotionally disturbed children', in C.E. Walker & M.C. Roberts (eds), *Handbook of clinical child psychology* (pp. 1069-1088), New York, Wiley & Sons.

10 A systematic approach to residential care

Erik KNORTH
Monika SMIT

Introduction

Although dissatisfaction with residential child care in the Netherlands has led to general improvement in the quality of services (Colton, Hellinckx, Bullock and Van den Bruel, 1991), much remains to be done. There is a need for increased professionalism, for improvement in the quality of care, and for a systematic approach. With the coming into effect of the new Dutch Child Care Law (*Wetgeving Jeugdhulpverlening*, 1991), this need has to some extent become statutory: residential child-care institutions are now required by law to plan and account for their activities. This requirement obliges institutions to prepare institutional documents, called "working plans", and individual treatment plans. In an institutional document, the nature of the institution must be made explicit through a description of the kind of children the institution can serve, and its specialties in terms of treatment potential. Individual treatment plans must be prepared as soon as possible, but not later than six weeks after intake. Ideally, these plans will contain a problem assessment report, treatment goals, specific treatment plans, and an evaluation schedule, as well as either a description of the ways the institution intends to involve parents, or a reason for not doing so.

In this chapter, we will first explore the reasons for the need for a systematic approach to residential child care. Next, we will discuss a particular aspect of systematisation at the level of individual treatment plans: goal-oriented care and the use of written, hierarchically-ordered treatment goals.

Why is a systematic approach needed?

The statutory obligation to work in a more systematic way has increased an existing interest in this topic. This interest originated at least in part from the worrisome findings of studies concerning various stages of residential child care.

In recent years, Dutch empirical studies have shown that child-care workers often make *intake* decisions on the basis of limited information (Knorth, 1987; Dubbeldam, Stapper and Knorth, 1994). Information in files is usually "problem oriented" and lacks details on, for example, earlier contacts with professional educators of one kind or another, the school situation, and relationships within the family (Van den Bergh, 1992). Moreover, many children are not well prepared for admission (Knorth, 1990).

Furthermore, it has become clear that *during the stay* in a residential institution, in some cases, individual treatment plans are not prepared. For example, a 1988 study covering over 400 adolescents in residential care showed that a treatment plan was available for only one third of the group under investigation (Vissers, 1988). Knorth (1987) found that, for almost one third of the 30 child-care homes under study, it sometimes took three months or longer before treatment plans were recorded. Even in 1991 and 1992, with the Child Care Law in effect, 29 per cent of the files in 14 residential institutions in the urban agglomeration of western Holland, did not contain treatment plans for the children concerned (Inspectie Jeugdhulpverlening Regio Zuid-West, 1992).

Furthermore, existing plans and goals for treatment are not always appropriate for the problems diagnosed. Besides, group workers and staff members on the one hand and children on the other hand seem to envision different treatment goals (Van der Laan, 1986). According to a study undertaken with more than 200 residents of child-care homes, in 60 per cent of the cases goals formulated by residential workers differed from those mentioned by the children, and in 30 per cent of the cases these differences were substantial (Smit and Wouda, 1986).

In almost 50 per cent of all cases, *discharge* is a unilateral initiative arising from either the institution, the parents, or the children. Moreover, even in cases of planned discharge, criteria for discharge are vague, and it is unusual for all treatment goals to be achieved (Smit, 1993). Furthermore, although approximately 60 per cent of the institutionalised children benefit from their stay, a review of Dutch follow-up studies pointed to many problems after discharge concerning, for example, the financial situation, housing, social contacts and delinquency (Smit, 1991).

Supposedly, residential child care benefits from a systematic approach. There is some empirical evidence supporting this assumption. An increase in the care taken with the intake procedure in *Die Gute Hand*, a German child care institution, led to a substantial decrease of premature discharges (Hebborn-Brass, 1989). According to the study conducted by Vissers (1988), the mean number of changes of the social worker is smaller when a treatment plan is available (3.4 versus 4.1), and the average duration of residential care is shorter (12.9 months versus 18 months). Also, according to Smit (1993), conscientious preparation for discharge has a positive effect on the way in which children who are about to return to their parental home perceive their impending discharge. This in turn correlates positively with a favourable situation after discharge.

In the Netherlands, the need for systematisation and improvement of the quality of the interventions is not restricted to the field of residential child care. Similar trends have been found in the areas of education (Kool and Van der Leij, 1985; Van Veen and Van Rijswijk, 1993) and care of the mentally handicapped (Van Pelt, 1990; Nakken, Vriesema and Van Gemert, 1993).

Characteristics of a systematic approach

A systematic approach to residential child care can be seen as a well thought-out pattern for action in all phases of the care process (intake, treatment and termination), which is reviewed regularly. The following features, which represent an elaboration of a previously presented model (Knorth and Smit, 1990; Smit and Knorth, 1992), are characteristic of a systematic approach:

(1) A well thought-out approach to the problem behaviour of children demands insight into the nature and background of that behaviour. For this purpose, a description and analysis of the problems is undertaken *(diagnostic **A**ssessment)*;

(2) Before care can be rendered, choices must be made, ranging from the type of treatment environment most suitable as a context for care to the specific interventions which may be appropriate, in, for example, the residential care unit. This requires well thought through decision-making *(**D**ecision-making)*;

(3) The choices made lead to a treatment plan in which the problems to be dealt with, the goals to be set, and the methods to be used are specified and provided with a timeframe *(**P**lanning)*;

(4) The actual implementation of the care means that a concrete intervention strategy is undertaken in accordance with the treatment plan *(Implementation)*;
(5) Implementation of the plan is monitored closely; regular evaluation makes it possible to review the plan and the implementation process, and, where necessary, to make adjustments *(evaluative Assessment)*.

The above-mentioned characteristics make up a cycle which can serve as a blueprint for a systematic approach to care and can be applied in each phase of the care process. This can be visualised as shown in Figure 10.1[1].

The three cycles presented in Figure 10.1 "revolve", so to speak, around the concept of assessment. At first, the focus of assessment will be on the analysis of the situation of the child and family (diagnostic assessment) but, as the care process continues, the assessment focus will shift to the question of whether changes and, if so, what changes, are occurring in the child and the family as a result of the applied interventions (evaluative assessment)[2].

As already noted, goal-oriented treatment in residential care is the primary subject of this chapter. In the following sections, we will highlight the content, the setting, and the evaluation of goals within the framework of individual treatment planning.

Treatment goals in Dutch residential care

What goals play a part in residential care in the Netherlands? In the project called *Tehuizen in beeld* (Residences portrayed), Van der Ploeg and Scholte (1988) explored this issue. The authors attempted to determine which treatment goals prevail in the residential care system. Their method was based on goals research in which 56 residential centres participated[3].

A principal component analysis of the collected data showed five basic clusters of goals. In Table 10.1, we can see these clusters. Moreover, this table shows the percentage of the participating institutions in which the goals subsumed under the factors played a large or a small role or no role at all.

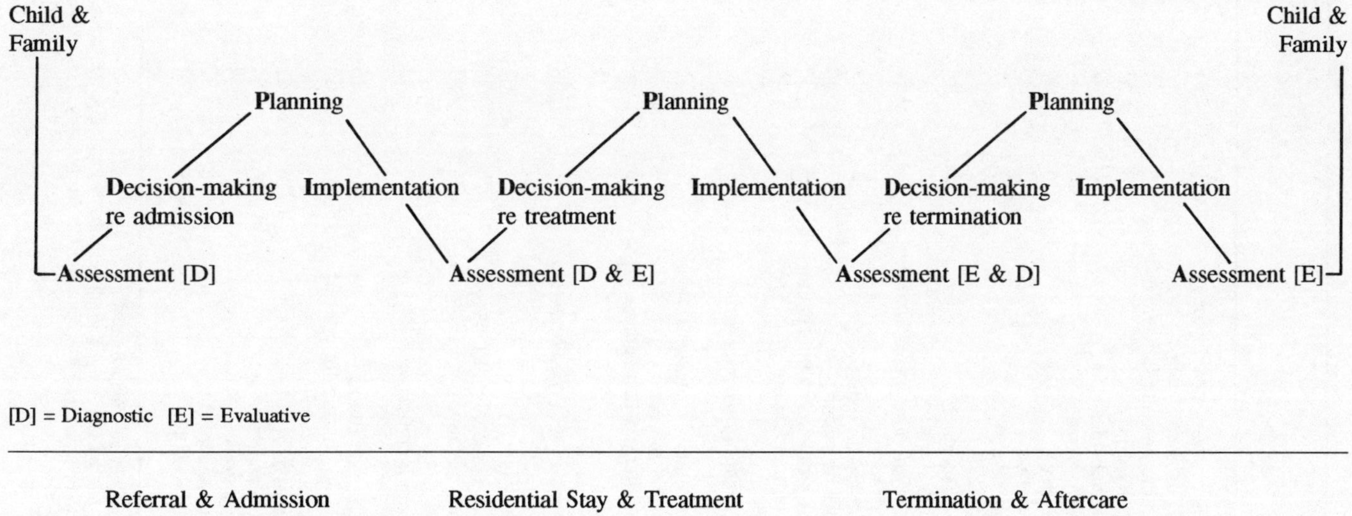

Figure 10.1: The ADPIA model

Table 10.1: Often or seldom/not used treatment goals in 56 institutions for residential care*

Goals	*often used* n	*often used* %	*seldom/not used* n	*seldom/not used* %
*Factor 1: Improving the problem behaviour** (α=.89, expl.variance=33%)*		*39*		*16****
changing/decreasing the problem behaviour	33	59	8	15
learning to start relationships	28	51	4	7
learning to accept social rules	26	47	4	7
stimulating personality growth	26	47	6	11
increasing responsibility	25	46	1	2
stimulating self-discipline	18	33	6	11
increasing communicative skills	17	31	9	17
increasing empathic skills	13	24	16	29
optimal adaptation to society	8	14	23	42
Factor 2: Optimizing the relationship with parents (α=.87, expl.variance=9%)		*34*		*31*
improving the parent-child relationship	24	44	13	24
maintaining contact with parents	22	40	12	22
helping parents with problems in upbringing	19	35	18	33
improving family communication	10	18	25	45
Factor 3: Creating a climate of basic security (α=.72, expl.variance=7%)		*70*		*4*
creating a climate of mutual confidence	42	75	2	4
offering acceptance and respect	41	73	-	-
supporting the emotional development	35	64	4	7
offering security	33	60	4	7
Factor 4: Enhancing intra-psychic functioning (α=.84, expl.variance=6%)		*53*		*5*
increasing personal insight	34	62	4	7
learning to cope with personal conflicts	28	51	1	2
learning to cope with feelings	26	47	3	5
Factor 5: Upgrading social competence (α=.80, expl.variance=5%)		*48*		*15*
offering an outlook on the future	41	75	-	-
increasing the ability to manage for oneself	36	66	1	2
increasing social skills	33	60	3	6
learning to take initiatives	26	47	4	7
supervising independent living	24	44	20	36
learning to make decisions	24	44	5	9
learning to deal with leisure time	18	32	10	18
upgrading general education	8	14	25	45

* Data from Van der Ploeg and Scholte (1988)

** The percentages per factor are averages of all variables belonging to the factor concerned

*** Row-percentages do not add up to 100% because for simplification, one column (*moderately often used*) has been left out

Before the results in the Table are discussed, a preparatory remark is in order. It must be realised that the reported findings derive from interviews with directors and staff of residential centres, who answered the questions about whether the goals identified in the Table were used as guidelines often, moderately often, or seldom/not at all in the care of the children residing in their centre. These answers can represent nothing more than an average view, and a certain response bias can never be completely ruled out.

In this context, it is interesting to note that there is a difference in the amount of attention that the various goal areas receive. Most frequent use is made of goals that aim to create a climate of basic security (factor 3). Next, enhancement of the intra-psychic functioning of the admitted children (factor 4) and upgrading of their social competence (factor 5) are mentioned comparatively frequently. Less attention is paid to the first factor: improvement of problem behaviour. The fact that problem behaviour, on average, is given little to no attention in one out of six institutions raises questions. However, it may be that the various goals relate hierarchically to one another. In other words, certain immediate, short-term goals may, to some degree, be means of reaching other intermediate goals which, in turn, are means of reaching final or long-term goals. Perhaps staff formulate long-term goals aimed at "decreasing the problem behaviour" less frequently because they approach these through the short-term and intermediate goals. Hence, only immediate and intermediate goals may be mentioned explicitly, even though ultimate goals are also sought, and vice versa. This theory would also explain the high percentage of references to creating a sense of basic security - obviously a short-term goal (factor 3). Van der Ploeg and Scholte themselves have put forward a similar explanation.

Also remarkable is the finding that, in almost one in three homes, hardly any goals concerning improvement of the child's relationship with his or her parents have been included. In spite of the many references in the literature to the importance of family-oriented care (e.g. Hellinckx, 1983; De Ruyter and Van Weelden, 1986; Jenson and Whittaker, 1987; V-erzaal, 1992), there are a number of cases where family-oriented care might represent an impossible task. Furthermore, it is evident that identifying goals does not automatically mean that these goals are actually pursued (Van der Laan, 1986).

In the next sections, we will consider the question of how treatment goals can be determined and evaluated in the context of residential care.

Goal determination upon admission

Careful decision-making about admission is the first step in the drafting of a goal-oriented treatment plan. Knorth (1987; 1991) introduced a model for "vigilant intake decision-making", based on the *decisional conflict theory* formulated by Janis and Mann (1977), an approach aimed at reducing the chance that the decision-maker will later regret his decision about a placement. The method comprises four phases, namely:

(1) *Assessing the situation.* In this phase the main questions to be addressed are: which problem areas are the most important for the child in question; and, will there be a serious risk to the child or his family if an intervention or, in this case, an admission does not take place. Assessment also includes determining which problems and goals are to be given most urgent attention.

(2) *Surveying alternatives.* Here, there are two questions. The first is whether the institution that will potentially admit the child can make a care offer appropriate to the child's needs; that is, appropriate to the care demand. Three factors which may be used to evaluate an institution's care offer are: the population or kind of children at whom the offer is aimed, the goals that could be realised through the offer, and the methods or means that will be employed to reach those goals (Van der Ploeg, 1990). The second question is then whether there are alternative treatments which also offer possibilities for dealing with the identified problems and reaching the goals.

(3) *Weighing alternatives.* In this phase, the pros and cons of the various alternatives are compared. When the most attractive alternative has been selected, a check is made to see whether it meets the requirements and goals that are considered essential. In theory, this phase will result in a decision.

(4) *Preparing for implementation.* Here, consideration is given to the consequences of implementing the decision. For example, an effort will be made to identify the possible disadvantages or objections associated with the chosen alternative (in this case, admission to a certain home) and to think about how these might be dealt with.

These four decision-making steps relate to the ADPIA cycle presented earlier as shown below:

ADPIA cycle	Vigilant decision-making
Assessment [Diagnostic]	Assessment of (risk factors in) situation
Decision-making	Surveying of alternatives Weighing of alternatives
Planning	Preparation of implementation
Implementation	
Assessment [Evaluative]	

This comparison shows that the four steps in vigilant decision-making can be integrated into the model of a systematic approach in child care: they consitute an extension or "enlargement", of, in particular, the second block in the ADPIA cycle - Decision-making. In vigilant decision-making, a significant focus of attention in the first step (Assessing the situation) is an analysis of risk factors; and, in the fourth step (Preparing for implementation), much attention is paid to the question of how disadvantages or objections related to the choice made can be dealt with. Both these questions can be seen as a *sub-class of questions* which are characteristic of the blocks "[Diagnostic] Assessment" and "Planning" in the ADPIA cycle.

Vigilant decision-making during intake allows a thorough assessment of the child's problems and the goals which need to be achieved. These goals also provide a frame of reference to guide consideration of a placement request. Moreover, during the "preparation for implementation" phase, when the chosen treatment alternative is being thoroughly examined, a number of guidelines will emerge that will form the outlines of the treatment plan. All this can contribute to a shortening of the period in which help is being given without a treatment plan - something which seems to appear in everyday practice quite often, as already mentioned.

Working with treatment goals

Residential child care is finite: eventually, the children concerned will leave the institution. Therefore, treatment goals must be future-oriented. Heringa and Knaap (1988) studied 15 treatment plans in two child-care homes, and found that about half of the goals mentioned in these plans were ultimate goals and that, for half of these ultimate goals, no intermediate goals had been defined. However, child-care workers cannot begin work with ultimate goals, because these goals are formulated on an abstract level (Heringa and Knaap, 1988), and are usually only realisable over the long term. Ultimate goals can only be reached after attention has been paid to a series of immediate and intermediate goals, and after these goals have been at least partially achieved. These various kinds or levels of goal together form so-called *hierarchic chains of objectives* (Patton, 1986), which the present authors believe should be explicitly made part of individual treatment plans. To further clarify the various goals and their interrelationships, it is advisable to draw them on paper or *visualise* them. This can be illustrated with an example which concerns the fictitious case of Emiel and is described below:

> Emiel, a boy aged 15, lives with his parents, his brother aged 12, and his sister aged 6 in an apartment building in a large city in The Netherlands. Emiel's father is a salesman whose work often takes him away from home for several days in succession. Emiel's mother finds it difficult to take care of the children. She often goes out, leaving the three children alone at home. When the father is at home, he is usually tired and prefers to be left alone.
>
> Emiel was never an easy child. As a baby, he cried a lot and as a preschooler he demanded much attention. Also, he was very jealous after the birth of his brother. At this time, the parents consulted the regional institute for mental welfare, which offered pedagogic advice. During the last few months the old problems have increased and, on the advice of the school, the parents again consulted the regional institute for mental welfare. Emiel is a non-achiever at school. Although he repeated a class, his marks are unsatisfactory, he often plays truant and he has fights at school with peers and teachers. These fights have escalated a couple of times and he is in danger of being expelled from school. At home, Emiel fights with his brother and his parents. Several of these fights have turned into physical struggles. Emiel is referred to a treatment home and admitted.

Figure 10.2 shows how possible goals for Emiel's treatment can be visualised in a hierarchic chain of objectives.

In Figure 10.2, we can distinguish an immediate goal, intermediate goals, and an ultimate goal. The choice of specific goals, of course, depends on the outcome of the diagnostic assessment and on the available treatment alternatives. The figure presents a global overview of goals which experienced social workers can expand upon and fill in more specifically. We will not dwell upon these possibilities here, because the example is meant simply to illustrate a proposed procedure. However, we do want to emphasise one point: in our opinion, it is advisable, for each goal, to specify the person who is primarily responsible for the attainment of that particular goal, and to whom enquiries can be directed.

The (imaginary) y-axis in the figure is a time-axis: the higher the position, the later the point in time. Depending on needs and possibilities,

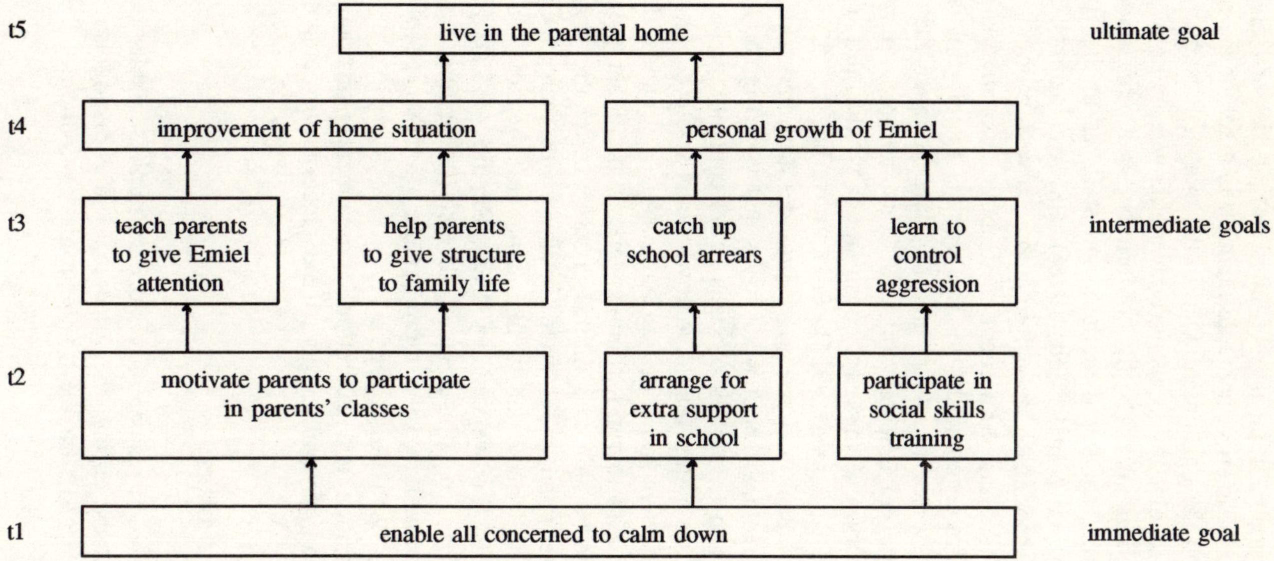

Figure 10.2: Hierarchic chain of objectives concerning residential child care

this axis can be divided into rough time intervals (for example: admission, treatment, termination, and aftercare), or detailed in terms of days, weeks, and months. In the course of time and if progress is made with the treatment, the immediate goal will become defunct, and intermediate goals will become immediate goals. It is also of interest that Heringa and Knaap (1988) reported that, in practice, sporadic mention is made of the estimated time required to reach the goals mentioned in the treatment plans.

As far as the choice of goals is concerned, we prefer a so-called "expanded participation model". In conformity with this model, the partners in consultation are social workers and staff (as in the "participation model" (Klomp and Van Oeffelt, 1978)), and also parents, referring agencies and, where possible, the children themselves. With the coming into effect of the Child Care Law mentioned above, consultation with the parties concerned became compulsory. This applies to referring agencies, to all minors aged twelve or older, and to some younger than twelve, depending upon their judgemental abilities. Consultation with parents is required unless a crisis occurs or consultation would hurt the child (*Wetgeving Jeugdhulpverlening*, 1991; Deel D, art. 5, lid 3).

The treatment plan and its goals provide an important way of preventing any disagreement about what it was that was originally decided. If a plan is put on paper, implicit changes in its content can be avoided. The existence of a plan means that anyone who chooses to depart from the planned course of action must do so on adequate grounds. However, planning should not lead to rigid, routine work. It is neither possible nor desirable to expect to be able to formulate a series of treatment goals that will remain unaltered and valid from intake to discharge. Children's development and the course of a treatment are dynamic and never completely predictable (Louwersheimer, 1991; Rietdijk, 1991). Therefore, evaluation may lead to an adjustment of the plan: changing, deleting or adding goals and methods, or the more precise specification of initially broad goals (see also Beenackers, 1986).

The implementation and execution of treatment plans will not be discussed here: instead, we will consider the evaluation of treatment plans.

Evaluating treatment plans

A systematic approach to residential child care implies regular evaluation of the treatment plans during the treatment. We distinguish between evaluation of separate goals for the treatment and evaluation of the plan as a whole.

Goal Attainment Scaling (Kiresuk and Sherman, 1968) is practicable with respect to the evaluation of separate goals. It is a method of goal definition and measurement, which uses a measurable scale for each goal to determine the extent to which these goals have been attained. The method is especially useful for the evaluation of concrete immediate and intermediate goals.

After evaluation of the separate goals has been regularly conducted, the overall picture can be re-examined. For the purpose of illustration we return to the case of Emiel. The following developments took place:

> Emiel has been in the treatment home for six months. After a period of adjustment lasting about a month, the group workers succeeded in talking to Emiel about his problems and working on some of those. Emiel goes to a school in the neighbourhood which has close ties with the child-care home. With the help of individual attention in the classroom and remedial teaching, Emiel made slow progress catching up the arrears in school. He also took part in a social-skills training programme and, in individual treatment sessions, his customary ways of coping with frustration and problems were discussed. Alternative coping strategies were offered and practised. Emiel became less aggressive. Instead of acting out, he now tries to explain what is bothering him or he withdraws from an encounter and jogs for a while. Emiel's parents were relieved when Emiel was admitted to residential care, but simultaneously felt guilty about it. In initial contacts, the parents were stand-offish. The contact has improved, but the suggestion to take part in a parents' classes was refused on the grounds of lack of time.

Based on an interim evaluation after six months, an overview of goals and objectives could be drawn up as shown in Figure 10.3.

A clear visual distinction has been made between the goals already attained (printed in half tone), and the goals still unattained. The figure shows clearly that, with respect to Emiel, important progress has been made in the realisation of intended goals. This is less true for the parents, who have refused to take part in parents' classes, under the pretext of lack of time, but in fact because of inhibitions.

An important advantage to the use of visualised hierarchic chains of objectives is that, after evaluation, it becomes clear to all parties concerned what still remains to be achieved before the treatment can be ended in a planned way. Further, if discharge occurs before all goals have been reached, the starting points for discharge preparation or for aftercare immediately become clear. Discharge preparation and aftercare can then be directed at supporting or compensating for the "weak points". In Emiel's case, it might be useful to show the figure to the parents to help them obtain a clear understanding of all developments. This understanding will hopefully make them realise the need for action on their part. Perhaps they can be persuaded to take part in parents' classes after all, or possibly the

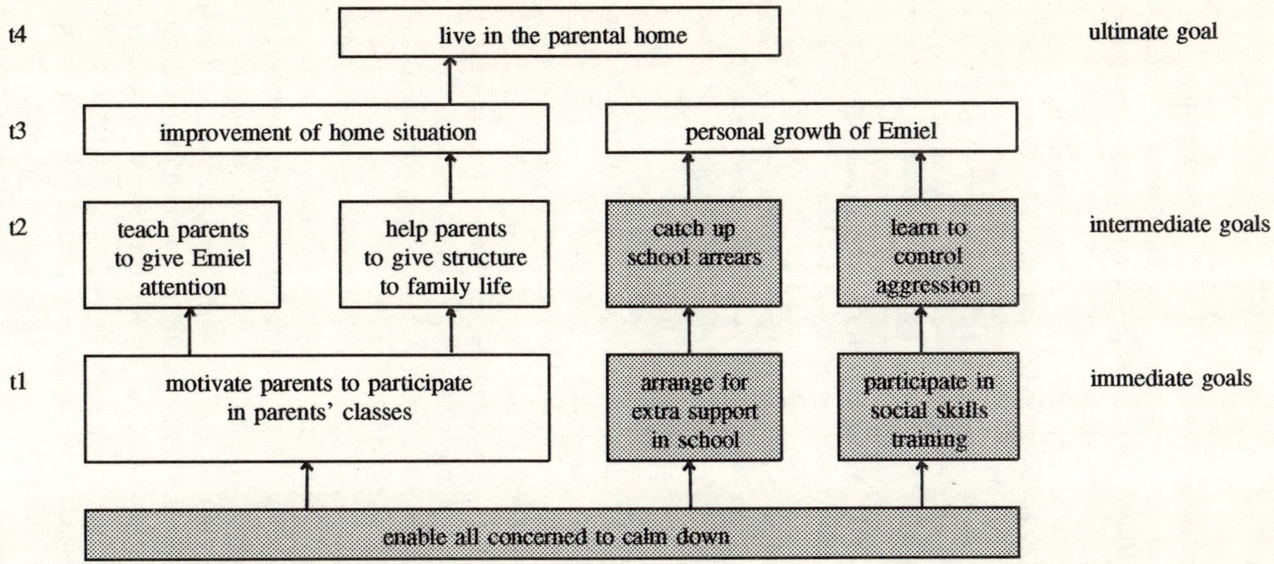

Figure 10.3: Hierarchic chain of objectives after evaluation

treatment plan will have to be adjusted to include a more individual and private way of supporting the parents. If Emiel were to leave the residential institution before the situation at home had changed, preparation for discharge and aftercare could, on the one hand, be directed at strengthening the family's social network to find sources of support and, on the other hand, consist of consultation with Emiel and his parents. This would create an opportunity to prepare for the return home, to discuss possible problems, and to point out ways of handling those problems adequately.

Summary and conclusions

This chapter has described aspects of a systematic, goal-oriented approach to residential child care. Careful decision-making at intake allows goals to be determined and constitutes the first step towards treatment planning. Next, the identified goals can be ordered in a hierarchical pattern and displayed on paper in a clear manner. This "visualisation" process helps to show what progress has been made toward the achievement of each individual goal. From time to time, it will be useful to undertake a complete review in order to determine which immediate and intermediate goals have already been reached and which remain to be achieved. The written plan or pattern of goals is a simple resource which can be used to show all those concerned what the residential placement has so far achieved and on which aspects the care process will focus from now on.

It has already been mentioned that the proposed, goal-oriented approach can be helpful when intervention decisions have to be made. However, there are additional practical advantages associated with this approach. For example, decision-makers are compelled to consider goals in relation to each other and to make starting-points explicit. This clarity of procedure can motivate group workers, staff members, and other professionals (Posavac and Carey, 1980; Van Coillie, 1993) as well as children and their parents. Another important advantage is that the inclusion of different types and levels of goals increases the chance of satisfying the interests or priorities of all parties concerned. Furthermore, the goal-oriented method can be productive with respect to planning for the residential institution itself as a whole. Aggregation of individual treatment plans and evaluation data generates important information which can be used to create or adapt an institutional working plan.

It is evident by now that there are some positive expectations with respect to the application of a systematic, goal-oriented approach in residential child care. There are empirical indications for the value of this approach as well but the evidence from research is still limited. Therefore, there is a definite need for more research in settings where experiments with elements of a systematic approach as described in this chapter can be carried out.

The present authors are preparing to conduct such research. First, the research will be aimed at a description of *the process* of the development and evaluation of individual treatment plans, with special attention to the formulation and operationalisation of treatment goals. Second, the *effects* of these plans on the course of the treatment process itself will be explored. Such a line of research could also be helpful in providing more insight into the valuable elements in the black-box of residential child care (Harinck and Smit, 1992; Hoghughi, 1992; Van der Ploeg, 1993).

Notes

1. The model for a systematic approach in child care presented in Figure 10.1 resembles the "regulative cycle" model conceived by Van Strien (1975; 1990) which can be used to characterise and systematise problem-oriented thinking in practice. Van Strien distinguishes five steps: formulation of the problem; diagnosis; planning; intervention; and evaluation. Compared with van Strien's cycle, the model presented here puts more emphasis on the role of decision-making.
2. It need hardly be said that working in practice along the lines of a systematic approach does not always follow as strict a sequence as implied here. Furthermore, by picturing only *three* cycles, we do not mean to imply that these cannot be worked through more often, as will presumably be the case in the stay and treatment phase.
3. The facilities concerned were: residential homes for "normal" children and adolescents, treatment homes, residential vocational training schools, centres for supervised lodging, and open and closed reception centres.

References

Beenackers, A.A.J.M. (1986), *Project-evaluatie in de geestelijke gezondheidszorg*, Delft, Eburon.

Colton, M., Hellinckx, W., Bullock, R. & Van den Bruel, B. (1991), 'Caring for troubled children in Flanders, The Netherlands, and the United Kingdom', *British Journal of Social Work*, vol. 21, 381-392.

De Ruyter, P.A. & Van Weelden, J. (1986), 'Taak en functie van de residentiële hulpverlening', in R. De Groot & J. Van Weelden (eds.), *Van gisteren over morgen. Een orthopedagogische overzichtsstudie* (pp. 176-198), Groningen, Wolters-Noordhoff.

Dubbeldam, J.W.E., Stapper, E.A.A. & Knorth, E.J. (1994), 'Aanmeldingsrapporten in de residentiële jeugdzorg. Een vooronderzoek naar het informatief gehalte', *Kind en Adolescent*, vol. 15, 46-51.

Harinck, F.J.H. & Smit, M. (1992, November), *Process evaluation in residential care*, Paper presented at the 2nd EUSARF Seminar on "Caring for Separated Children", Paris (pp. 1-15).

Hebborn-Brass, U. (1989), *Abschlussbericht zum Praxisforschungsprojekt 'Evaluation und Vorhersage des Behandlungserfolges bei psychisch gestörten Kindern und Jugendlichen eines heilpädagogisch-psychotherapeutischen Heims'*, Kürten-Biesfeld, Stiftung 'Die Gute Hand'.

Hellinckx, W. (1983), 'Gezinsgerichte orthopedagogische hulpverlening aan een emotioneel- en/of gedragsgestoord kind', in J. Van Weelden et al. (eds.), *Onvoltooid of onbegonnen? Hulpvragende kinderen I* (pp. 185-205), Groningen, Wolters-Noordhoff.

Heringa, H. & Knaap, M. (1988), *(Be)handelbare plannen. Een praktijkgericht onderzoek naar behandelingsplannen*, Leiden, Rijksuniversiteit, Vakgroep Orthopedagogiek (Doctoral thesis).

Hoghughi, M. (1992, November), *Inside the black box. What is involved in Intervention Process Research?* Paper presented at the 2nd EUSARF Seminar on "Caring for Separated Children", Paris (pp. 1-30).

Inspectie Jeugdhulpverlening Regio Zuid-West (1992), *Dossiers in de jeugdhulpverlening*, Rijswijk, Inspectie Jeugdhulpverlening.

Janis, I.L. & Mann, L. (1977), *Decision making. A psychological analysis of conflict, choice and committment*, New York/London, The Free Press.

Jenson, J.M. & Whittaker, J.K. (1987), 'Parental involvement in children's residential treatment: from preplacement to aftercare', *Children and Youth Services Review*, vol. 9, 81-100.

Kiresuk, T.J. & Sherman, R.E. (1968), 'Goal Attainment Scaling: a general method for evaluating comprehensive community mental health programs', *Community Mental Health Journal*, vol. 4, 443-453.

Klomp, M. & Van Oeffelt, P.W.H.M. (1978), 'Residentiële behandelingsplanning als proces', *Pedagogisch Tijdschrift*, vol. 30, 387-404.

Knorth, E.J. (1987), *Opname op maat. Een verkennend onderzoek naar de intakeprocedure als begin van residentiële jeugdhulpverlening*, Leuven/Amersfoort, Acco.

Knorth, E.J. (1990), *Ingenomen met opname? Ervaringen van jongeren met de opname in een tehuis* (KLOP-reeks 1), Leiden, Rijksuniversiteit, Vakgroep Orthopedagogiek (2nd. ed.).

Knorth, E.J. (1991), 'Vigilant decision-making in connection with residential admission of juveniles', in W. Hellinckx, E. Broekaert, A. Vanden Berge & M. Colton (eds.), *Innovations in residential care* (pp. 195-210), Leuven, Acco.

Knorth, E.J. & Smit, M. (1990), 'Planmatig werken in de residentiële jeugdhulpverlening', in E.J. Knorth & M. Smit (eds.), *Residentiële jeugdhulpverlening. Mogelijkheden voor planmatig werken* (pp. 13-27), Leuven/Apeldoorn, Garant.

Kool, E. & Van der Ley, A. (1985), 'Planmatig handelen', in A. Van der Ley (ed.), *Zorgverbreding, bijdragen uit speciaal onderwijs aan basisonderwijs*, Nijkerk, Intro.

Louwersheimer, F.W. (1991), 'De praktijk is niet eenvormig. Werken met behandelingsplannen', *Tijdschrift voor Jeugdhulpverlening en Jeugdwerk*, vol. 3, 48-53.

Nakken, H., Vriesema, P.L. & Van Gemert, G.H. (1993), 'Planning in de zorg voor verstandelijk gehandicapten', in G.H. Van Gemert & R.B. Minderaa (eds.), *Zorg voor verstandelijk gehandicapten* (pp. 235-250), Assen/Maastricht, Van Gorcum.

Patton, M.Q. (1986), *Utilization focused evaluation*, Londen, Sage.

Posavac, E.J. & Carey, R.G. (1980), *Program evaluation: methods and case studies*, Englewood Cliffs (N.J.), Prentice-Hall.

Rietdijk, L.E. (1991), 'Het behandelingsplan voor het kind in de leefgroep', *Tijdschrift voor Jeugdhulpverlening en Jeugdwerk*, vol. 3, 36-42.

Smit, M. (1991), 'De situatie van jongeren na een tehuisverblijf. Resultaten uit een literatuuronderzoek', *Tijdschrift voor Orthopedagogiek*, vol. 30, 476-492.

Smit, M. (1993), *Aan alles komt een eind. Een onderzoek naar de beëindiging van tehuishulpverlening*, Dissertation University of Leiden.

Smit, M. & Knorth, E.J. (1992), 'Doelgericht werken in tehuizen', *Nederlands Tijdschrift voor Opvoeding, Vorming en Onderwijs*, vol. 8, 101-113.

Smit, M. & Wouda, L. (1986), 'Dropping out of residential care homes for juveniles: some tentative results', in R. Soisson (ed.), *Aktuelle Probleme Jugendlicher in der Heimerziehung in Europa* (pp. 213-220), Zürich, Fice.

Van Coillie, M. (1993), *Burnout in de hulpverlening*, Leuven/Apeldoorn, Garant.

Van den Bergh, P.M. (1992), 'Information about the client', in J.D. Van der Ploeg, P.M. Van den Bergh, M. Klomp, E.J. Knorth & M. Smit (eds.), *Vulnerable youth in residential care. Part II: Clients, staff and the system* (pp. 45-57), Leuven, Garant Publishers.

Van der Laan, P.H. (1986), 'Een wet van vraag en aanbod? Over residentiële hulpverlening aan allochtone jongeren', in P. Adriani (ed.), *Interculturele jeugdhulpverlening. Ervaringen met en gedachten over hulpverlening aan allochtone jeugdigen* (pp. 77-90), Utrecht, WIJN.

Van der Ploeg, J.D. (1990), 'Residentiële hulpverlening: jeugdigen, doelstellingen, methoden en kwaliteit', in E.J. Knorth & M. Smit (eds.), *Residentiële jeugdhulpverlening. Mogelijkheden voor planmatig werken* (pp. 29-39), Leuven/Apeldoorn, Garant.

Van der Ploeg, J.D. & Scholte, E.M. (1988), *Tehuizen in beeld*, Leiden, Rijksuniversiteit, Vakgroep Orthopedagogiek/Centrum Onderzoek Jeugdhulpverlening.

Van der Ploeg, J.D. (1993), 'Some concluding remarks concerning current research on youth care', *EUSARF News*, vol. 1, 6-10.

Van Pelt, G. (1990), *De zwakzinnigeninrichting. Leefgemeenschap en organisatie*, Lochem, De Tijdstroom.

Van Strien, P.J. (1975), 'Naar een methodologie van het praktijkdenken in de sociale wetenschappen', *Nederlands Tijdschrift voor de Psychologie*, vol. 30, 601-619.

Van Strien, P.J. (1990), 'Theorie, methodologie en ethiek van het praktijkdenken en -handelen', in P.J. Van Strien & J.F.H. Van Rappard (eds.), *Grondvragen van de psychologie* (pp. 307-324), Assen, Van Gorcum.

Van Veen, A.F.D. & Van Rijswijk, C.M. (eds.) (1993), *De proef op de som. Kwaliteitsverbeteringsprojecten in pedagogische werkvelden*, Leuven/Apeldoorn, Garant.

Verzaal, H. (1992), 'Family-oriented treatment in a residential institute for adolescent girls', in J.D. Van der Ploeg, P.M. Van den Bergh, M. Klomp, E.J. Knorth & M. Smit (eds.), *Vulnerable youth in residential care. Part II: Clients, staff and the system* (pp. 119-129), Leuven, Garant Publishers.

Vissers, J. (1988), *De residentiële carrière van jongeren in de kinderbescherming* (J en J Reeks 12), 's Gravenhage, CWOK.

Wetgeving Jeugdhulpverlening. Wet op de jeugdhulpverlening. Algemene maatregelen van bestuur. Ministeriële besluiten (1991), Rijswijk/Den Haag, Ministerie van Welzijn, Volksgezondheid en Cultuur/Ministerie van Justitie.

11 Evaluating family support services

Matthew COLTON
Charlotte DRURY
Margaret WILLIAMS

Introduction

Between 1969 and 1989, at least 20 Acts of Parliament with a child law theme were enacted in the United Kingdom. These, together with the pre-1969 material, comprised a daunting bulk of legislation which was comprehensible for the most part only to lawyers. The 1989 Children Act brought together, in a single, reasonably clear code of law, all the public and private laws concerning the care, protection and upbringing of chldren and the provision of services to them and their families. The Act was heralded by the Lord Chancellor, Lord Mackay, as "the most comprehensive and far-reaching reform of child law...in living memory". Packman and Jordan (1991, p.323) described it as "a quantum leap from the old restricted notions of 'prevention' to a more positive outreaching duty of support for children and families". There is no doubt that the 1989 Children Act has great potential, not least with respect to the establishment of a genuine partnership between parents and local authorities. Part III of the Act redefines the general powers and duties of local authorities in relation to children, on the principle that parents and local authorities should work together in "voluntary partnership" for the benefit of the children concerned (Bridge, Bridge and Luke, 1990).

However, the results of a study conducted by the present authors suggest that the Act's potential is not being realised, largely because of an inherent contradiction between the all-embracing spirit of the Act and current political and social realities. The study focused on the ways in which Welsh social services departments operationalise the concept of need contained in Part III of the Act. Data with respect to key issues were collected from the eight social service departments in Wales through analysis of policy documents and interviews with lead child care managers. Other data sources included interviews with social workers and service users, and questionnaires completed by senior officers from voluntary and other statutory agencies, and community groups. (For further details, see Colton, Drury and Williams, 1994a and 1994b.)

This chapter identifies the key dilemmas in the implementation of the Children Act and highlight the conflicts facing local authorities. The three issues considered here are pertinent not only to Wales but to the whole of the United Kingdom and Europe: definitions of need, identification of children in need, and family support services.

Operational definitions of need

Two notable features of Part III of the Children Act are its recurrent reference to "children in need" and its firm emphasis on the functions of social services departments (SSDs). A first important question must therefore be: How do SSDs define "children in need"? Since the expression "children in need" is a legal term bearing a restricted meaning whenever it appears in the Act, SSDs are essentially obliged to follow the definition given. The definition as it appears in Section 17(10) is as follows:

"a child shall be taken to be in need if

(a) he is unlikely to achieve or maintain, or to have the opportunity of achieving or maintaining, a reasonable standard of health or development without the provision for him of services by a local authority under this Part;

(b) his health or development is likely to be significantly impaired, or further impaired, without the provision for him of such services; or

(c) he is disabled."

The words "disabled", "development" and "health" are themselves more completely defined in the Act but there is no precise definition of the phrases "reasonable standard of health and development" and "significantly impaired". Seven of the eight SSDs examined incorporate these last two concepts into their policy documents but they do not define them either. Nor do the SSDs provide guidance to social workers on how the concepts ought to be interpreted when making decisions with respect to clients. It may be argued that they do not do this for the very good reason that they are between a rock and a hard place. "Reasonable" and "significant" are relative concepts just as the concept of poverty is relative. Probably, no-one in the U.K. is poor in the way that people in the Third World may be poor, but a large, and seemingly increasing, proportion are poor nevertheless in that they are denied access to a quality of life enjoyed by others in their society (Oppenheim, 1990). In the same way, "reasonable standards" cannot be meaningfully defined without an agreed basis of comparison. Is a child living in a disadvantaged community to be compared with others in that same community or with children living somewhere else who are enjoying greater benefits?

Since every possible answer to this question is likely to elicit vociferous criticism, SSDs can hardly be blamed for avoiding the issue. Social workers, however, are not in a position to avoid it. Our data indicate that their response is an uneasy compromise. In the first place, they provide service to children who are disadvantaged *with respect to their own community* because these children fall into a particular category of need (for example, they are at risk of abuse or neglect, or they are disabled). Since social workers are rarely in a position to serve an entire community, they must perforce restrict service to children who are in need with respect to that community. However, the *level of service* they provide may - and, according to the study data, often does - surpass community standards. A number of parents who were generally satisfied with the services provided to them by the SSDs remarked that children of theirs who were being accommodated received far more in the way of material goods, opportunities and general support than did siblings who had remained at home. Since accommodation in many cases had resulted from police involvement, parents felt that bad behaviour was essentially being rewarded and there was justification for the resentment and jealousy often exhibited by siblings. One mother remarked that, if her youngest threw a brick through a window as her eldest had, he'd get a holiday too.

Social workers can hardly be blamed for trying to raise the quality of life for children in need to what they themselves perceive as "a reasonable standard". Nevertheless, the evidence suggests that some social workers define "reasonable" in a way that creates dissension in the natural families of the children being served. Of course, this does not apply to all social workers. Some provide a level of service which is more consistent with community standards and is therefore lower than the level received by other families in the same community who are served by other workers. Dissension is created here as well, this time between community members.

It may be argued that SSDs have essentially three choices. First, they can allow the situation to continue as it presently exists. This is doubtless the safest choice from a political standpoint since they will not then involve themselves in the kind of controversy that has raged for so many years around the issue of poverty (see, for example, Townsend, 1979; Oppenheim, 1990). Second, they might issue guidance to social workers to the effect that children being served must not receive goods or opportunities which would normally be denied to other children in the community. Furore would doubtless result since such a policy would amount to an official endorsement of continued disadvantage for children from troubled environments. Third, they might encourage all social workers serving a particular community to decide among themselves what levels of service are appropriate in commonly-encountered situations, adding the proviso that the *family* should be served and not only the child. A decision to provide a higher level of service to all would naturally have resource implications. A decision, in the name of equality, to deprive some children of services presently being offered would inevitably provoke dissension.

Gardner and Manby (1993) have observed that the social justice definition of need (as opposed to the individual pathology definition) recognises the inequalities inherent in society, on the basis of which whole areas rather than individual families could be defined as needy. These authors also refer to the working group, co-ordinated by Jane Tunstill at National Council of Voluntary Child Care Organisations (NCVCCO), which set out the basis by which need could be assessed in a holistic way using the powers as well as the duties set out in the Act. However, pressures on family support have increased since then and the present data suggest that the individual pathology definition of need is still, by far, the most prevalent.

The same issues arise with respect to Section 17(1) of the Act, which reads:

> "It shall be the general duty of every local authority (a) to safeguard and promote the welfare of children in their area who are in need, and (b) so far as is consistent with that duty, to promote the upbringing of such children by their families, by providing a range and level of services appropriate to those children's needs."

Not surprisingly perhaps, lead child care managers expressed some dissatisfaction with this Section which was felt, in general, to be too broad and open to interpretation. There is no doubt that the Section is of the highest significance, paving the way for a wide spectrum of new services for families and children. There is also little doubt that its practical value is limited since it expresses a general philosophy with no specific definitions of important terms. What are the services which ought to be provided? What is the meaning of "appropriate", bearing in mind that "appropriate" too is a highly relative term? SSDs in Wales have offered no guidance to social workers on these matters, possibly because they are aware that the Section imposes a political rather than a legal duty upon them and they are not sure what this duty is.

A political duty must be viewed in a political context. The 1980s saw major changes in social policy in Britain which together amount to the most fundamental re-evaluation of the welfare state since the 1940s. Johnson (1990, p.4) relates:

"...After the war a mixed economy of welfare emerged in which the state predominated with smaller roles allotted to the voluntary and commercial sectors and in which domiciliary care was left largely to families. A broad consensus concurred with the balance struck between the statutory, voluntary, commercial and informal sectors. Mrs. Thatcher and her colleagues sought to overturn these arrangements by reducing the role of the state..."

It may be argued that the role of the state, as perceived by service providers, plays a major part in determining the operational definitions of such concepts as "providing appropriate services" and "safeguarding and promoting the welfare of children in need". The SSDs represent the state. Is it now their function to continue to play a reduced role, perhaps focusing on facilitating the provision of services by the voluntary and commercial sectors? This question assumes a particular importance in light of the fact that the current political thrust is towards the community care purchasing/care manager model which encourages the targetting of services towards individuals.

Alternatively, are the SSDs themselves supposed to be the primary providers? If they are supposed to provide - as of course they are, if only by funding others - what level of provision is politically expected? Is it a low level, in tune with current residualist policies, or is it the all-embracing level implied by the wide definition of need contained in the Act? If SSDs could answer this question, they might know whether they should provide services to children in poor communities in line with the standards of those communities or whether they should aim for higher standards. They might know, in short, whether to interpret the concept of need in relative or absolute terms.

Reflected here is the old dilemma of collective versus individual responsibility (see, for example, George and Wilding, 1976; Pinker, 1979). Is it the function of the state to achieve and maintain material equality, or should those who are able to prosper be permitted to prosper while providing a modicum of care for those less well equipped? Which of these philosophies is currently predominant in Britain? Is the present aim of the state collectivism or residualism: or even perhaps an expedient compromise between collectivism in theory and residualism in practice? It may appear that residualism is the victor but, of course, residualism cannot exist unless there is an underclass to receive the residue. Murray (1990) argues that there is an emerging British underclass, while others have vigorously disputed this claim (Field, 1990; Brown, 1990; Walker, 1990; and Deakin, 1990). However, Bradshaw (1990) has documented the growing evidence that the post-war trend towards greater equality in the distribution of income and wealth came to a halt and was reversed during the 1980s. For example, he reports that from 1979 to 1987 the share of final income of the bottom 20 per cent dropped by 11 per cent and that of the top 20 per cent increased by 11 per cent (Bradshaw, 1990, p. 17-18).

In addition to growing inequality, a significant increase in child poverty occurred in the UK during the 1980s. Between 1979 and 1987, for instance, the proportion of children living below 50 per cent of average income more than doubled from 12.2 per cent to 25.7 per cent. Over the same period, moreover, there was also a doubling of the number of children living in families dependent on supplementary benefit and on family income supplement (Bradshaw, 1990). According to Bradshaw (1990, p. 51) children have...

> "...borne the brunt of changes that have occurred in the economic conditions, demographic structure and social policies of the UK. ...There is no evidence that improvements in the living standards of the better off have 'trickled down' to low income families with children."

Few people are in a better position to observe the effects of increasing inequality and child poverty than lead child care managers in Welsh SSDs. Wales labours under a relatively high degree of social disadvantage. Indeed, the former coal mining area of South Wales is one of the most disadvantaged regions in the UK (Day, Rees and Read, 1991). Welsh SSDs - in common with their counterparts in England - are therefore faced with a profound dilemma. On the one hand, there is the Children Act 1989 which the Lord Chancellor, Lord Mackay, has rightly heralded as "...the most comprehensive and far reaching reform of child care law in living memory." On the other hand, there are flourishing social policies, both inside and outside the child care field, which would seem to blatantly contradict the spirit of this reform. Hardiker (1991, p.356) comments that "the language of 'needs' contained in the 1989 Act, is usually associated with a collectivist model of welfare, and... sits oddly in our new residualist era." Likewise Packman and Jordan (1991, p.315) note that "...concepts...like sharing responsibility between parents and the state, reaching agreements and partnerships...have a surprisingly communitarian or even collectivist ring about them..."

The conflict is perhaps most tellingly reflected in the area of resources. If a wider definition of need is to be translated into increased service provision, then obviously additional resources will be required. However, resource constraints were much in evidence in the 1980s and the situation does not appear to have changed. Johnson (1990) observed that, at the time of writing, the resources of SSDs were stretched to breaking point owing to a growth in child abuse referrals, the rise in unemployment since 1979, the increasing level of crime, policies of deinstitutionalisation, and demographic factors (Johnson, 1990, p. 183-184). He reports that:

> "Over the period from 1980/81 to 1984/85 net expenditure...on the personal social services increased by 2 per cent less than was required to meet increased demand, and gross

expenditure increased by 3 per cent less than was required. Between 1980/81 and 1985/86 almost two-thirds of local authorities fell short of the target increases of 2 per cent a year, and the most recent expenditure plans indicate that between 1988/89 and 1990/91 real expenditure on the personal social services will fall by 0.7 per cent..." (Johnson, 1990, p. 184).

There is clear evidence that resource constraints are adversely affecting the quality of services for children and their families. For example, in London alone an estimated 600 children at risk are unsupervised as a consequence of staff shortages (Johnson, 1990, p.184). The results of the present study confirm this general position. All the lead child care managers interviewed stated quite categorically that their departments were under-funded, and that resources for implementing Part III of the 1989 Act were inadequate. None could give specific information on the scale of the shortfall but all indicated that the extent of underfunding was significant. Social services chiefs in West Glamorgan have subsequently stated publicly that they are already £1 million short of the funds they need to carry out critical and far-reaching demands under the Children Act. Lead child care managers further pointed out that child and family services do not have a sufficiently high political profile within certain Welsh counties to attract adequate funding, and that, in order to effect a shift away from accommodating children towards family support, greater political commitment to children in need was required.

In the wake of inadequate resources and philosophical and political confusion, it is hardly surprising that the study found Welsh SSDs to be experiencing difficulties in formulating operational definitions around the concept of need. A not unusual response to difficulties associated with reform is to retreat to a more familiar position. For example, Section 17(1) of the Children Act replaced Section 1 of the Child Care Act 1980 which has guided SSDs for the last decade. The study found that some Welsh SSDs were approaching the Children Act in the same way as they approached the Child Care Act rather than seeking to operationalise the much broader concept of family support which the Children Act contains. The lead child care managers of all SSDs said that they planned to provide guidance for social workers regarding the interpretation of Section 17(1) as a whole in assessing need. Section 17(1) as a whole of course includes the ten sets of provision set out in Schedule 2, of which the first is *identification of children in need and the provision of information.*

Identification of children in need

Schedule 2 of the 1989 Act requires local authorities to take reasonable steps to identify the extent to which there are children in need in their areas. It is hardly necessary to point to the difficulty of identifying a population which has not been clearly defined, particularly as the legal definition encompasses children who are likely to be in need in the future. Nevertheless, it was found that most Welsh SSDs had taken various steps to identify overall needs. These steps had not involved attempts to gather new kinds of information, but were limited to the collation of data already collected under the old legislation, such as information contained in child abuse registers or gathered for reviews of services.

Lead child care managers were asked to provide statistics on the following categories of need which, with the exception of children leaving care, were derived from the University of Leicester/ Department of Health (1991) guide for child care managers on Part III of the Act.

- children with disabilities;
- children at risk of abuse or neglect;
- children who are delinquent or at risk of becoming delinquent;
- children separated from their parents;
- children with serious family problems;
- children whose home conditions are unsatisfactory;
- children living in poverty; and
- children leaving care.

Information on the number of children subject to neglect or abuse was generally available but little reliable data could be produced with respect to the other categories. All departments had encountered difficulties in identifying children with disabilities. Managers of five of the eight Welsh SSDs provided data on the total number of children with disabilities but most had no information about the estimated or registered number of children in the individual categories of disability given in the 1989 Act. Although local authorities are required to open and maintain registers of children with disabilities, none of the departments had done so 12 months after the Act came into force. This was attributed in part to insufficient time and staff, yet some managers also revealed a distinct lack of enthusiasm for the task, which one described as ... "an exercise in futility".

There are three issues here. First, the primary purpose of identifying children in need is to enable preparations to be made for providing services to them. Preparation will normally begin with deciding what services should be provided, at what level, and who should provide them. The political and philosophical difficulties associated with such decisions have already been discussed. Preparation will also include ensuring that the necessary resources are available - another difficulty - and training staff to perform the agreed-upon tasks. It is possibly not surprising that Welsh SSDs have been slow to identify a population whose needs - both present and potential - they are unlikely to be able to meet.

The second issue concerns the actual process of identification. Children in need, as defined in the Act, comprise a broader population than before and therefore cannot be identified merely by collation of existing data. New needs assessments are indicated, involving a formidable amount of work for which local social service departments do not have the time, the funds, or possibly the skills.

Third, there is the matter of who is to provide the identification data. Parents can hardly be expected to complete a questionnaire - no matter how anonymous - to the effect that their children are at risk because of abuse, neglect, family problems or unsatisfactory home conditions: such data would have to come from education, health and police authorities and local community groups. However, parents might be expected to admit to having children with disabilities, since the tragedy of disabled children is not associated in British culture with either class or the level of parental skills. Findings from interviews with parents of disabled children indicated that these parents had not yet been asked to register their children. The majority said that they would register them if asked to do so. Indeed, one woman with a hyperactive child felt that the parenting difficulties associated with hyperactivity were not sufficiently appreciated and having her child formally listed as disabled might entitle her to more appropriate and extensive service. A substantial minority of parents, however, expressed hesitation, one mother remarking very sensibly that she could not decide until she knew what information would be included in the register, who would have access to it, and whether she would be permitted to withdraw her child's name at a later date. Other parents showed reluctance, partly because they did not anticipate any advantages from having their child's name on a list, and partly because they considered the list to be stigmatising.

It should be noted that the parents interviewed were drawn from social workers' caseloads so that, insofar as they perceived association with social services to be stigmatising, they were already burdened with this stigma. A disabled children's register seemed to present an *additional* stigma for reasons which could not be determined since the parents themselves did not appear to know quite why they felt that way. Only a small proportion of the total number of parents interviewed had disabled children, so the findings do not provide a good indication of the feelings of this population in general. However, they do provide *some* indication, and if parents already receiving services perceive the list to be stigmatising, parents not presently involved with local authorities may be even more reluctant. This is even more likely when it is considered that disability, in and of itself, *is* considered stigmatising in some cultures. A list from which some children are excluded on the grounds of culture or parental pride is surely an inadequate basis for service provision.

Lead child care managers remarked during interview that they need to decide themselves exactly what function the register serves other than fulfilling a legal requirement. Department of Health Guidance, Volume 2, suggests that the register will be useful as an aid to planning the right level and mix of social services to help children with disabilities. In the long term, it will also assist in planning services for when the children become adults. Registration should be encouraged on the grounds that, while it does not lead to an automatic right to service, it may improve access to other agency resources such as those provided in the voluntary sector and financial benefits such as social security benefits, tax relief (if registered blind) or assistance with text telephones (if registered deaf). Managers suggested in addition that the register could be used as a contact or mailing list for providing information.

The situation with respect to registering disabled children reflects the interplay between resources, skills and attitudes which underlies the implementation of the Children Act in its entirety. The study found that some of the Act's requirements are not being met, or are only partly being met, because resources are lacking: identification of children in need is only one of numerous examples. Other requirements have not been met to date because service providers do not perceive them as having practical worth and therefore assign them a low priority. Identification of children is need is again an example, since there is little point in identifying a need which cannot be satisfied. Of course, it may be argued that identification is useful in itself since it will enable shortfalls in funding to be estimated and may uncover serious cases of actual or potential risk. Nevertheless, perceptions on the part of service providers - and sometimes on the part of clients - do determine the speed and adequacy with which a task is performed and even if it is performed at all.

Finally, the data suggest that some of the Act's requirements are not being met because of lack of skills on the part of service providers. For example, many of the staff in Welsh SSDs do not speak Welsh, with the result that difficulties are encountered in catering fully to the needs of Welsh-speaking clients. It must be emphasised that the reference to skills is not intended to reflect in any way upon the inherent fitness and abilities of social service staff. One definition of "skill" is an expertness that comes from training; and the issue over training is the funding needed to provide it. In the long term, it may be a matter of reviewing the skills required, in co-operation with educational institutions, and adjusting employment criteria to reflect these skills. An aspiring social worker, for example, who needed to speak Welsh in order to be appointed would be very likely to take lessons in Welsh (see Colton et al., 1994b, for a discussion of linguistic, ethnic, and cultural issues pertaining to children in need).

Competence in Welsh is an asset only in Wales, but competence in research methods appears to be increasingly important, particularly with respect to implementation of the Children Act. New data on clients and client characteristics can only be acquired through research; routine monitoring and more rigorous evaluative efforts will both require research skills. More relevant data will be gathered in the long run - and the probability of utilisation will be higher - if social service departments themselves are able to undertake this research. Again, there will be resource implications but the primary questions have more to do with opinions and attitudes. What kinds and degrees of skill should be expected from a person who is going to make a career out of serving other people? Should such a person be expected to evaluate his or her own work, keep abreast of current research, and contribute to the gaining of new knowledge? If no, then what skills are required? If yes, is the average level of attainment seen at present adequate? And if no, what might be done to improve it?

It may be argued that social workers are already expected to keep abreast of current issues, including research findings, but do not have the time to do so. Whilst case loads soar ever higher and cases go unallocated, is it reasonable to suggest that social workers should spend time reading when they could be serving clients? A balanced answer will involve consideration of many factors, but in essence it is a matter of priorities. To what degree should quality be sacrificed for quantity? How important is it that social workers should understand and practice the basic research methods that will allow them to evaluate their work with clients? Does it matter that this type of practice is increasingly required of social workers in other countries, particularly in Canada and the United States, but it is rarely required in Britain?

The interplay between attitudes, skills and resources is much in evidence with respect to the kinds of difficulties encountered by most SSDs in identifying children in need. These difficulties appeared to centre on the lack of adequate systems for collecting and collating the sort of data required, exacerbated by the fact that children move in and out of being in need and may be counted more than once because they are identified by several different agencies. Lead child care managers recognised that other agencies should be involved in the process of identifying overall need, although the extent to which this occurred in practice varied. Most SSDs had agreed joint protocol for identifying children in need with other statutory agencies, primarily education, housing and health authorities. SSDs in Wales are less likely to have similar agreements with voluntary agencies since these agencies have a weak base in most Welsh counties.

Establishing inter-agency protocols for any reason is a process fraught with difficulty. Jealousies concerning territory, the perceived status of various disciplines in the professional hierarchy, conflicting structures, traditions, objectives, values, powers and duties, and the persistence of stereotypes are only a few of the problems which beset the most well-intentioned attempts to establish communication channels between agencies. Almost twenty years ago, Webb (1975) wrote:

> "Better co-ordination and teamwork are a perennial desire of planners, administrators, teachers and researchers in the social services. It is unfortunate that in Britain we have hardly begun to analyse what it is we are urging on practitioners; why it is we are doing so; how much we think it is worth paying for better co-ordination, or how we might recognise good co-ordination - or teamwork - when we see it."

The questions raised by Webb still remain to be answered from a theoretical research perspective. In the absence of a guiding framework, social service administrators themselves must answer the questions on an ad hoc basis. What specific objectives do protocols hope to achieve? How will success be measured? How much autonomy will have to be surrendered, and are departments prepared - and even permitted - to relinquish control in certain areas? Above all, what are the prevailing attitudes of social service staff towards co-operative work with other agencies? Is education needed to acquaint staff with the problems and aspirations of professionals from other disciplines?

In sum, the identification of children in need is a complex matter, requiring resources, skills, motivation, and time not only for performance but for conceptualisation. In this respect, it might be noted that the first phase of the study reported in this paper was conducted only a year after the Children Act came into force. It is therefore not surprising that Welsh SSDs were found to be still struggling with the very difficult task of fulfilling new duties and accommodating new perspectives.

Family support services

Schedule 2, paragraph 4, of the 1989 Act states that local authorities must take reasonable steps, through the provision of Part III services, to prevent children suffering ill-treatment or neglect. A connected duty in paragraph 7 stipulates that authorities must reduce the need to bring proceedings which might lead to children coming into care, and discourage children from committing criminal offences. Emphasis is thus placed on working with children at risk of abuse or neglect; but there is an equal emphasis on providing services to families suffering severe problems in order to avert the most serious consequences of family breakdown. The study explored the degree to which these emphases are equal when the two connected duties are translated into practice.

Lead child care managers were asked to rank the nine categories of children previously specified in two ways: first, in order of the actual service priority each category receives; and, second, in the order which each category, in the manager's opinion, should ideally have. Table 11.1 shows the average (mean) ranks assigned by lead child care managers to each category of need, in descending order of priority.

Table 11.1: Priority given to categories of children in need

	Actual Priority	Ideal Priority
Sexual Abuse	1.50	2.75
Other abuse/neglect	1.88	3.00
Delinquency	4.31	5.94
Leaving Care	4.38	4.56
Disabilities	5.88	5.75
Separated from Parents	6.13	6.81
Severe Family Problems	6.38	4.63
Unsatisfactory home conditions	6.94	6.00
Poverty	7.81	5.56

Table 11.1 suggests that SSDs in Wales are currently concentrating their efforts on children at risk of abuse and neglect, and that these children are seen as the major priority whatever the circumstances. Managers indicated that they are now compelled to prioritise more stringently, and this is reflected in the wide band of ratings for 'actual' priorities, which ranges from 1.50 (sexual abuse) to 7.81 (poverty). When asked how they would prioritise under ideal circumstances, managers were far more likely to give equal rating to a number of categories. Hence the band of 'ideal' ratings - from 2.75 (sexual abuse) to 6.81 (children separated from parents - is narrower than that for 'actual' priorities.

The differences between the actual and ideal rankings reflect a desire on the part of managers to move away from simply prioritising child protection towards putting more emphasis on areas which might reduce the need for statutory intervention. For example, poverty moves up from an actual rank of ninth to an ideal rank of fifth; and severe family problems similarly moves from seventh place to fourth. Several managers indicated that ideally all children's needs should be given equal priority, but limited resources mean that priority has to be given to some categories over others. The following comment is typical.

> "We have to respond to abuse of children as a priority ... [But] beyond that we ought to be doing a lot more preventive work with families. If we did, they wouldn't reach crisis point."

The findings indicate that SSDs in Wales are prioritising child protection work in order to fulfil their duty under the Children Act to prevent children from suffering ill-treatment and neglect. The parallel duty outlined in the Act - to work with families suffering severe family problems in order to avert the most serious consequences of family breakdown - is not given the prominence that managers would like it to have because of limited resources. This appears to confirm the conclusions drawn by Aldgate, Tunstill and McBeath (1992) to the effect that child protection will take a major share of resources under the 1989 Act, with insufficient left for the provision of family support services.

Nevertheless, SSDs in Wales have provided family centres under Schedule 2 of the Act, often in co-operation with voluntary and other statutory agencies and after consultation with service users. As is the case with other family support endeavours, these centres are intended to facilitate a flexible, multi-disciplinary approach to problem solving and to promote the idea that children, parents, communities and the state will henceforth work together in partnership. However, the essence of partnership is equality. The difficulties associated with attaining an equal relationship between server and served are familiar, particularly if those served are perceived - in their own eyes or in the eyes of others - as being of lower status, more dependent, more vulnerable, or all three.

All SSDs in Wales ascribe to the philosophy that parents and children should be included in conferences, reviews and planning meetings, should be consulted about all major decisions affecting them, and should be informed about all relevant procedures, including complaints procedures. Lead child care managers reported that policies with respect to these matters are available to staff and are understood but are not always implemented. Indeed, participation by children in decision making was described by one manager as "patchy".

Interviews with parents and children yielded mixed data. Some parents said that they attended meetings frequently, expressed their opinions openly and felt that their needs and wishes were taken into account. Others felt that they were invited solely for the purpose of expressing their agreement: the decisions had been made already and protest would not be countenanced or even heard. Doubtless, both perceptions are correct, at least in part. Parents who are articulate, appreciative and co-operative from the social worker's perspective are more likely to be accepted into a genuine partnership than parents who fall short in any of these areas. Social workers are trained to engage not only those who demonstrably conform to expected norms but also those who do not, and some of the difficulties may be resolved through additional training in engagement techniques. However, there will always be times when parents are not able to perceive their own limitations, mutual agreement cannot be reached, and parents wishes must be overruled for the safety of the child. Such instances are part of the normal fabric of social work, and perhaps the only difference under the Act is an increased emphasis on keeping parents informed and involved and working with them to try to improve their parenting skills.

However, increased emphasis on parental involvement may not be appropriate in every case. One mother interviewed on a late Friday afternoon was in a visible state of dread because she was expecting her eldest son, who was fostered during the week, to come home for the weekend. She expected, she said, that he would damage the house and intimidate her and her younger children, perhaps to the point of physical assault. This happened every weekend, and sometimes during the week, and she was unable to convince the social worker that she was totally unable to cope.

The Children Act places the child at the centre. It promotes services for, and decisions about children, young people and their families that are more child centred than was the case under the old law (Open University 1990). In the case cited, the child's wishes had certainly been taken into account. He returned home as scheduled, agreed to be interviewed and expressed satisfaction about the fact that his foster home was near enough to his mother's home to allow him frequent visits. Other parents with behaviourally disturbed children also expressed the view that emphasis on increased contact and involvement had exposed them and the child's siblings to tension and fear and sometimes physical risk.

The question, perhaps, is one of balance. The Act replaces "parental rights" with "parental responsibility" but parents still do have rights and one of these rights is surely to be protected from children who are stronger than they are. Neither should the emphasis on parental responsibility mean an abrogation of social services' own responsibility. The purpose of the Act is to find a balance between children and parents, the state and families, the courts and local authorities and, where power is unequal, to safeguard the weak. It should not be assumed that it is always the children who are weak.

One question posed to parents concerned their degree of comfort in approaching social services for help. Some professed themselves to be entirely comfortable; some expressed reluctance because of anticipated social worker "interference". A substantial minority, including most of the male respondents, perceived any such approach to reflect negatively upon their own competence as parents and providers. In short, they perceived the approach, and the resulting association, to be stigmatising.

Lead child care managers in Wales are very aware of the need to provide non-stigmatising services in order to maintain service to existing users and to encourage others to come forward. Steps taken to ensure that family support services are provided in a non-stigmatising way include working in partnership with voluntary agencies, setting up open-access services, appropriate planning and monitoring of services, and consultation with service users. However, the managers interviewed did not, on the whole, believe that non-stigmatising services can realistically be provided within the current budget constraints. Indeed, one manager argued that in order to ration resources, services may have to become more, rather than less, stigmatising.

Stigma and privilege - opposite sides of the same coin - both have to do with receiving services denied to other society members. It follows that the fewer the number of recipients, the more prestigious or stigmatising receiving the service becomes. Providing service to greater numbers is not a real option in the current economic climate and, in any case, it does nothing to solve the underlying problem. Many existing and potential service users do not *want* to be served and may not have to be served if they had employment income sufficient to supply their needs. Provision of non-stigmatising services is not an aim which can be achieved by local SSDs, or indeed by anything short of a comprehensive national strategy involving employment, housing, wages, taxation and social security policies at the very least.

None of this absolves social service departments from their immediate duty to try to reduce the perception of stigma, particularly where it is associated with poor parenting skills. Few parents with adolescent children have travelled the turbulent waters entirely unscathed. Community parent support groups are less an admission of failure than a method of self-defence; and as such they are in an excellent position to provide non-stigmatising assistance to all parents, whether served by SSDs or not. Reduction of stigma through liaison with community groups may prove to be one way in which local authorities can "facilitate the provision by others of services..." as required by Section 17, paragraph 5.

Conclusions

This chapter has described findings with respect to key issues drawn from an examination of the eight social services departments in Wales. The data suggest that difficulties are being encountered in operationalising the concept of need and that these difficulties stem from an inherent contradiction between the all-embracing spirit of the Act and current political and social realities. The contradiction is reflected in the interplay between resources, attitudes and skills which underlies the formulation of polices, both official and unofficial, and the performance of related activities.

For example, the concept of need as defined in the Act embraces all children who might benefit from the provision of services. However, in the context of residualist national policies, "need" must be defined in terms of child protection, with little left for the parallel duty of family support. Since social services departments are hardly in a position to formulate official policies which seem to contravene the spirit of the Act, it is not suprising that policies were found to be non-specific or even lacking, and that contradictory, informal policies were also found to exist. Findings also gave some indication that social workers operating in the midst of the confusion were interpreting "need" according to their own convictions, and that differences in the attitudes of individual social workers were creating dissension within and between the families and communities being served.

The populations to be served have not generally been identified, partly because they have not been officially defined, partly because social services personnel see little point in identifying needs which cannot be met, and partly because of insufficiencies in the resources, skills and inter-agency agreements required for data collection. Since services are inherently stigmatising in the present residualist context, despite the best efforts of social service departments to reduce the perception of stigma, it may be anticipated that some potential users will be reluctant to come forward. Data indicate that this may be the case with respect to parents of disabled children.

Service to existing users again reflects the interwoven influence of attitudes, skills and resource constraints. Difficulties have been encountered in establishing service protocols with voluntary agencies because of inadequate monitoring systems, insufficient funding and some lack of mutual understanding. Even in areas such as parent and child involvement, where little conflict might be expected between theory and practice, the data indicate that the shift towards parental responsibilities is occasionally prejudicing parental rights.

In closing, it is worth highlighting that the development of adequate monitoring and evaluation systems is still in its infancy. Here too, resources, motivation and research skills will be the primary factors determining progress. In this general atmosphere of gloom and doom, it should not be forgotten that the Children Act 1989 *does* represent "a quantum leap from the old restricted notions of 'prevention' to a more positive outreaching duty of support for children and families." (Packman and Jordan, 1991, p.323). In an era that is generally residualistic, here is a major piece of legislation that is not.

References

Aldgate, J., Tunstill, J. & McBeath, G. (1992), *National Monitoring of the Children Act: Part III section 17 - the first year*, Oxford University/NCVCCO.

Bradshaw, J. (1990), *Child Poverty and Deprivation in the UK*, London, National Children's Bureau.

Bridge, A., Bridge, S. & Luke, S. (1990), *Blackstone's Guide to the Children Act 1989*, London, Blackstone.

Brown, J.C. (1990), 'The Focus on Single Mothers', in C. Murray, *The Emerging British Underclass*, London, Institute of Economic Affairs.

Children Act 1989, London, HMSO.

Colton, M. Drury C. & Williams, M. (1994a), 'Policies for Children in Need', *Applied Community Studies*, (forthcoming).

Colton, M., Drury, C. & Williams, M. (1994b), 'Policies on Ethnic, Linguistic and Religious Needs in Wales Under the Children Act 1989', *Social Work and Social Sciences Review*, (forthcoming).

Day, G., Rees, G. & Read, M. (1991), *Contemporary Wales*, Cardiff, University of Wales Press.

Deakin, N. (1990), 'Mr Murray's Ark', in C. Murray, *The Emerging British Underclass*, London, Institute of Economic Affairs.

Department of Health (1991), *The Children Act 1989 Guidance and Regulations; Volume 2, Family Support, Day Care and Educational Provision for Young Children*, London, HMSO.

Field, F. (1990), 'Britain's Underclass: Countering the Growth', in C. Murray, *The Emerging British Underclass*, London, Institute of Economic Affairs.

Gardner, R. & Manby, M. (1993), 'The Children Act and family support: a crisis of values', *Adoption and Fostering*, vol. 17, no. 3.

George, V. & Wilding, P. (1976), *Ideology and Social Welfare*, London, Routledge and Kegan Paul.

Hardiker, P., Exton, K. & Barker, M. (1991), 'The Social Policy Contexts of Prevention in Child Care', *British Journal of Social Work*, vol. 21, 341-359.

Johnson, N. (1990), *Restructuring the Welfare State: A Decade of Change*, London, Harvester-Wheatsheaf.

Murray, C. (1990), *The Emerging British Underclass*, London, Institute of Economic Affairs.

Open University (1990), *The Children Act: Putting it into Practice*, Open University Press.

Oppenheim, C. (1990), *Poverty: The Facts*, London, Child Poverty Action Group.

Packman, J. & Jordan, B. (1991), 'The Children Act: Looking Forward, Looking Back', The *British Journal of Social Work*, vol. 21, no. 4.

Pinker, R. (1979), *The Idea of Welfare*, London, Heinemann.

Townsend, P. (1979), *Poverty in the United Kingdom*, London, Penquin.

University of Leicester & Department of Health (1990), *Children in Need and Their Families: A New Approach; A Manual for Senior Managers on Part III of the Children Act 1989*, University of Leicester.

Walker, A. (1990), 'Blaming the Victims', in C. Murray, *The Emerging British Underclass*, London, Institute of Economic Affairs.

Webb, A. (1975), *Co-ordination between Health and Personal Social Services: A Question of Quality*, Unpublished paper presented to European Seminar on Interaction of Social Welfare and Health Personnel in the Delivery of Services: Implications for Training.

12 Multi-problem families: investigating the client perspective

Pol GHESQUIÈRE
Walter HELLINCKX
Herman BAARTMAN

Introduction

In 1988, the Orthopedagogics department of the Catholic University of Leuven began to develop a home-based treatment program for multi-problem families who had been referred to a child abuse assistance centre (Ghesquière, 1989). In this article, we will discuss a number of aspects of a research study linked to this project, focusing particularly on the meaning of the term "multi-problem family". First, we will develop our own definition of "multi-problem family". Next, we will give an overview of the research design. Finally, we will discuss some of the results of one part of the research which are particularly relevant to practice[1].

Meaning of the term "multi-problem family"

The origin of the term "*multi-problem family*" is linked to a study that was carried out in 1948: the "*St. Paul Family Unit Report Study*" (Buell et al., 1952). This study investigated the ways in which families in the city of St. Paul, Minnesota, USA, were making use of public and private support agencies. *"[The] most striking finding was that 6 per cent of the families studied suffered from such a compounding or vicious circle of problems that they absorbed well over half of the combined services of all agencies"* (Leiby, 1978, p. 284). The term "*multi-problem family*" was coined to describe these families.

The term "*problem family*", the English counterpart of the American term, originated at about the same time and has a rather similar meaning (Women's Group on Public Welfare, 1948; Spencer, 1970). This term also found acceptance in the 1980s in the Netherlands (Baartman, 1988), Flanders (Ghesquière, 1989), Germany (Goldbrunner, 1989), and Italy (Cancrini, 1992). In these countries, the terms "multi-problem family" and "problem family" are now used interchangeably. The most frequent Anglo-Saxon alternatives are "*disorganised family*" (Malone, 1966), "*hard-to-reach family*" (Thinker, 1959) and "*multi-agency family*" (Minuchin et al., 1967).

There is little agreement in the literature about the definition of the term "multi-problem family". A number of authors use an *administrative definition*, through which families can be categorised based on the administrative characteristics of the support services they receive (Dax, Gosden and Hagger, 1980). Selig provides a simple summary of these administrative definitions: "*A multi-problem family is defined as one that is in contact with a variety of agencies in the community*" (Selig, 1976, p. 526).

Other scholars use the presence of a minimum number of *preconceived characteristics* as a criterion for deciding whether a family can be classed as "multi-problem" (Mazer, 1972). These characteristics often include concrete problems as well as more theoretical aspects of the family's functioning; and there is little agreement as to which particular characteristics should be present in order to warrant a "multi-problem" assessment.

Despite the diversity of definitions to be found in the literature, research by Baartman et al. (1987), has shown that helping professionals have very largely reached agreement as to what they mean by a "multi-problem" family. We can come to a clearer understanding of the nature of this agreement by analysing the literature to determine in what context the various definitions usually appear. Such an analysis shows that definitions are usually formulated with respect to two key elements of the problem situation: the problems experienced by the families themselves; and the problems inherent in the care system.

A multi-problem family is characterised as experiencing multiple, complex, serious, and chronic problems, which are resistant to help. These problems mostly have to do with a combination of socioeconomic factors, such as housing, employment and finances, and psycho-social difficulties (Rutter and Madge, 1977). The problem most frequently identified as characteristic of multi-problem families is poor parenting skills (Baartman and Dijkstra, 1987).

However, as Philp (1963) remarks: "*...the problem cannot be understood by looking at the families only and ignoring the services which have drawn attention to them. These families appear as "problems" to social administration partly because of the nature and aims of the social services themselves.*" (Philp, 1963, p. 16). Of the problems inherent in the care system, the first is concerned with the care system's organisation. Many authors have mentioned the dispersion and lack of co-ordination in service provision (Philp, 1963; Geismar and La Sorte, 1964; Spencer, 1970; Selig, 1976; Carson, 1986; Kaplan, 1986; Rothery, 1990). Second, it has been noted that the support methods used are not appropriate to the nature of the multi-problem families for whom they are intended. They are often too verbal, occurring only in the consulting room and disregarding the practical socioeconomic problems of the family. It is accepted in the literature that well-established therapeutic methods of all schools fail when treating these families (Rothery, 1990); and it is remarkable that almost no scientific research has been undertaken on this issue.

Because of the double theme that exists in current definitions of the term multi-problem family, it would appear that the term "multi-problem family" can never be used solely as a diagnostic category in which to place families. Instead, we need to seek a definition which includes the characteristics of both the family and the care system. This seems an insoluble paradox. Based on our analysis of the literature, we conclude that the real meaning of the term "multi-problem family" is to be found in the *problematic relationship between the families in question and the helping professionals*. Hence, the term "multi-problem family" does not refer to the family or to the care system but to a system on a higher level, a system in which the family and the care system constitute sub-systems.

However, the decision about whether the term "multi-problem family" is appropriate in a particular situation is not made mutually by both sub-systems. The label is assigned by one sub-system - the helper - to the other sub-system - the family. The family's problems are "resistant to help" only in the helping professionals' experience; and, in fact, the term "multi-problem family" has a meaning only for the helping professionals. For them, the term describes families who are grappling with a *chronic complex of socioeconomic and psychosocial problems resistant to help.*

Research design

Definition of the problem

Through our research, we have tried to provide a complete and clear description of the "multi-problem" phenomenon. In accordance with our view that a "multi-problem family" is really a multi-problem relationship between the helper and the helped, we begin our analysis by considering that relationship. The relationship between a professional helper and a family is, in theory at least, a support process. The support process can be viewed as a socio-cybernetic system of which the family and the care system constitute a sub-system[2].

As the support process continues, the family members will behave towards the helper in accordance with the meaning which the support process has for them. If they perceive it to be irrelevant, they will probably disregard the helper; if they perceive it to be interfering or otherwise harmful, they will be hostile; if they perceive it to be beneficial, they will be co-operative. Depending on the helper's reactions to their behaviour, their perceptions may change and so may their subsequent behaviour.

Similarly, the helper's initial actions will be guided by his or her own understanding of the meaning of the support process. If he believes that the purpose of the support process is to help a "deviant" member of society conform more closely to societal rules, he will behave differently to the way he would if he believed that the purpose of the process was to help family members set and achieve their own goals. His beliefs regarding the support process are probably just as firm and definite as those of the family members, but both sets of beliefs have the potential to change depending on changes in the other. Hence, the multi-problem phenomenon is "*a meaning-processing system in which the interacting participants maintain and transform the identity of themselves and of their network through a more or less shared understanding of both themselves and the world*" (Bråten, 1984, p. 193).

The interaction between the helper and family members constitutes just one aspect of the meaning-processing system. Others are also involved in the support process - policy makers, for example - and each player interacts with every other player in a complex dance of shifting perceptions and behaviours. In the present study, however, we have confined ourselves to examining just the interaction between helping professionals and family members. With respect to this specific interaction, our research question can be expressed as follows:

> *How can the support process with multi-problem families best be described in terms of meaning-processing social systems?*

Research methodology

Since very little is known about the support process as it applies to multi-problem families, research at the exploratory level is appropriate. The aspects of the support process to be explored are: first, the helping professional's perspective; second, the family's perspective; and, third, the circular process through which both perspectives are linked. These aspects are illustrated in Figure 12.1.

The helping professional's perspective was ascertained by means of a literature review (Ghesquière, 1993). Since the literature is written by professionals and not by clients, it would follow that the perspective presented in it is that of professionals, not of clients. This applies to both the research and practice literature and accounts for the connotations associated with the term "multi-problem family".

The family's perspective was obtained by means of interviews with the parents of five families designated "multi-problem" by professionals. The approach was non-interventive, essentially comprising *qualitative empirical research* as defined by Smaling (1987). This research design was selected primarily on pragmatic grounds but is also appropriate to the exploratory nature of the study.

The circular process through which the two perspectives are linked was examined through an in-depth case study of one multi-problem family. The objective here was to obtain a concrete view of the way in which the family's perspective and the helping professional's perspective had taken shape and affected each other during the support process.

In this article, we shall focus on just one aspect of the study: the family's perspective, contributed by the five "multi-problem" families who were interviewed. In order to select the five families, three experienced helping professionals were first chosen, all from different organisations vital to the support process. The first professional was employed in a housing project for the underprivileged and hence was primarily concerned with the socioeconomic problems of the family. The second was employed in the mental health sector and represented psycho-social support. The third worked in a child abuse centre and was concerned with parenting problems, among other aspects of abuse.

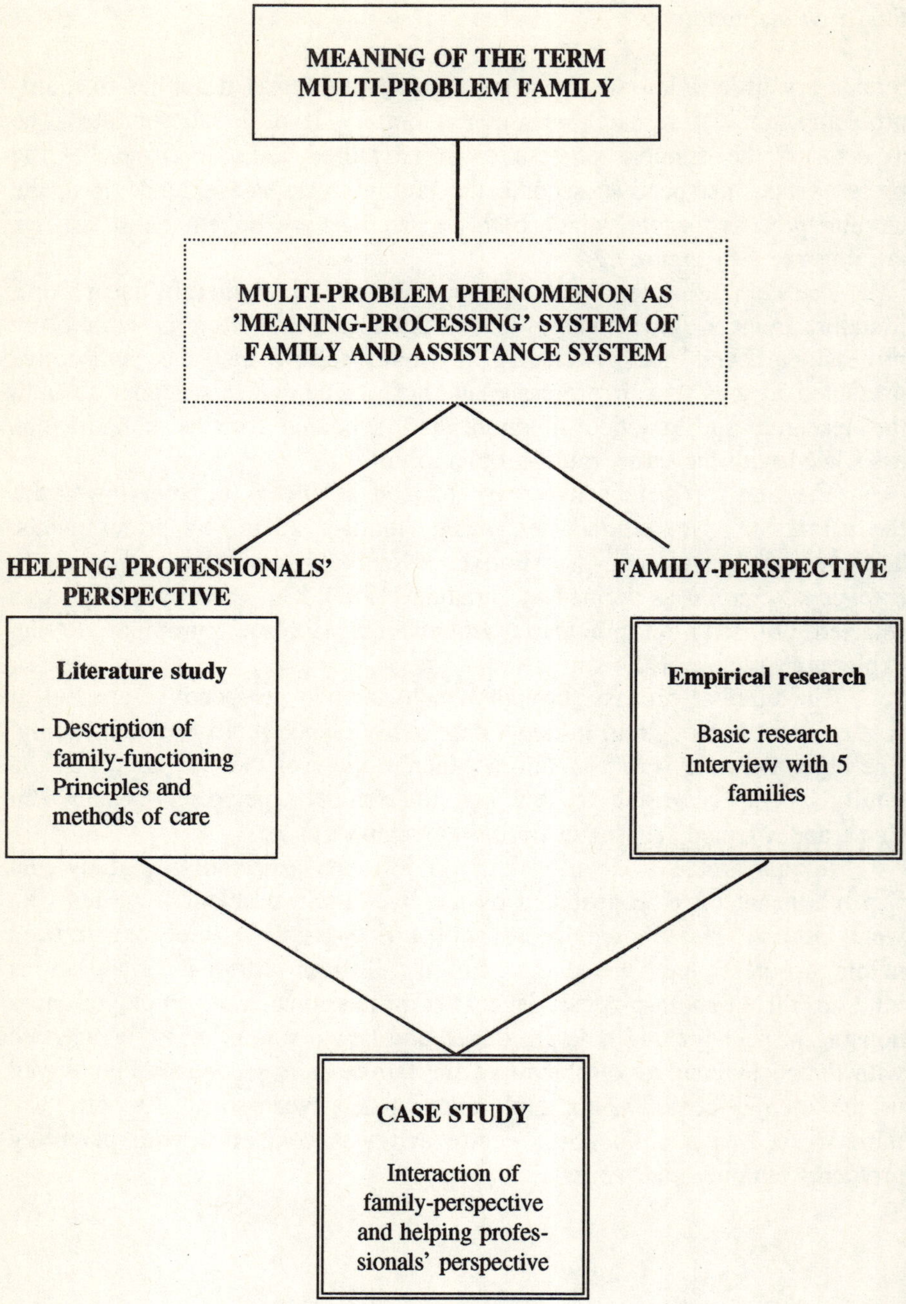

Figure 12.1: Overview of the research

These three helping professionals were asked to designate families from their respective client populations with whom they had experienced difficulties in bringing about change. Two additional criteria were set: first, the families had to be grappling with a chronic complexity of socioeconomic and psycho-social problems; and, second, they had to have been reported as having serious parenting problems. Although the helping professionals were asked to justify their selection of families on the basis of these three criteria, their decisions about which families fit the criteria were not questioned. In this way, a population of families which were "multi-problem" from the helping professionals' perspective was obtained. Five families were then selected from the helping professonals' population of families according to the principles of *theoretical sampling* (Guba, 1981).

The interviews with the families were conducted in three stages. The first stage utilised a semi-structured interview schedule, which tapped the family's perceptions of the support process with respect to a number of pre-determined elements. The supportive elements included in the schedule were derived from a conceptual model which takes into account various theoretical aspects of support, such as the problem theory, the change theory and the result theory, and a number of interactional aspects, such as agreement and mutual understanding. This conceptual model was constructed on the basis of recent research in the area of psychotherapy (Lazare and Eisenthal, 1989; Lazare, Eisenthal and Frank, 1989; Dormaar, 1990).

In the second stage, the different elements examined in the first interview were explored more thoroughly. This process sometimes required a number of interviews, structured on the basis of material from the first stage but sufficiently open to allow the family's perspective to be considered in all its variety.

In the third stage, the material so far gathered was synthesised and submitted to the parents concerned to allow them to make corrections to both facts and nuances. This feedback or *back-to-the-field* procedure (Ely et al., 1991, p. 156) increases the reliability of the qualitative data.

The data analysis was also conducted in three stages. First the background of the family and the history of the support process were reconstructed on the basis of the interview material. Next, the material was reviewed and the most important aspects of the family's perspective were identified. Finally, the interviews were coded on the basis of the conceptual model and a content analysis was performed.

These three stages were undertaken, first for each family separately - the vertical analysis - and then for the five families together - the horizontal analysis. The results presented in the remainder of the article are drawn from the horizontal analysis[3].

Aspects of the family perspective

In all the families examined, the central concern was the placement of children outside the home. Families rated as negative any element in the support process which increased the probability of one or more children being placed, or which resulted in an effective placement, or which delayed the children's return home after placement. A helping professional who was associated with any of these three elements was distrusted.

As would be expected, any element in the support process which gave rise to the opposite of these effects was rated as positive; and the associated professionals were trusted. Families used this three-tiered criterion for evaluating professionals not only with respect to those professionals who were involved directly with the placing authorities, but also with respect to professionals from other sectors.

Rating a placement as negative is particularly remarkable in light of the fact that parents who had themselves been placed in their youth (about half of the research group) had a very positive view of that placement. They saw their placement as an important opportunity which they had been given. One parent, for example, who was allowed to return home when he was seventeen on the condition that he would finish his last grade in high school - which he did not - explained that a longer placement would have meant a diploma for him. Despite this, all parents wanted to avoid their own children being placed.

One explanation of this seeming paradox may lie in the parents' desire to be recognised as better parents than their own parents were.

The single need to be viewed by themselves and others as competent parents may result in two quite different behaviours. These behaviours lie at opposite ends of a continumm which runs from *engagement* with the support process at one end to *disengagement* at the other.

At one extreme, some families act in a way which emphasises their engagement with the support process. They very often contact various helping professionals in order to report problems and to suggest ways in which appropriate help might be given. In this way, they try to take control of the support process so that placement can be avoided. Kaplan (1984, p. 325-327) calls these families *professional clients* because they are skilled in manipulating helping professionals towards the achievement of their own goals.

At the other extreme, there are families who emphasise distance. They fail to keep appointments with helping professionals and are consistently out when visited. By staying out of sight, they hope to postpone the placement of their children for as long as possible. These families fit the traditional image of multi-problem families: distrusting, unmotivated and hostile.

Study findings showed that a family's position on the engagement-disengagement continuum is largely determined by the first experience with supportive intervention. A family which has a positive first experience will tend to engagement, while a negative experience results in distance or disengagement. Once an attitude towards professional help is established on the basis of the first experience, change will only occur if subsequent experiences are markedly different from the first.

A third recurring theme from the family's perspective is the inadequacy of *information exchange*. Various factors contribute to this inadequacy. In the first place, parents have almost no conception of how the various supporting agencies fit with each other and who is responsible for what. Since the agencies themselves can often not agree about who should provide what service under what circumstances, this is hardly surprising. However, it does lead to a good deal of frustration when a parent is referred from one helping professional to another and back again.

Second, when supportive efforts have been co-ordinated by the agencies involved, the parents may not be informed. Often, they receive incomplete or distorted information second-hand with the result that they are not only ill-informed but their trust is eroded. For example, a mother told us that she had heard in the hospital that various people had come together in order to organise a placement for her children. Probably, what had really happened was that all the involved professionals had come together in order to integrate their helping efforts, not to organise a placement. However, the mother believed what she had heard, with a consequent erosion of trust.

Finally, parents complained that they were not informed about the professionals' own opinions of the family and its problems. Hence, they were not in a position to refute the professionals' views, based on the reality of the family as they themselves saw it. Helping interventions, in the parents' judgement, were often based upon the professionals' erroneous beliefs, not upon the real problems being encountered by the family.

A fourth theme emerging from the family's view of the support process concerned the *hierarchical relationship* between the family and the helping professionals. On the one hand, an equal partnership was expected. Professionals who emphasised partnership were appreciated most. On the the other hand, parents did expect the professionals to know more than they themselves did about a number of things and to be able to offer concrete help, advice and information. In other words, parents expected that professionals would take the first step in helping family members to obtain their entitlements.

Interview data suggested that professionals can win a family's trust by meeting concrete needs: for example, by providing housing or unemployment benefits. However, such material assistance must be provided in a way that does not diminish the family's sense of its own competence, privacy and independence. Parents who feel patronised place less trust in the professional than they otherwise would.

Finally, study findings showed that families attach much importance to *continuity* in the support relationship. Continuity here refers both to the frequency of contact and to the person with whom the contact is made. Many parents complained about infrequent contact, such as one visit every six months. They were also disturbed by organisational upheavals and ever-changing social workers and other helping professionals. They would have preferred a relationship with a limited number of individuals over a longer period of time; and they did not consider staff turnover to be any excuse. Neither did they consider that they should have to change from one agency to another because they themselves had moved.

This desire for more continuity raises questions about the length of time for which support can legally be provided by some services. A second concern is inconsistency in the attitudes of different authorities towards the same types of families and problems. A family receiving a service in one area may be worse served after moving because the new authority has different priorities and considers the family less deserving.

Conclusion

The results of the present study identify the areas of most concern to "multi-problem" families and give some indication of the ways in which support for these families can be optimised. First, it is important to provide complete, accurate and timely information and to strive for continuity of service. Next, helping professionals need to commit themselves to an equal partnership with parents, in which concrete assistance is provided without undermining the parents' own sense of competence and independence.

Finally, we need to understand that the fear of losing their children may lead parents to become professional clients on the one hand or elusive and hostile on the other. Professional concern for the safety and wellbeing of children must be balanced against the need of parents to demonstrate that they are good parents: better parents than their own parents were, and the kind of parents who should not lose their children. Professionals who understand this very basic need may win the parents' co-operation; professionals who do not are more likely to encounter a prolonged and losing battle.

Notes

1. For the complete report of this research, refer to the doctoral thesis of the first author (Ghesquière, 1993).
2. The epistemiological presuppositions of these ideas are outside the scope of this chapter. Interested readers can refer to the literature about this system-theory (Bateson, 1972; Keeney, 1983; Bråten, 1984; von Glaserfeld, 1984; Keeyney and Ross, 1985).
3. It is outside the scope of this article to illustrate the different aspects of the family's perspective with fragments of the interviews. For this, the reader is referred to the complete report of the research (Ghesquière, 1993).

References

Baartman, H.E.M. (1988), 'Intensieve thuishulp voor multi-problem gezinnen' [Intensive home-based treatment of multi-problem families], *Nederlands tijdschrift voor opvoeding, vorming en onderwijs*, vol. 4, no. 6, 310-322.

Baartman, H.E.M. et al. (1987), *Multi-problem gezinnen. Sores en scores. Een onderzoek bij Amsterdamse hulpverleningsinstellingen [Multi-problem families. A research in helping agencies of Amsterdam]*, Amsterdam, Vakgroep Pedagogiek, Vrije Universiteit.

Baartman, H.E.M. & Dijkstra, J.S. (1987), 'Multi-problem gezinnen. II: De opvoedingsproblematiek' [Multi-problem families. II: The parenting problems], *Tijdschrift voor orthopedagogiek*, vol. 26, no. 1, 2-20.

Bateson, G. (1972), *Steps to an Ecology of Mind. A Revolutionary Approach to Man's Understanding of Himself*, New York, Balantine Books.

Bråten, S. (1986), 'The Third Position: Beyond Artificial and Autopoietic Reduction. -In F. Geyer & J. Van der Zouwen (Eds.), *Sociocybernetic Paradoxes. Observation, Control and Evolution of Self-steering Systems* (pp. 193-205), London, Sage.

Buell, B. et al. (1952), *Community Planning for Human Services*, New York, Columbia University Press.

Cancrini, L. (1992), *L'adolescente nella famiglia multiproblematica*, 2° Congresso Internazionale della Società Italiana die Psicologia e Psicoterapia Relazionale: "L'adolescente e i suoi sistemi", Rimini, 9-12 aprile 1992.

Carson, A.T. (1986), *A Professional Challenge. Working with Multi-Problem Families*, San Diego (California), San Diego State University, Project IINTACT.

Dax, E.C., Gosden, S.D. & Hagger, R. (1980), 'A Comparison between Recidivists from Problem Families and Recidivists currently in the Tasmanian Prison', *Austalian and New Zealand Journal of Criminology*, vol. 13(2), 124-132.

Dormaar, J.M.M. (1989), *Consensus in Psychotherapy*, Maastricht, Datawyse (Doctoraatsproefschrift).

Ely, M. et al. (1991), *Doing Qualitative Research: Circles within Circles*, London, The Falmer Press.

Geismar, L.L. & La Sorte, M.A. (1964), *Understanding the Multi-Problem Family. A Conceptual Analysis and Exploration in Early Identification*, New York, Association Press.

Ghesquière, P. (1989), 'Multi-problem gezinnen: eigen-aardige cliënten vragen een eigen-aardige hulpverlening' [Multi-problem families. Peculiar clients ask for peculiar help], *T.O.K.K.*, vol. 14(4), 157-170.

Ghesquière, P. (1993), *Multi-problem gezinnen. Perspectieven op een problematische hulpverleningssituatie [Multi-problem families. Perspectives on a problematic helping situation]*, Leuven, Katholieke Universiteit (Doctoral thesis).

Goldbrunner, H. (1989), *Arbeit mit Problemfamilien. Systemische Perspektiver für Familientherapie und Sozialarbeit* (Edition Psychologie und Pädagogik), Mainz, Matthias-Grünewald-Verlag.

Guba, E.G. (1981), 'Criteria for Assessing the Trustworthiness of Naturalistic Inquiries', *Educational Communication and Technology Journal*, vol. 29(2), 75-91.

Kaplan, L.W. (1984), *The 'Multi-Problem' Family Phenomenon: An Interactional Perspective*, University of Massachusetts. (Doctoral Dissertation)

Kaplan, L. (1986), *Working With Multiproblem Families*, Massachusetts/Toronto, D.C. Heath and Company/Lexington.

Keeney, B.P. (1983), *The Aesthetics of Change*, New York, Guilford.

Keeney, B.P. & Ross, J.M. (1985), *Mind in Therapy. Constructing Systemic Family Therapies*, New York, Basic Books.

Lazare, A. & Eisenthal, S. (1989), 'Clinican/Patient Relations. I: Attending to the Patient's Perspective. -In A. Lazare (Ed.), *Outpatient Psychiatry. Diagnosis and Treatment. Second Edition* (pp. 125-136), Baltimore, Williams & Wilkins.

Lazare, A., Eisenthal, S. & Frank, A. (1989), 'Clinican/Patient Relations. II: Conflict and Negotiation. -In A. Lazare (Ed.), *Outpatient Psychiatry. Diagnosis and Treatment. Second Edition* (pp. 137-152), Baltimore, Williams & Wilkins.

Leiby, J. (1978), *A History of Social Welfare and Social Work in the United States*, New York, Columbia University Press.

Malone, C.A. (1966), 'Safety First: Comments on the Influence of External Danger in the Lives of Children of Disorganized Families', *American Journal of Orthopsychiatry*, vol. 36, no. 1, 3-12.

Mazer, M. (1972), 'Characteristics of Multi-Problem Households: A Study in Psychosocial Epidemiology', *American Journal of Orthopsychiatry*, vol. 42, no. 5, 792-802.

Minuchin, S. et al. (1967), *Families of the Slums. An Exploration of Their Structure and Treatment*, New York/London, Basic Books, Inc.

Philp, A.F. (1963), *Family Failure. A Study of 129 Families with Multiple Problems*, London, Faber and Faber.

Rothery, M. (1990), 'Family Therapy with Multiproblem Families', in M. Rothery & G. Cameron (Eds.), *Child Maltreatment: Expanding Our Concept of Helping* (pp. 13-32), Hillsdale, New Jersey, Lawrence Erlbaum Associates.

Rutter, M. & Madge, N. (1977), *Cycles of Disadvantage. A Review of Research*, London, Heinemann Educational Books.

Selig, A.L. (1976), 'The Myth of the Multi-Problem Family', *American Journal of Orthopsychiatry*, vol. 46, no. 3, 526-532.

Smaling, A. (1987), *Methodologische objectiviteit en kwalitatief onderzoek [Methodologically objectivity and qualitative research],* Lisse, Swets & Zeitlinger (Doctoral thesis).

Spencer, J.C. (1970), 'The Multi-Problem Family', in B. Schlesinger (Ed.), *The Multi-Problem Family. A Review and Annotated Bibliography. Third Edition* (pp. 3-54), Toronto, University of Toronto Press.

Thinker, K.H. (1959), 'Casework with Hard-to-Reach Families', *American Journal of Orthopsychiatry*, vol. 29, no. 1, 165-171.

von Glaserfeld, E. (1984), 'An Introduction to Radical Constructivism', in P. Watzlawick (Ed.), *The Invented Reality. How Do We Know What We Believe We Know? Contributions to Constructivism* (pp. 17-40), New York, Norton.

Women's Group on Public Welfare. (1948), *The Neglected Child and His Family. A Study Made in 1946-7 of the Problem of the Child Neglected in His Own Home*, London, Oxford University Press.

13 Exploring parenting roles

Paul DURNING

This chapter explores the processes involved in bringing up children in residential institutions, away from their families. Such "processes" include not only the roles and tasks of the involved adults but also their relationships with the children at an emotional level. Residential processes are next compared with similar processes within the family group in an attempt to answer two questions:

(1) In what ways does research into residential settings increase understanding about the processes involved in bringing up children?
(2) In what ways does an international comparison between the child-care philosophies and activities prevalent in France and Great Britain throw light on these processes?

Residential institutions and the child's natural family comprise the opposite extremes of a continuum of care. Various other child-care options lie at different points along the continuum. When a child must be removed from his family in France, he may be placed by a juvenile magistrate in the care of a reliable person who does not play a professional role but only the very basic role of caring for the child. Conversely, care by professionals may be considered more appropriate. Foster parents in France are accorded high professional status and most children brought into care are placed in foster homes. Alternatively, placements may be found in group homes or in smaller or larger residential settings. The very diversity of the available options points up the necessity of knowing more about parental and professional methods of raising children.

Diversity is also increasingly found in the natural families themselves. There are families where both parents, married or not, take equal responsibility for raising their mutual children, families where the main responsibility falls upon one parent, usually the mother, and single-parent families where responsibility is necessarily carried solely by the resident parent. In addition, there are blended or reconstituted families where some combination of the wife's children by a previous marriage, the husband's children, and the couple's mutual children live together under the same roof. There are also arrangements, involving thousands of children in industrialised countries, where it is difficult to identify the biological parents: the child has been adopted, or is a test-tube baby, or has otherwise come into being through a medically-assisted birth.

The emotional issues inherent in parenting at both the professional and personal levels give rise to the following questions:

Who counts as a parent?

Can a foster mother who has raised another woman's child from birth claim to be that child's mother? Can an adoptive father, or a stepfather, or a divorced father who is completely absent from the home really claim to be a father? And are such questions significant?

Can or should a professional "parent" feel love towards the child?

The view that all children need to be loved gives rise to some sensitive issues when children are being raised by adults other than their natural parents. Does a substitute or professional parent have the right or the duty, or even the ability, to love another person's child? How can we define the kinds of feelings which might be viewed as "love"?

Can residential care be beneficial?

Opinions on whether or not a child can actually benefit from some form of institutional care vary between nations and classes and may be different at different points in history. For example, boarding school education is currently valued by a high proportion of the British upper classes whereas, in France, this kind of education is reserved for handicapped or problem children, almost all of whom come from modest or low-class social environments. The degree to which matters concerning children spark public concern is reflected and often fuelled by media over-attention to conflicts concerning adoption, the abuse of children by their families, and most fostering issues. The actions of social workers are systematically questioned both when they remove children from their homes and when they return them. The debate concerning the quality of community care does not take place only in the public arena but is also of much concern in professional circles.

Such a debate calls into question the very foundations of parenthood and professionalism. The definition of a "parent" or a "professional" in the child-care field can only be based on a complex interplay between qualities such as instinct, love, choice, skill and status. These qualities come into play when we consider such matters as adoption, or the difference between a father and a stepfather, or the relationship between professionals and parents when both are involved in caring for the child.

By and large, current research does not give answers to questions of what is meant by parenting or being a parent or being a professional parent. This chapter attempts to clarify these questions by describing a research study into parenting in foster and family situations. The study includes attention to the roles and activities of adults who are trying to parent, and the framework in which the act of parenting occurs. First, however, it is necessary to say something about the methods used in the study, and about the translation difficulties arising from conceptual and linguistic differences with respect to parenting between Great Britain and France.

Translation difficulties

Translation difficulties are particularly apparent when we try to assign names or labels to adults fulfilling specific parental roles. For example in French, the term "beau-père" applies both to a husband who is not a parent (stepfather in English) and to the wife's father (father-in-law). In English, a professional who takes care of a group of children in a residential setting, is called a group worker. The term "group worker" does not say anything about the actual child-care activities of the worker but only about the context in which the care occurs, and it has no parallel in French. Similarly, the word "education", in English, is mostly used in connection with school activities and does not evoke an immediate image, as it does in French, of a wider kind of education, including socialisation, which is not necessarily school-based. The word "parenting" has been used already in this text to signify the entire complexity of emotions and activities involved in raising a child, whether one's own or someone else's. However, "parenting" cannot be directly translated into French and, when the English term is used, it is not adequate to describe professional parenting activities.

As the German researcher Schulteis (1988) has noted, translation difficulties are not only linguistic but also conceptual. If an English word has an exact French parallel, or vice versa, it is easy to assume that the respective words mean the same thing in the French and English cultures, whereas in fact this may not be the case at all. In some instances, it aids translation if there is no word, since the absence of a word will point to a difference in patterns of thinking. Philosophers tell us that it is difficult to think about something without being able to give it a name. In Western countries, we think using seven basic colours which are more fully described by adjectives. People in other cultures use two basic colours and then introduce shades. It is the shades and nuances associated with words which are most easily lost in translation; and it is these same, fragile nuances which are most important to a true understanding of the concept being discussed.

The word "parenting" has already been cited as an example of a complex concept which cannot readily be translated. Consider in addition the word "care", translated into French as "soin", which is also the translation of the English word "cure". It is not difficult to see that "care" in French would carry a medical connotation and would be associated with the care of the body by professional medical staff rather than with the care of the whole person, in this case a child, by professionals and non-professionals alike. Thus, the French language has no global words such as "caretaker" or "primary caretaker" which, in English, encompass the entire function of caring by any person, whether a natural parent or a professional or non-professional parent substitute. When the French adopt the English meaning of the word "care", the term refers to care outside the family, in a foster, group, or residential placement. Similarly, "residential care", in the English usage, may include treatment, whereas the French prefer to distinguish between "residential treatment" which implies that a specific treatment is being implemented and "residential care" which denotes placement without planned treatment.

The research study

Much of the material on which this study is based was obtained through observation of the activities in five residential settings for children in France over a period of a year. The aim was to explore, from a psychological perspective, the processes involved when youngsters are brought up in a group away from their families. Such an approach enables commonalities to be identified between the child-care processes in institutions catering for different types of children: that is, children who have been placed in care for different reasons, ranging from problems in school to physical or mental illness to serious social and delinquency problems. Commonalities in the care afforded by institutions may then be compared with the care generally given in a foster or family home with respect to certain key activities.

Data in the five institutions were gathered through regular recording of staff meetings, periodic interviews with the team manager, the staff and some of the children themselves, and daily logbook entries.

Identification of key activities

The complexity and diversity of the tasks involved in rearing children necessitates an attempt to identify and categorise the key activities involved. In this study, seven key activities were drawn from the traditional model of parenting within the family and comprised: household tasks, such a cooking and cleaning: technical tasks, such as maintenance; child minding; physical care and nursing sick children; general socialisation tasks, such as instilling values or teaching social skills; co-ordination with agencies or groups outside the family, in connection with education, health, leisure, and so forth; and social reference tasks, concerning choices which the adult must make on behalf of the youngster, such as allowing an abortion or a surgical procedure.

Household and technical tasks

Bringing up children involves a number of household tasks, such as cooking, washing clothes and cleaning. There are also more technical tasks, such as making repairs, mending or making toys, decorating bedrooms, and so forth. Although highly necessary, both these types of tasks are somewhat peripheral to the central business of helping the child develop to his full potential, although they may have developmental value when they are performed by the child himself. However, they can also be performed in the absence of the child and, in better-off families, are often undertaken by a maid or handyman.

In large residential settings, household and technical tasks are performed by specialised staff who are divided into three teams: cooking staff; cleaning staff; and maintenance staff. In the five institutions studied, cooking and cleaning chores are undertaken by women, while maintenance and outdoor tasks, even gardening, are carried out by men. This dichotomy between "women's jobs" and "men's jobs" can also be seen to differing degrees in family environments but it is not so absolute there as it is in residential institutions.

Child minding

As every parent knows, a young child cannot be left alone, and household tasks are often performed at the same time as the child is being minded. However, in a residential setting, the staff member responsible for minding the child does not have household duties. Instead, the duties are likely to be incompatible with child minding: attending a staff meeting, for example, or writing a report. In a residential institution, there is thus a differentiation between actually minding the child and other tasks, which does not occur in a family setting. Such a differentiation has important consequences which are rarely identified or even considered. If it is a question of either attending a meeting or interacting with the child, which will the staff member choose? Do staff members in fact have choices in such matters and, if they do, what do their choices reveal about their perceptions of their roles?

Nursing tasks

Nursing tasks include everything to do with providing for the child's physical needs. The proportion of the parent's time spent in physical care - washing, feeding, dressing and tending to minor ailments - obviously decreases quite substantially as the child progresses from infancy through childhood to adolescence.

General socialisation tasks

General socialisation refers to the huge, multi-faceted task of teaching the child to function in society. The content of socialisation includes everything from instruction in how to use the bus or underground, to table manners, to moral imperatives about stealing or acceptable social behaviour, to higher ethical or religious values. Socialisation methods may include stimulating activities, such as games, discussions and outings, verbal commands, role-modelling, various forms of correction, and many others. Thus, when "socialisation" is identified as a parenting task, no assumptions are made with respect to what will be taught, how it will be taught, or how obliged the parent feels to teach it.

"Socialisation" in this sense includes the two roles of "parent educator" and "parent teacher" which are differentiated in American literature. A parent may be a teacher when he is explaining something concrete - how to use a bus timetable, for example - and an educator when he is explaining something more nebulous - why the child should do his chores or obey school rules or conform with a family or national tradition. The task of socialisation can be, and usually is, combined with other tasks. For example, when a mother exhorts a child to eat his dinner and not waste food, she is combining the tasks of child minding, nursing - in the sense that she is meeting the child's nutritional needs - and socialisation.

Co-ordination tasks

Co-ordination refers to activities, often involving a parent, in which the child interacts with others outside the immediate family. Such activities may be related to health - visits to the doctor, dentist, hospital and so forth - school, relationships with extended family members, or leisure or vocational pursuits.

The sociologist, Kellerhals (1991), has quite rightly suggested the term "co-ordinating" in order to emphasise that the parent's task with respect to socialisation occurs on two levels. At the first level, the parent exerts a direct socialising influence, personally teaching acceptable social behaviour. At the second level, the parent exerts an indirect influence, monitoring, correcting or co-operating with the efforts of other actors who are also trying to socialise the child. Some second-level socialisation activities may be undertaken with the child: the parent and child may watch a television show together, or talk to a school teacher or psychologist together. However, much of the interaction between the parent and other socialising actors will not involve the child. This allows an opportunity for concerned adults who do not live with the child to also become involved: non-custodial parents or, in residential institutions, professionals who do not participate in everyday care.

Social reference tasks

Social reference tasks refer to the different decisions a parent must make on behalf of a child. For example, parental consent is required before a child can go on a school trip or participate in various school programmes, such as abuse prevention education. Consent is also required for marriage, for abortion in the case of girls under 16 years, and for surgical and other medical procedures. In addition, parents may choose a child's school and contribute to his later choices about his life-style, training and future.

When a child is reared at home, it is the parents - and often, traditionally, the father - who assume social reference tasks. However, when a child is placed in care, some or all of these tasks devolve upon the adults connected with the child's new living situation. The first decision to place the child in care may have been made by the parents or by the juvenile magistrate if legal measures were required to protect the child (Corbillon, 1993). Later decisions may be made by residential staff, the court, foster parents, adoptive parents, natural parents, or any combination of these depending on the situation. However, looking at parenting in terms of social reference tasks does allow us to distinguish quite clearly between a foster family and an adoptive family, since adoptive parents have decision-making powers which, in a foster family, may fall within the province of either the natural parents or the juvenile magistrate.

Identifying the roles and responsibilities of involved adults

We have identified seven parenting tasks which have been distinguished from each other somewhat artificially in that the normal course of child rearing demands co-ordination between them. However, the task-oriented approach does allow us to establish a relationship between the roles and responsibilities of the different adults concerned with parenting in different types of family and residential situations. The allocation of parenting tasks in different settings is summarised in Table 13.1.

Division of tasks in natural families

As Table 13.1 shows, all seven tasks are performed by the father or mother in a traditional family. Although gender roles are changing rapidly, mothers have traditionally assumed certain parenting tasks while fathers have undertaken others: for example, the mother does the housework, child minding and nursing, while the father looks after the technical side and assumes some of the socialisation tasks. Kellerhals (1991) has pointed out that the mother supervises school work much more frequently than the father. On the other hand, the father may take a greater part in co-ordination and social reference tasks which require interaction with people outside the family. Whatever the particular division of labour, all seven tasks are performed by only two people, or by one in the case of a one-parent family.

In more complex family structures, such as divorced or reconstituted families, a non-resident father is still likely to take some part in socialisation, co-ordination and social reference tasks. The new husband or wife of the natural parent living with the child more often participates in household, child-minding and nursing tasks and, to some extent, in the direct socialisation of the partner's child.

Division of tasks in care

When a child is placed away from his family, the seven identified tasks are often divided between a large number of care givers. This is true even when the term "care givers", as in the present study, is limited to primary care givers and does not take into account teachers, psychiatrists, psychologists, psychotherapists, re-educators and workshop leaders who play specific roles in the child's care or treatment but have no general responsibility.

In a residential children's home, as shown in Table 13.1 and described by Durning (1986), group workers carry out child-minding, nursing, socialisation and co-ordination tasks, while household and technical tasks are

Table 13.1: Parenting tasks in families and foster settings

Settings / Tasks	Ordinary Family	Blended Family	Foster Family	Residential Nursery	Group Home	Residential Home
Household	Parent (Mother)	Mother Step father	Foster parents	House staff	Group worker or House staff	House staff
Technical	Parents (Father)	Mother Step father	Foster parents	Odd job man	Group worker or Mainten. staff	Maintenance staff
Child minding	Parents (Mother)	Mother Step father	Foster parents	Assistant nurse	Group worker	Group worker
Nursing	Parents (Mother)	Mother Step father	Foster parents	Assistant nurse	Group worker	Group worker
Socialisation	Parents	Mother Father	Foster parents	Educator	Group worker	Group worker
Co-ordination	Parents (Father)	Mother Father	Social worker	Staff	Group worker	Group worker
Social Ref.	Parents (Father)	Father Mother	Parents or Magistrate	Parents or Magistrate	Parents or Magistrate	Parents or Magistrate

undertaken by others. Social reference activities are the province of the parents or the juvenile magistrate, and input is provided on various occasions by the director of the home, parents, the magistrate and the social welfare inspector.

In a children's psychiatric ward, observed by the author and colleagues, psychiatric nurses undertook tasks related to nursing and socialisation, while pedagogical and therapeutic activities in small groups were supervised by other specialists. In a residential nursery, also observed by the author and accommodating 20 children, three adults were responsible for household matters, supported by a handyman. Assistant paediatric nurses carried out the tasks of looking after and nursing the children, and also assumed some educational responsibilities in association with an educator (residential social worker). Co-ordination activities were essentially the responsibility of the director and other professionals, such as psychologists. Social reference was the province of the parents if they had made the decision to place the child and of the juvenile magistrate if not. Thus, in the residential nursery, only two of the seven parenting tasks were carried out by the same people, and attempts to limit the number of adults interacting with the same child were effective only in the child-minding and nursing areas.

Conversely, efforts to limit the number of adults interacting with the child are far more successful in a group or foster home. In a foster home, as shown in Table 13.1, the foster parents are responsible for five of the seven tasks and other adults are involved only with respect to co-ordination and social reference. The situation is more complex in group homes where some household and technical tasks may be undertaken by support staff.

The involvement of many adults with the same child raises the question of what name should be given to each adult consonant with his or her role and status. For example, assistant pediatric nurses are not entitled to be called educators or group workers. Their status is associated with a designation which, in French, emphasises their role as assistants or auxiliaries[1].

Love is necessary but not enough

As G. Snyders explains, if it is difficult to love our own children, it is obviously even more difficult to adequately love other people's children (Tomkiewicz, 1989; Durning, in press). In residential settings, over-emotional relationships between children and adults occur rarely. Emotional outbursts in accommodated youngsters are more frequently expressed in violence than in emotional demonstrations of affection, except in the case of some adolescent girls.

Criticisms of residential settings often emphasise the inadequate emotional relationships between children and adults, especially where very young children are concerned. The converse seems to be true in foster care, where most disagreements, at least in France, are related to requests by foster parents to keep and possibly adopt a child whom they have raised and love as their own. Attempts to avoid such situations are made by the overall foster care organisation which reviews problematic issues arising out of residential nurseries.

The aim of professional aptitude tests, and of the training and management provided to foster parents by psychologists and social workers is to help such parents develop into educative professionals. While this may be perceived as desirable, it must not be forgotten that children are placed in foster homes and not in residential homes *because* the adults in foster homes are parents, living with their families.

Love as I tell you!

Earlier in the chapter, reference was made to a residential nursery run by children's social welfare. Over a three-year period, together with D. Fablet, it was possible to observe the very difficult position of assistant pediatric nurses with respect to small babies who were being reared by them. The children were not grouped into small living units, as is the case elsewhere, and the system was such as to intimately involve the assistant pediatric nurses in the children's treatment. Each nurse was designated to care for one or two children during the entire placement period. The nurses were much criticised by the educator or psychologist when they allowed the children to call them "mother" or when they referred to a colleague as the "mother" of a particular child. This behaviour, indicative of a high personal investment, was condemned because of the fear that it would create confusion in the mind of the child.

A privileged relationship with a caregiver

A book which has been the reference in residential nursery circles in France for nearly 20 years clearly summarises two visits by M. David and G. Appel (1973) to an experimental residential nursery in Budapest (see also Vince, 1984). This nursery was organised by Pikler into small living groups which offered better stability for the children's staff during the entire period of the children's care. Activities which facilitated autonomy on the part of the children were very well developed. However, the fundamental contribution of Pikler's approach was to systematise the fostering situation by demanding that a staff member be completely involved with a child and completely devoted to him during certain specified periods. During other periods, however, the staff member must maintain only limited verbal contact with the child and no physical contact. The book explaining this approach was published in France at the same time as B. Bettelheim's book concerning life on a Kibbutz. It was looked upon as a kind of bible and was unanimously accepted by pediatricians, psychoanalysts, administrative heads and training staff[2].

This situation may be examined from the point of view of all potentially concerned: the child, the fostering professionals, the child's natural or adoptive family and the social organisation providing the care. It is undeniably true that a very small child cannot develop adequately without a loving environment. He may even refuse to eat and die. He therefore needs love and attention from someone, whether the assistant nurse in an institution or the parent in a foster home. On the other hand, because the placement is temporary, it is important not to hinder and indeed to facilitate the relationship between the child and the family which will eventually give the child a permanent home. When a child is abandoned, attempts must be made to minimise potential conflict between adoptive parents and assistant nurses during the period prior to adoption.

This need for a balance between enough love but not too much has resulted in an attempt on the part of social organisations to impose supposedly adequate relational systems upon the assistant nurses working in residential nurseries and also upon foster parents. Conformity with the rules pertaining to relationships is reinforced by pressure from the head of the team which supervises the appropriateness of affective interactions[3]. An alternative way of obtaining an emotional balance is to provide training to staff, through psychotherapy or otherwise, to allow them to develop their own intuitive knowledge of when affection should or should not be demonstrated. However, if it is admitted that such intuitive knowledge may not be adequate in all situations, another solution is to set up meetings in which staff themselves decide in what circmstances affection should and should not be given for the mutual benefit of staff, children, and families.

Characteristics of fostering organisations

Much of the work in this study has been devoted to examining the effects of organisational processes on the socialisation of children in care. For a long time, the provision of care for children placed away from their families has been increasingly supervised, if not actually provided by the State. Since the State has responsibility for children in care, authorities who cannot themselves provide care must entrust the children to other organisations from whom guarantees about the quality of care are required.

Work and everyday life

When a child is cared for by paid staff, it is inevitable that the care process will be professionalised in the sense that it will be affected by the factors involved in working life: for example, time management, the division of tasks and hierarchical responsibilities.

The length of the working week obviously increases the number of adults interacting with the children; and this increase in the number of caregivers is clearly prejudicial to the child's development, especially in residential nurseries. In recent years, part-time work has been the general practice for women employed by the French civil service. This tendency to part-time work has run counter to efforts to be better organised, particularly with respect to working in teams.

In addition, the routine of the children's daily life must be planned around the staff's working day. In a hospital, getting-up times, meal times, and so forth seem incomprehensible from the patient's point of view but make much more sense if the shifts and meal times of staff are taken into account. Other examples of daily routine planned around staff requirements may be drawn from organisations providing temporary accommodation, such as holiday camps, where time management is an important factor. Smaller group homes attempt to get around the timetable problem by suggesting that accommodated youngsters and involved adults live together on a continual basis.

The division and importance of tasks in residential settings

The division of parenting tasks into the seven categories mentioned earlier allows us to analyse the boundaries imposed upon staff members with respect to their interaction with accommodated children. In a family, the decision as to which parenting task will be performed by which parent is made by the couple themselves. In residential settings, on the other hand, the special functions of each staff member are dictated by the system and assume a great importance. In many establishments, a maintenance worker would not be allowed to go shopping with a young person, nor discuss his future with him. In many foster care organisations, foster parents are asked not to make any contact with the school: co-ordination with the school is the function of the head social worker of the organisation.

The "care"[4] which is provided to handicapped children, old people or infants is particularly revealing with respect to the underlying power stakes. In a residential nursery, an educator for young children cannot bottle-feed a child nor bathe him. Physical care of this kind is the sole prerogative of assistant pediatric nurses, just as a medical prescription can only be given by a doctor.

The requirement that a prescription must be provided by a doctor is based on the assumption that only a doctor has the specialised knowledge to perform the task. It is difficult to apply this same argument to the requirement that only a pediatric nurse must feed or bathe a child, even if it is accepted that some nursing procedures are more easily accomplished during bath time[5]. The reality is that doctors prefer assistant pediatric nurses to perform this task in order to preserve the power base of the medical profession. Doctors have always protected the specific functions of paramedical staff against interference by outsiders while exerting absolute authority over the activities of paramedics[6].

An unevenly developed hierarchical system

Different official managers assume responsibility for ensuring that specialised tasks such as medical attention are carried out in accordance with the practices of the profession concerned and are co-ordinated with other areas of child care[7]. The frequent division of a residential setting into distinct departments, such as healthcare, education and general development often leads to an increase in the number of managers and thus to the potential for conflict. In residential settings, such issues may assume particular importance, especially with respect to the role of a deputy manager. In foster care services, hierarchical levels are fewer but more pronounced. Such levels systematically differentiate the primary provision of child care, by such people as foster parents, from the management or supervision of these primary providers, often undertaken by social workers or by the heads of children's villages.

The importance of a relational approach to educational processes

The study of the tasks, roles and feelings of the parents and other actors involved in foster care has allowed us to identify a dual and contradictory tendency: on the one hand, towards greater diversification of child-care practices; and on the other hand, towards a more restrictive form of parenting associated with practices prevalent in the professions and entering even into foster care, which is supposed to be more flexible and less bureaucratic than traditional residential settings.

In short, there appears to be a basic contradiction between the way that parenting tasks are performed in natural families and the way that these same tasks are performed in any child-care situation outside the natural family. This perceived contradiction may be usefully explored by analysing the relational processes involved in the different forms of family groups in various fostering services.

Notes

1. The assistant pediatric nurses often call themselves "the girls" whereas the other professionals shorten their vocational title, calling them "the assistants". Foster parents are often called "nanny". For the child who is faced with a complex network of relationships, there is an obvious difficulty in sorting out who is who and who does what with reference to the names assigned to the various adults concerned.
2. The contrast between the Hungarian nursery and the abortive attempt to establish a kindergarten based on the psychoanalytical approach in Moscow is remarkable. For example, Vera Schmidt has noted that the educators were called "nanny". In the Loczy institution and in France, such a practice is unacceptable (see Schmidt, 1969; Korczak, 1978).
3. The career pattern of many social workers, particularly educators, is quite standard. After leaving one of the declining number of residential settings, they become foster care managers, supporting the foster parents in their efforts to maintain the desired emotional balance in relationships with the child. The foster parents are recruited and trained by the educators, who critically evaluate cost-efficiency and look for any counter transference being exhibited by the foster parents. The everyday activities of foster parents are monitored through unexpected home visits and direct contact with children. Foster parents contribute only to major decisions so that the focus remains on the child's relationship with the natural family. This allows conflicts between the natural family and the foster family to be minimised. However, it also means that foster parents are deprived of a frame of reference which would help them to more effectively fulfil their role.
4. It will be recalled that, in French, "care" and "cure" are translated using the same word, "soin". In English, there is no ambiguity between the terms "to cure" and "to care".
5. The same conflicts concerning division of labour arise around such taks as treating cuts and scratches, taking temperatures, bathing physically handicapped children, and so forth.
6. The assistant pediatric nurse has no responsibility for the children's care within the medical hierarchy. Her principal task is to care for the children's everyday physical needs. The medical monopoly has no basis in reality and makes an art of medicalising the children's education.
7. A concrete application of the present study could concern the training of these managers. Training should emphasise the absolute necessity of an approach based on the relationship between different methods of caring for children outside the natural family. This could counteract the present approach, in which managerial policy focuses upon the association of the residential setting or school with a professional organisation, such as medicine or education.

References

Colton, M.J. and Hellinckx, W. (1993), *Child Care in the EC. A country-specific guide to foster and residential care*, Aldershot, Arena.

Corbillon, M. (1993), 'The nature of residential and foster care provisions', in M.J. Colton & W. Hellinckx (Eds), *Child Care in the EC. A country-specific guide to foster and residential care*, Adershot, Arena.

David, M. & Appell, G. (1973), *Loczy ou le maternage insolite*, CEMEA Scarabée, Paris.

Durning, P. (in press), *Violences et climats socio-émotionnels en institution. Du symptôme au tableau d'alerte*, Violences en institution, 2 - Outils, CREAI Rhône-Alpes, 1er trimestre 1994.

Durning, P. (1991), 'A psychological approach to foster-parenting in residential care', in W. Hellinckx et al. (Eds), *Innovations in Residential Care* (pp. 227-235), Leuven, Acco.

Durning, P. (1992), 'Crisis in a residential home, a case study', in J.D. Van der Ploeg et al. (Eds), *Vulnerable youth in residential care. Part 2 - clients, staff and the system* (pp. 250), Leuven: Garant.

Durning, P. (1986), *Education et suppléance familiale: psychosociologie de l'internat spécialisé* (pp. 275), Paris: CTNERHI.

Durning, P. (1992), 'L'enfant, enjeu des interactions entre familles naturelles, milieux de suppléance familiale et travailleurs sociaux', *Communautés éducatives*, vol. 80, 51-60.

Kellerhals, J. & Montandon, C. (1991), *Les stratégies éducatives des familles. Milieu social, dynamique familiale et éducation des pré-adolescents*, Paris: Delachaux et Niestlé.

Korczak, J., (1978), *Comment aimer un enfant*, Paris: R. Laffont.

Moss, P. (1975), 'Residential care of children: a general view -In J. Tizard et al., *Varieties of Residential Experience*, London: Routledge & Kegan Paul.

Schmidt, V. (1969), 'Education psychanalytique en Union Soviétique, trad. française', *Temps modernes*, vol. 273, 1626-1647.

Schulteis, F. (1988), 'Pour une reconstruction critique d'un objet de recherche et d'intervention: un exmeple allemand', in P. Durning (Ed.), *Education familiale, un panorama des recherches internationales*, (pp. 225-243) Paris: Matrice.

Tomkiewicz, S. (1989), 'Violences institutionnelles', *Lien social*, vol. 39, 4 ff.

Vincze, M. (1984), 'Répercussions du changement de climat éducationnel. Réflexions à propos d'une post-enquête à Loczy, Hongrie', *Les Cahiers du CTNERHI*, vol. 26, 73-82.

14 Integrating research, policy and practice

Matthew COLTON
Pol GHESQUIÈRE
Walter HELLINCKX
Margaret WILLIAMS

Aristotle believed that women have fewer teeth than men. Although he was twice married and the number of teeth possessed by women was a contentious issue, it would never have occurred to him to ask his wives to open their mouths so that he could count their teeth. Aristotle did not engage in empirical research studies. He evaluated his theories by recourse to authority, or, where no suitable authority existed, by dialogue and meditation. So did his peers. So did the majority of thinkers until about the seventeenth century (Russell, 1961).

We of the twentieth century set far more store by observation. We are more inclined to approach "truth" through measurement, which provides the necessary link between theory and reality. Further, it may be argued that we are less interested in truth for its own sake than in the use we can make of the truth once we have come upon it. We are interested in atoms, for example, because they are the building blocks of all we see around us. However, sceptics would hold that funding for atomic research has not been based on the inherent fascination of the atom: it lies instead in the atom's potential as a power source and weapon. Increasingly, in the physical sciences, pure research has become the handmaid of technology.

To some degree, the same may be said of the social sciences, although, as Bullock and Little have pointed out, many countries still lack the tradition of seeking remedies to pressing social problems by reviewing empirical evidence (Bullock and Little, see Chapter 2). In the same vein, Casas (Chapter 1) comments on the general dissatisfaction expressed at the 1991 European seminar in Madrid with respect to the link between research and social action programmes. Nevertheless, in the past few decades an increasing effort has been made to forge a practical dimension to research work. We may be interested in the developmental stages of childhood just for the sake of knowing, but we are even more interested if we can use these developmental stages to persuade parents to have realistic expectations of their children and to improve their parenting skills. Funders are mostly concerned with the practical applications of research. Managers of social service agencies are usually only interested in research if it can provide them with information to guide them in making decisions. It seems something of a paradox, therefore, that all the chapters in this book are concerned with the *dichotomy* between research and practice - with the undoubted fact that practice is rarely research-based and the results of research studies are rarely used (Colton and Hellinckx, 1993).

Why is this? Casas (Chapter 1) draws our attention to the difficulties and antagonisms which have existed and continue to exist between five key groups of social actors in the child-care field: practitioners, researchers, policymakers, the media and public. Each of these five groups adopts a different perspective towards child-care issues. Practitioners are concerned with the immediate problems of individuals and communities, and tend to be wary of politicians, defensive about research and suspicious of the media. Researchers focus on methodological rigour, approaching truth slowly, through careful observation, accurate measurement and ongoing verification. The media need novelty - spectacle and drama. The public need information relevant to their daily lives and need, moreover, to feel that they are consulted and involved. Politicians often have their own agenda but their basic task is to integrate the needs of the other actors into a coherent, legal framework, establishing priorities, standards and procedures. One obstacle to the integration of research, policy and practice is thus the number of different social actors with conflicting perspectives.

This theme of the diversity of social actors is continued in Chapter 2, where Bullock and Little observe that many professionals concerned with child care, such as guardians ad litem, judges and court clerks, work in isolation and are not part of the networks, weak though they are, in which social work research findings are disseminated and discussed. Casas' "practitioners" group is thus seen to comprise a wide variety of subgroups, each with their particular functions and interests and each participating to varying degrees in the different child-care networks. Researchers also have their subgroups, particularly with respect to the tensions which exist between theoreticians, who have always had a higher status in the academic community, and applied researchers, whose empirical studies are sometimes perceived as just collecting figures. Similarly, "the public" includes not only varied and often conflicting special interest groups but also foster parents and childminders (who might also now be classified as "practitioners"), and those individuals and communities whom practitioners are trying to help. Media representatives take very different standpoints, and the perspectives of politicians and policymakers at national and local levels reflect a spectrum of fairly basic philosophical conflicts. We should also bear in mind that "policy" and "practice" are not the same thing, and that the concerns of policy makers are not necessarily shared by practitioners. This certainly appears to be the case with regard to child-care research and its application (see Parker, 1989).

Casas suggests that the convergence of research and practice might best be facilitated by a forum where key social actors can come together at national and international levels. Bullock and Little (Chapter 2) adopt a complementary approach, focusing on the relationship between research and development, with particular attention to dissemination. They note that realisation of the need for a link between research, policy and practice has only quite recently occurred, and that in the United Kingdom such links are tenuous and varied. For example, there has not been any mechanism in social work by which intermediary bodies, such as the Royal Colleges in medicine, could co-ordinate and publicise research findings. At central government levels, there is a system of research liaison which ensures discussion between researchers and policy makers, but at a local level the relationship is far more fragile.

Research links with local practitioners are even weaker, exacerbated not only by the failure of staff to read research material but also by the lack of any tradition in which practitioners undertake investigations as part of their work. Thus, even if research findings are available, they are often viewed as irrelevant and alien. More serious still is the patchy adoption of research evidence in child-care training courses. The reasons for this are complex but partly stem from the difficulties of incorporating material that seems agnostic and critical into courses which seek socialisation and consensus. Another reason may lie perhaps in a dearth of the requisite expertise on the part of social work tutors. In turn, this may owe something to the fact that most social teachers are necessarily recruited direct from practice. Many may have received little by way of up-to-date formal training in research methodology and the application of research to practice.

Bullock and Little thus point to a number of reasons for tenuous links between research, policy and practice in the United Kingdom. They further note that it is only within the last decade that dissemination has assumed importance as a means of establishing such links. In 1985, a landmark in dissemination occurred when the Department of Health, a major research funder in the child-care field, produced *Social Work Decisions in Child Care*. This publication, affectionately known as the Pink Book, summarised the results of nine recently completed child-care projects and was circulated to every child welfare agency in the country. It was followed by a series of national seminars for social workers at all levels of seniority, and gave official, government approval to dissemination, paving the way for subsequent research programmes to undertake developmental work.

While most researchers do not expect research to have clear cut and positive effects on policy and practice, the influence of research nevertheless remains significant. Even in countries like Spain, where research is rather limited, measures taken to improve the quality of residential care and to restructure the community-based framework of services for children have often been based on fairly comprehensive research studies (Colton and Hellinckx, 1993). Indeed, in the United Kingdom, the impact of research on policy and practice is relatively impressive. The Children Act 1989, which is widely seen as the most far reaching reform of child care law in England and Wales this century, was informed by the series of government-commissioned research projects referred to above.

However, although the programme of child-care research outlined and its subsequent dissemination represent the largest exercises of their kind ever undertaken in Britain, the dissemination of British child-care research has been hampered by a number of factors. These include the fact that while the government initiatives described were clearly effective in disseminating research findings and incorporating them into government policy and legislation, insufficient emphasis has been placed on ensuring that the necessary changes in ethos, structure and practice occur in child welfare agencies. Furthermore, the research and development initiative was a one-off exercise. The single broad sweep obtained from the set of complementary studies cannot offer much more than a sophisticated natural history. It can lay out processes, typologies and outcomes but can only offer tentative causal explanations. Thus, the tools derived from research to help social workers make assessments and to select appropriate strategies are not yet validated sufficiently for them to gain uncritical acceptance (Colton and Hellinckx, 1993).

The dissemination of research findings in a useful and attractive way is only one dimension of developmental research. A second dimension involves drawing out policy and practice implications from research results and making recommendations about guidance and procedures, often in the form of a code of practice. A third dimension is the production of indicators or checklists to help those making decisions. These can be limited in scope, such as aide memoires, or can have predictive possibilities in that they enable decision makers to be more aware of the consequences of their actions. Clearly, different types of research will have different relevance for different types of development work, and vice versa. Bullock and Little provide examples of the usefulness of developmental work in linking research, policy and practice through a discussion of two projects undertaken by the Dartington Social Research Unit: the Foster Care Breakdown project, leading to the publication *Lost in Care*; and the *Going Home* project.

The *Looking After Children* programme described by Sonia Jackson in Chapter 3 is another, superb example of what can be achieved when researchers, policy makers and practitioners combine their expertise. The *Looking After Children* programme developed in parallel with the enactment and implementation of the 1989 Children Act, and the work of the development team had considerable influence on the content of the Guidance and Regulations issued in association with the legislation (DH, 1991). The core of the scheme and the means through which its philosophy is expressed is a set of six Assessment and Action Records, colour-coded by the age of the child, which are designed to provide a method of recording and evaluating outcomes of residential and foster care. In relation to individual children, they enable supervisors and managers to assess in detail the quality of care being offered and to identify problems. When the data are aggregated, they provide evidence for policy formation and strategic planning. Thus, the materials that make up the scheme are designed to help social workers and carers to fulfil the requirements of the Act by providing information which can feed directly back into practice.

Rink, in Chapter 5, takes a somewhat different approach to the assessment of children and the establishment of appropriate methods of care. His work originated from the need to provide more effective supervision for delinquent youngsters in prisons and better care for juveniles with serious behavioural problems in residential institutions. The Reaction Pattern research studies he describes concern the attitudes of juveniles to social limits: that is, to the laws, rules and expectations of others about behaviour. Rink and his colleagues have developed and used a standard reaction instrument (SRI) for the purpose of identifying juveniles who tend towards delinquent behaviour and suggesting appropriate treatment methods for them based on their attitudinal flexibility towards social limits. Here, we note the focus on the relationship between the process and outcomes of care, based on the characteristics and situations of the children concerned.

In the following chapter, Colton, Heath and Aldgate dwell more fully upon the outcomes of care in their examination of the possible relationship between educational attainment and behaviour. Evidence presented by the authors suggests that abuse and neglect before entry into care had lasting and profound effects on both the children's educational attainment and on their behaviour. Children admitted into care for other reasons fared somewhat better but were still below the national average in their attainment, even after long-term, settled placements with foster parents who showed every indication of providing an environment - emotional, social, cultural and material - conducive to educational progress. The authors conclude that something more than "normal" family life and "normal" parental interest is required to compensate for earlier deprivation. In other words, the "normalisation" goals which we often aim to achieve may not be enough.

We are interested in the outcomes of care because we genuinely wish to know how best to care for children; and we try, through research, to attain some knowledge of the human and systemic "truths" upon which such care should be based. However, while the ultimate goal of research may be truth, research is also part of the wider political agenda, as Bullock and Little have perceptively remarked, and knowledge is ammunition. Over the last 20 years, this duality of truth and weaponry has given rise to a field of endeavour which holds a great deal of potential for creating and nurturing research-policy-practice links. This new field - evaluation research - has come into being in a time of recession when accountability is at a premium and the emphasis is on the highest possible quality at the lowest possible cost. Even the concern with quality is relatively new, in the sense that we are now asking questions about the process and outcomes of child care which we did not ask before. As Madge observes in Chapter 6, in the early days of extrafamilial care, questions about outcomes were not asked. If the goal of care was merely to rescue children from abandonment or to remove them from "bad" families, then any institution providing food and shelter was bound to meet that goal.

In the present day, however, we have come to realise the importance of meeting the emotional and developmental needs of individual children, fostering their relationships with their natural families, minimising stigma, and ensuring the availability and relevance of after-care support. In other words, we are interested in the outcomes of care, with respect to goals which are more complex, more specific and harder to achieve than the "rescue" goals of former days. In her examination of the short-term and long-term outcomes of extra-familial care, Madge begins by drawing attention to the difficulties both of defining and of measuring "success". She observes that success for any individual child is usually measured in terms of number of placements, whether or not the placement broke down, or whether the placement goals were achieved. However, in the absence of suitable controls, it is still not possible to isolate the effects of care from extraneous effects, such as maturation or personal relationships. In particular, it is not possible to address the central issue of whether coming into care was better for the child than remaining in the family home.

With regard to longitudinal studies, Madge makes the further point that changing philosophies and organisational structures in residential care have created significant difficulties in generalising the results of past studies to present-day conditions. Nevertheless, past studies have been important in documenting the potential dangers of institutional care and influencing change, particularly with respect to the age of the children placed and to their need for a stimulating environment, affectional bonds, a sense of identity and the maintenance of family links. In other words, we see here that increased knowledge of children's needs, provided by research, has to some extent effected changes in policy and practice in residential care. This echoes the experience of Jackson and of Bullock and Little in their developmental work aimed at improving the outcomes for children in residential and foster care.

Of course, much remains to be done, both short-term and long-term, especially regarding the *process* of care. Madge remarks that the main gaps in our knowledge concern what goes on between the time a child is received into care and the time he or she is discharged. Much of this information might be collected by practitioners themselves, who are in the best position to document day-to-day procedures and to witness the effects of such procedures on the different types of children they are meant to help. The research-practice link could thus be used to explore the process-outcome link, providing policy makers with relevant data upon which to base decisions.

Madge reviews the findings of a number of outcome studies, drawing our attention to factors which are particularly influential in affecting outcomes, such as the age and characteristics of children, family links, length of time in care, realistic goals, patterns of placement, preparation for care and after-care, and the training and experience of staff. In her discussion of realistic goals, she notes that there are limits to what can reasonably be expected from both residential and foster care. For example, there is evidence (Parker, 1980; Rowe et al., 1989; Utting, 1991) that residential care is best suited to fulfilling short-term functions such as preparing young people for foster placements or for leaving care. It is less successful with longer-term or more ambitious goals such as treatment. Similarly, foster care is not always appropriate for children with behavioural difficulties, particularly when it is not preceded by extensive preparation and support (Berridge and Cleaver, 1987).

The point here is that care facilities fall upon a continuum, from light to heavy, or from less restrictive to more restrictive, and the most appropriate place on that continuum for any particular child will depend on the child's own situation and characteristics. It may therefore be inappropriate to try to show that one type of care is inherently "better" or "worse" than any other type. It would also appear unwise to react to problems by eliminating a whole section of the continuum, as did one county council in England which closed all its children's homes in 1986.

The decline of interest and belief in residential care in the United Kingdom is reflected in the low status and skills of residential staff. In the U.K., the adults looking after children are more likely than not to be untrained and isolated from fellow professionals. Such factors appear to have played a part in the recent controversy surrounding malpractice in children's homes in various parts of the country (Levy and Kahan, 1991; Utting, 1991). These scandals were followed by calls for improved status, training, supervision and conditions for care workers and more careful selection procedures (CCETSW, 1992; Department of Health, 1992; Howe, 1992). It may be significant that the main profession involved in residential child care within and beyond the E.U. - that of the social pedagogue or *educateur specialise* - does not exist in the U.K. Instead, residential care is undertaken by a variety of groups, including social workers, youth and community workers, and teachers. Consequently, in the U.K., the learning, scholarship and vocabulary associated with a distinctive residential child care profession is largely missing (Davies Jones, 1991, p.16). The concept of "social educator" may have a good deal to offer in terms of helping to resolve the current crisis in residential care in the U.K., and ensuring that high quality residential care forms part of a comprehensive range of child-care services.

The care continuum is addressed more fully by Scholte in Chapter 7 through his discussion of the application of longitudinal research studies to three major trends in care services in West European countries. These trends are: the establishment of a continuum of care; an increasing awareness of the complexity of the problems of children at risk; and an increasing demand for outcome evaluation. Through meta-analysis of a number of research studies, Scholte explores the links between the child's problems at intake, the type of care provided, and the outcomes of care as reflected in the degree of resolution of the assessed problems.

The thrust of Scholte's argument is that, before care can be effective in resolving problems, care workers must know what kinds of settings with what kinds of interventions produce what kind of developmental outcomes on what kind of children and their families. In other words, they must be able to relate a known process-outcome link to a problem situation which has been assessed in a standardised way. Scholte suggests that assessment might be based upon a uniform conceptual model - the socio-ecological model - which enables a child to be described in terms of his or her behaviour, personal characteristics and family, school and peer-group situation. The child's development within the framework of this model might then be measured at standard intervals during the process of care. At the same time, the care process itself might be measured through conceptual models which describe the nature of the care provided: the degree of restrictiveness, for example, as well as special treatment strategies, such as behavioural therapy, social-skills training, educational-vocational training, or psychotherapy. Internally and externally valid research studies which measured these variables would enable data to be gathered, across care settings and nations, from which a process-outcome link might be established in relation to the various problem situations of different types of children at risk.

In Chapter 8, Hellinckx and van den Bruel take the process-outcome relationship further in their discussion of the meaning and place of quality evaluation in residential child care. They provide us with an overview of the difficulties of defining and measuring quality, together with reasons for the growing interest in quality evaluation, not only by funders, researchers and child care workers but also by the public and the children and families who are the recipients of care. While making reference to the contribution of Harinck and Smit in the next chapter, Hellinckx and van den Bruel take us through the different types and functions of quality evaluation on the macro, meso and micro levels, stressing the point that the aim of quality evaluation is to improve practice, not just with respect to obtaining desired outcomes but also in relation to raising the standard of process elements. As Harinck and Smit also remark (Chapter 9), treatment elements should be of quality quite apart from their contribution to outcome: preparation for discharge, for example, should be planned with care even if careless planning does not result in maladjustment in later life. Likewise, high quality day-to-day care practices do not require justification in terms of measured outcomes. Kindliness and consideration, an environment in which children are respected as persons, treated as individuals, and given variety of experience are important irrespective of whether they can be shown to benefit children in measurable terms (King et al., 1971, p. 199).

Harinck and Smit, in Chapter 9, focus on process evaluation in residential care, drawing our attention to the dangers of attempting to evaluate outcome before the care programme has reached a developmental stage in which outcome evaluation would be appropriate. They point out that programmes, like people, go through developmental stages, and the questions relevant to the earlier stages of development have little to do with outcome. For example, at the programme's inception, the most relevant questions have to do with the needs the programme is being designed to meet, and the most appropriate way of answering such questions is through a needs assessment. In all, Harinck and Smit discuss six types of evaluation research: component analysis; monitoring; underlying process evaluation; implementation evaluation; clarifying practitioners' concepts; and formative evaluation. Since residential care is of primary interest in many E.U. countries, examples of each type of evaluation are drawn from research in the field of residential care. The focus here is on *evaluability*: that is, on the degree to which a programme has reached that developmental stage in which its resources, activities and intended outcomes are clearly defined, logically linked and demonstrably appropriate to the needs of the individual client, the local community and society as a whole.

Harinck and Smit point to the need for a systematic approach in evaluating programmes. Knorth and Smit, in Chapter 10, adopt the same approach in their discussion of a particular aspect of systematization: goal-oriented care and the use of written, hierarchically-ordered treatment goals at the level of individual treatment plans. At the individual level, systematic care is reflected in a plan for action which encompasses all phases of the care process (intake, treatment and termination), and is regularly reviewed. Such a plan might be based upon the ADPIA model previously developed by the authors (Knorth and Smit, 1990; Smit and Knorth, 1992), in which diagnostic assessment, decision-making surrounding placement, treatment planning, implementation, and evaluative assessment are systematically undertaken.

With respect to the treatment goals themselves, the authors make the point that ultimate goals can only be reached after attention has been paid to a series of immediate and intermediate goals, and after these goals have been at least partially achieved. These various kinds or levels of goal together form hierarchic chains of objectives which can be usefully displayed on paper and included in individual treatment plans. Goals can thus be visualised in relation to each other, making it easier for care workers, children and parents to see what progress has been made and in what areas further attention is required. Another important advantage is that the inclusion of different types and levels of goal increases the chance of satisfying the interests or priorities of all parties concerned. Furthermore, the goal-oriented method can be productive with respect to planning for the residential institution as a whole. Aggregation of individual treatment plans and evaluation data generates important information which can be used to create or adapt an institutional working plan.

We see here that the scientific method essential to research can be usefully employed not only to improve service to children and their parents but to meet the needs of practitioners and to provide information to policy makers at an institutional level. Although it is true that policy makers and practitioners generally have different priorities and wrestle with different kinds of problems (Parker, 1989), it is nevertheless quite possible to produce data which will benefit both. The last three chapters of the book illustrate this point by presenting studies which draw together issues of concern to practitioners and issues which are important at institutional and national levels.

In Chapter 11, Colton, Drury and Williams describe key dilemmas in the implementation of the 1989 Children Act in the U.K., and highlight the conflicts facing practitioners and local authorities. They draw our attention to the difficulty of operationalising the concept of need in the light of limited resources and an inherent contradiction between the all-embracing spirit of the Act and current political and social realities. For example, the concept of need as defined in the Act includes all children who would potentially benefit from services now or in the future. However, in the context of residualist national policies, "need" must be defined in terms of child protection with little left for the parallel duty of family support. Since social service departments are not in a position to formulate official policies which seem to contravene the spirit of the Act, it is hardly surprising that the study found policies to be non-specific or even lacking, and that contradictory, informal policies were also found to exist. Findings also gave some indication that social workers, operating in the midst of the confusion, were interpreting "need" according to their own convictions, and that differences in the attitudes of individual social workers were creating dissension within and between the families and communities being served.

The results of this study point to the difficulties of establishing any unified policy with regard to child care when resource limitations mean that priorities must be set and conflicting philosophies make it hard to agree on what those priorities are. Good practice in child care is thus not just a matter of formulating links between research, policy and practice to evolve a better system. It is a matter of accommodating within an *existing* system the different philosophies which will inevitably result from changes in government, new legislation, new research findings, novel practice techniques, changing social attitudes, and even changing fads and fancies. It seems that what is needed is an ability to compromise, to avoid knee-jerk responses, to be open to change while holding fast to what has worked well before.

Ghesquiere, Hellinckx and Baartman (Chapter 12) continue with the topic of definitions, not with reference to policy but with respect to the meaning of the term "multi-problem family" in practice. They too are concerned with the need for compromise, in their case with the need to balance the safety and wellbeing of children against the needs of parents to demonstrate that they are good parents, the kind of parents who should not lose their children. These authors take us through the diversity of definitions of a multi-problem family to be found in the literature, and remark that, notwithstanding this diversity, practitioners have very largely reached agreement as to what they mean by a multi-problem family. Such agreement provides an excellent illustration of the mutual education which might ideally exist between research, policy and practice. Practitioners are directed by policy and informed by research, but it is they who seem best able, from sheer practical necessity, to cut through the knot of political and academic conflicts and arrive at workable solutions for the benefit of clients. Perhaps we should begin to look upon training from a different viewpoint: not just training for practitioners, but training of policy makers and researchers *by* practitioners with respect to practice issues.

Ghesquiere, Hellinckx and Baartman further remark that a multi-problem family is really a multi-problem relationship between the helper and the helped. In part, the problems arise from different perspectives about the purpose of the relationship and the roles of the different participants in it. The authors' study found that the predominant concern of parents is to avoid the placement of a child outside the home whereas helping professionals may be more concerned with poor parenting skills, mental health or socioeconomic conditions, depending on their particular professional focus.

Durning, in Chapter 11, is also concerned with the tasks, roles and feelings of parents as opposed to other actors, this time in foster and residential care. Much of his work in the study he describes is devoted to examining the effects of organisational processes on the socialisation of separated children in France. He points out that there appears to be a basic contradiction between the way that parenting tasks are performed in natural families and the way that these same tasks are performed in any child-care situation outside the natural family, particularly with respect to the division of labour and the continuity of care. In residential settings, for example, the special functions of each staff member are dictated by the system and seem to be designed to benefit the system rather than the child. In many foster care organisations, foster parents are asked not to make any contact with the school, as a natural parent would, because co-ordination with the school is not considered to be the foster parent's function.

Durning also remarks upon the conflict between policy and practice in the very sensitive area of providing love to a child in residential care which is sufficient to facilitate development but not so much as to impede a later attachment between the child and foster or adoptive parents. Rules concerning appropriate affective relationships tend to be broken by caregivers with a personal investment in their work who allow the children to call them "mother" or who refer to another caregiver as the "mother" of a particular child. One way of obtaining an emotional balance is provide training to staff, through psychotherapy or otherwise, to allow them to develop their own intuitive knowledge of when affection should or should not be demonstrated. However, if it is admitted that such intuitive knowledge may not be adequate in all situations, another solution is to set up meetings in which staff themselves decide in what circumstances affection should and should not be given for the mutual benefit of staff, children, and prospective parents. Durning suggests here that one way of linking policy and practice is to allow practitioners substantial input in determining policy. This suggestion runs parallel to the idea considered earlier that practitioners might be instrumental in providing training to policymakers.

So far, we have considered a number of obstacles - and a number of possible solutions - to the integration of research, policy and practice. The first obstacle is the sheer diversity of social actors in the child-care field, each with their different perspectives, agendas and needs. To some degree, this problem may be addressed through increased attention to communication, through local, national and international forums and through the dissemination of written material in a relevant and attractive manner. Researchers bewail the fact that practitioners ignore their findings, but it is presently often the case that the dissemination of research results stops with a report to the funder, and books and journal papers aimed at other academics. Little attention is paid to presenting the information in a way that is attractive, relevant and available to the practitioners who are supposed to apply it. The general pressure exerted on most academics to publish takes practically no account of what is published, for whom it is published, and through what mechanisms it is made available. The result may be, and very often is, the establishment of a clique of researcher-writers, who are talking almost solely to each other.

There are, of course, a large number of other reasons for the non-use of research findings by practitioners, ranging from the attitudinal to the purely practical. At an abstract level, there is a wide-spread belief in the uniqueness of the individual, a feeling among social work practitioners that the generalizations obtained from research cannot and should not be applied to the individual problems of children and parents. As Parker (1989, p.262) remarks, "social work practice...has a long history of according pride of place to the exercise of judgement, to the application of experience and to the use of insights...Indeed, there were long periods during which social work training was mainly aimed at sharpening students' sensitivities to individual predicaments."

One important difficulty thus has to do with the reluctance of practitioners to apply science to people. It may be argued that this reluctance stems from five related sources: first, the feeling that the application of the scientific method to human services reduces people to the status of objects; second, turf and territory considerations in that practitioners who have developed an understanding of the people they serve may resent any perceived interference with *their* judgements of *their* clients; third, lack of knowledge on the part of practitioners about research findings relating to their field; fourth, doubt about the worth of the research itself, with respect to both relevance and quality; and fifth, lack of commitment on the part of managers to the use of research by practitioners.

The first three of these sources of reluctance might be addressed through training, both in college and at the place of work. At the very least, educators should emphasise that individuals are not in fact diminished, and may be helped, through the application to them of knowledge gained about the thoughts, feelings, situations and behaviours of similar others. Judgements made by social workers on the basis of their own experience employ just such an application of acquired knowledge. With respect to considerations of turf and territory, it has never been suggested that the results of research can replace the wisdom and experience of practitioners in the field. Research is a helper, not a master. It provides guidance and information, not directives and not, unfortunately, ready-made or easy-to-apply solutions.

The third source of reluctance - lack of knowledge about relevant research findings - might be partly addressed through providing mandatory research methods courses to social work students, teaching them, first, how to read and understand the work of others and, second, how to conduct their own research around the problems they encounter in the field. As Parker (1989, p.263) has observed, "...there is much simple research that could (and should) be carried out by social workers alongside their daily practice." Courses to help social workers do this are provided routinely in the United States and Canada but currently appear to be afforded less importance in Europe.

A second, complementary approach is training in the work place, facilitated by managers who are themselves committed to solving their own problems by collection and interpretation of their own data. Such data will mostly have to do with evaluation, particularly in light of the present concern with quality and accountability. The word "evaluation" is connected in many minds with the measurement of outcomes, or with the emergence in the U.K. of efficiency audits, which have entailed enquiries into the methods and costs of child care in local authorities, using the methods of management consultants. In this context, it may be interesting to note that the meaning and place of "efficiency" in social programmes has excited considerable controversy in North America. The argument that efficiency in terms of time and cost is an insufficient and sometimes inappropriate measure of the worth of human services has resulted in more evaluation activity by social workers and considerably less by management consultants.

Evaluation activity should be seen as a hallmark of professional social work practice. Such activity may play a dual role. First, it may go some way to allaying the concerns of practitioners about the worth and relevance of research with respect to themselves and their clients. Second, their increased involvement may allow them a greater voice in asking for the kind of research they want, organising their requirements through some representative body - for example, the British Association of Social Workers in the U.K. - and using this same body to negotiate with management for the necessary funding. The research units which presently exist are largely devoted to providing a service to management, and no-one would wish to deny their considerable contribution to improvements in this field. However, they might be of equal use, not so much in providing a service to practitioners, but in assisting practitioners to formulate researchable questions and to collect, analyse and interpret their own data. The largest obstacle here, of course, is the under-funding and lack of support which besets child care along with so much other social research: the forever-present problem of resources.

Another advantage of research activity by social workers is the contribution they might make to developing a consensus about the desired outcomes of child care. As our society struggles out of the industrial age into the post-industrial age - or the post-modernist age or the information age, or whatever we choose to call it - the only even partial certainty we have is that our children will not think, or do or be or want, the same as us. We are not passing on to the next generation an ordered and accepted social system in which roles are defined and authority symbols such as church and state are comfortably in place. Many people today - at least in the U.K. - do not believe in God or government or in each other or even in themselves. Men who hold doors open for women are not sure whether they are being patronising or polite: women who make coffee for men are not sure whether they are making the coffee or betraying the sisterhood. Neither are sure whether a father is an absent genital, or any caring, participating male; or whether a career-oriented mother is a mother is any real sense; or what the functions of the family are; or even - given the increasing diversity of households associated with such factors as single parenthood, divorce, remarriage, ethnicity and religion - what a modern family is.

The point here is that we have very little to socialise our children *into*. We are on shaky ground when we try to perform the traditional parental functions of instilling values and behaviours, modelling gender roles, guiding life choices, and generally teaching conformity with social norms. Perhaps the success of the new generation will be found in the extent to which it jettisons rather than accepts the precepts and examples of the old. If this is the case, or even partially the case, we need to think through very carefully what it is we are doing when we aim to "improve a child's adaptive functioning" or help a child "adjust" to his or her environment. In other words, we need to give added thought to the desired *outcomes* of child care. Practitioners, who tackle these problems on an everyday basis together with their clients are possibly in the best position to translate the prevailing social confusion into the kinds of questions which can be addressed by research.

We must not forget, in this context, the very real contribution that can be made by consumers of social services and by community groups. Sonia Jackson, in Chapter 3, remarks upon the growing emphasis on consumers' rights, including the right to have their opinions heard and taken into account. Symptomatic of this new emphasis is the change in the terminology of British social work, from "client" to "service user" and the idea of working in partnership with people who need help. Such partnership is increasingly being extended to the various local and national organisations who are able to provide important insights into the needs of people with disabilities and people from different ethnic, linguistic and religious groups.

Child-care services sometimes develop a *modus vivendi* of their own, displacing the needs of clients, being reluctant to change and seeking continuity. Welfare interventions themselves can also generate problems for participants. There is a need for more research which exposes bureaucracies to external scrutiny, and which seeks to redress the emphasis on issues proposed by policy makers with studies that begin with the problems as perceived and approached by other groups, not least service users or consumers. Far more studies should be carried out on the views of children and their parents with regard to all aspects of the care experience.

Parker (1989) argues that efforts must be made to break free from the constraints imposed on child care research by existing child care categories. The practical value of not confining the definition of a problem to a particular administrative or service context is twofold; first, it is more likely to correspond with the way that children and parents actually experience their problems; second, it may reflect more realistically the case management approach in social work in which the most relevant package of help is assembled from diverse sources.

Before concluding, it might be useful to turn our attention to the statement made by Casas in Chapter 1 that technological advances in the physical sciences have a more immediate and greater public impact than advances in the human and social sciences. In other words, we use the results produced by physical scientists whereas the findings of social scientists are very largely ignored. One obvious reason for this is that technological innovations attract investment while social research and applications are usually dependent on the public purse. A second reason cited by Casas is that studies in the social sciences are often fragmented into numerous schools and theoretical paradigms, with the result that discussions about real social dilemmas tend to turn into abstract debates, far removed from ordinary citizens and the practitioners who are trying to serve them. A third reason, paradoxically, is the relevance of the issues raised to ordinary citizens: questions about relationships, value systems, rights and obligations. Physical scientists also have their factions, but most of us would not feel competent to enter a debate about the advantages and limitations of hot fusion, say, as opposed to cold fusion. If the debate were about parenting, on the other hand, everyone who has had a child and many who have not might feel that their own opinions were just as valid as those of "experts". Indeed, since their opinions form the basis of traditional and cherished lifestyles, they might, as Casas points out, be extremely reluctant to accept research evidence which shows them to be wrong. Social change is achieved more slowly than technological change because more people have a larger, personal investment in the status quo.

To some degree, the tardiness of social change is also a reflection of the status of the social sciences in the scientific hierarchy. Natural scientists, in the present age, possess authority. It may not be far from the truth to say that science *is* authority. It symbolises power; it is the modern god. Authority derives in part from the possession of knowledge which is denied to others; and it obviously follows that quantum mechanics, say, which is understood by few, will be accorded more status than sociological phenomena which are more familiar, and child care in particular, with which most people are intimately acquainted. As Casas remarks, low status and limited resources are naturally associated with the low popular impact of scientific achievements in the child-care field, even though these achievements may be of the greatest importance.

In conclusion, then, the authors who have contributed to this volume have identified and explored a number of obstacles to the integration of research, policy and practice in the child-care field. They have remarked upon the low status of child care with its concomitant effect on the researchers themselves, the amount, quality and type of research produced and the limited impact of that research on practitioners, policy makers and the public in general. A suggestion for improvement made by several is increased attention to dissemination, orally, and through the media, and by the production of written material which is attractive, relevant and specifically aimed at one or other of the many diverse actors in the child-care field.

Attention has also been drawn to the processes of research, particularly with respect to current concerns about evaluation and quality. Although, in our recessionist economy, evaluation has much to do with cost efficiency, it might also provide a vehicle whereby practitioners can devise questions and collect data which will address their own concerns as well as those of managers and funders. Central to this is the matter of relating evaluative efforts to the developmental stage of the programme under review. While practitioners can contribute to outcome studies, their usefulness with respect to process may be even greater, and it is in the area of process that some of the largest knowledge gaps exist.

Narrowing the gap between research and practice through concerted education aimed at attitudes as well as knowledge levels, may have the added effect of narrowing the policy-practice and policy-research gaps. Managers who are involved with practitioners in the effort to produce data of interest to funders will necessarily become more familiar with research endeavours and possibly more sympathetic to the ethical and methodological difficulties experienced by researchers working in the field. In addition, the input provided by practitioners with respect to the outcomes to be measured and the child-care methods to be explored may be influential in shaping policy around those same methods and outcomes. In short, the policy-practice-research triangle may be strengthened as a whole by attention to the practice-research side. However, it is apparent that the links will be even stronger if attention is simultaneously given to co-operation between the practice and policy and the policy and research levels.

In producing this book we have attempted to integrate the physical with the spiritual, the abstract with the actual, and the empirical with the contemplative in the field of child care. We have endeavoured to show how the art and science of child care can be brought together for the betterment of our children and ourselves.

References

Berridge, D. and Cleaver, H. (1987), *Foster Home Breakdown*, London, Basil Blackwell.

CCETSW (1992), *Setting Quality Standards for Residential Care: A Practical Way Forward*, London, Central Council for Education and Training in Social Work (CCETSW).

Colton, M.J. and Hellinckx, W. (1993) (eds), *Child Care in the EC: A Country-specific Guide to Foster and Residential Care*, Aldershot, Arena.

Davies Jones, H. (1991), 'Some Problems of Communication in Residential Child Care', in M. Gottesman (ed) (1991), *Residential Care: An International Reader*, London, Fice International.

Department of Health (1992), *Choosing with Care* (the Warner Report), London, HMSO.

Howe, E. (1992), *The Quality of Care* (The Howe Report), Local Government Management Board.

King, R.D., Raynes, N.V. and Tizard, J. (1971), *Patterns of Residential Care: Sociological Studies in Institutions for Handicapped Children*, London, Routledge and Kegan Paul.

Parker, R. (1980), *Caring for Separated Children*, London, Macmillan.

Levy, A. and Kahan, B. (1991), *The Pindown Experience and the Protection of Children: The Report of the Staffordshire Child Care Inquiry, 1990*, Staffordshire County Council.

Parker, R. (1989), 'Theme and Variations' in B. Kahan (ed.) *Child Care Research, Policy and Practice*, London, Hodder & Stoughton.

Rowe, J., Hundleby, M. and Garnett, L. (1989), *Child Care Now*, London, British Agencies for Adoption and Fostering.

Russell, B. (1961), *History of Western Philosophy*, London, George Allen & Unwin Ltd.

Utting, W. (1991), *Children in the Public Care: A Review of Residential Child Care*, London, HMSO.

Index

About the authors

Jane ALDGATE (Great Britain) is Professor of Social Work at the University of Leicester. She is an experienced child care researcher, and is co-editor of *Direct Work with Children*, (Batsford, 1988), and *Adolescents in Foster Families*, (Batsford, 1989).

Herman BAARTMAN (the Netherlands) is Special Professor in Child Abuse and Neglect, Department of Paedagogic, Free University of Amsterdam. He is author of a historical study on violence at home and at school, and is co-editor of a manual on Child Abuse and Neglect (with Dr. A. Van Montfoort). He has published many articles on multi-problem families.

Roger BULLOCK (Great Britain) is Senior Research Fellow at Dartington Social Research Unit, University of Bristol. His many publications (in conjunction with colleagues from the Dartington Social Research Unit) include *Chance of a Lifetime?* (Weidenfield amd Nicolson, 1975); *After Grace - Teeth* (Human Context Books, 1975); *Locking up Children* (Saxon House, 1978); *Learning to Care* (Gower, 1980); *Issues of Control in Residential Care* (HMSO, 1981); *Lost in Care* (Gower, 1986); *Access Disputes in Child Care* (Gower, 1989); and *Going Home* (Gower, 1992).

Ferran CASAS (Spain) is Professor of Applied Social Phychology in the Faculties of Psychology and Pedagogy, and of the doctorship course on Child Welfare and Quality of Life at Barcelona University. He is the President of the Experts Committee on Childhood Policies of the Council of Europe, and the President of Childwatch International, network for child research. He was Director of the Childhood Studies Centre (Centro de Estudios del Menor) of the Spanish Ministry of Social Affairs from 1990 to 1993, and Director of the Programme for Children in Risk Situations of the Autonomous Government of Catalonia, from 1985 to 1988. He has published articles and books on children's problems, social services, quality of life and social and psychosocial indicators.

Matthew COLTON (Great Britain) is Senior Lecturer in Applied Social Studies, University of Wales, Swansea. He is author of *Dimensions of Substitute Child Care: A Comparative Study of Foster and Residential Care Practice* (Avebury, 1989), and is co-editor of *Innovations in Residential Care* (ACCO, 1991), and *Child Care in the EC* (1993), and has published many articles on child care. He is a member of the Executive Committee of the European Scientific Association on Residential and Foster Care for Children and Adolescents, and is a member of the editorial board of *Community Alternatives: International Journal of Family Care*. He is a professionally qualified social worker, and has substantial practice experience with separated children.

Charlotte DRURY (Great Britain) is a researcher at the Department of Social Policy and Applied Social Studies, University of Wales, Swansea. Her main interests lie in evaluative and research studies in the field of child care, and working with adult survivors of child sexual abuse.

Paul DURNING (France) is Professor at the department of Educational Sciences of the University Paris-X Nanterre, where his research and teaching interests centre on family education and child care. He is member of the Executive Committee of the European Scientific Association on Residential and Foster Care for Children and Adolescents. He has published many articles on residential care, child abuse and family education.

Pol GHESQUIÈRE (Belgium) is Senior Research Fellow at the section of Orthopedagogics, University of Leuven. From 1986 to 1993 his research was focused on home-based treatment of parenting problems, especially in abusive multi-problem families. He has published many articles on parenting problems and family care. He is the author of a recent and exhaustive book on multi-problem families (Garant, 1993). He has been director of the University Home-based Treatment Centre for Special

Youth Care. At present he is doing research on children with learning disabilities.

Frits HARINCK (the Netherlands) is a member of Leiden University, Department of Special Education. He was involved in the development of a screening device for early childhood autism and investigated process and outcome questions in play therapy with children. More recently he published several papers on evaluation methodology. Presently he is conducting research projects concerning the quality of care institutions for the mentally retarded.

Anthony HEATH (Great Britain) is an Official Fellow of Nuffield College Oxford, and Fellow of the British Academy. He is co-author of *Origins and Destinations: Family Class and Education in Modern Britain* (Clarendon Press, 1980), and has published extensively on the sociology of stratification, the sociology of education and political sociology.

Walter HELLINCKX (Belgium) is Professor at the Section of Orthopedagogics, University of Leuven, where his teaching interests centre on work with troubled children. He is president of the European Scientific Association on Residential and Foster Care for Children and Adolescents, and a member of the editorial board of *Community Alternatives: International Journal of Family Care*. He has published widely on treatment for troubled children, and the different forms of care for such children - residential and foster care, and their alternatives - and on innovations in residential care. Recently, he published the results of a nationwide epidemiological research project on children with emotional and behavioural problems in Flanders.

Sonia JACKSON (Great Britain) is Professor of Applied Social Studies, University of Wales, University College of Swansea. She has previously been a primary school teacher, a child psychologist, a local authority social worker, and Director of Educational Service Advice (Advisory Centre for Education). Her publications include *Childminder* (with Brian Jackson)(1979), Routledge and Kegan Paul; *Other People's Children* (1981), BBC; and *The Education of Children in Care* (1988), Bristol Papers No. 1, University of Bristol, School of Applied Social Studies.

Erik KNORTH (the Netherlands) is Lecturer in Child and Youth Care at the Centre for Special Education and Child Care, Leiden University. He has published many articles and several books, including *Vulnerable*

Youth in Residential Care, I & II as co-editor (Garant, 1992). Dr. Knorth is engaged in research on out-of-home placement of troubled children, and in research on treatment planning for children in residential care. He is a member of the Executive Committee of the European Scientific Association on Residential and Foster Care for Children and Adolescents.

Michael LITTLE (Great Britain) is a researcher at the Dartington Social Research Unit, University of Bristol. He is author of several books and reports on the situation and experience of difficult and deprived children.

Nicola MADGE (Great Britain) is head of the European Children's Centre at the National Children's Bureau in London. Dr. Madge is a Chartered Psychologist and author, inter alia, of *Cycles of Disadvantage* (with Michael Rutter), *Ask the Children: Experiences of physical disability in the school years* (with Muriel Brown), *Families at Risk* (as editor), *The National Childhood Encephalopathy Study: A ten-year follow-up* (with others), and *Children and Residential Care in Europe*.

Ko RINK (the Netherlands) is Professor at the University of Groningen, where his teaching interests centre on treatment of neglected and/or criminal children. At present, he is working on the development of a standardised reaction instrument, to evaluate the social limits of juveniles. He is also active in the domain of helping multi-problem families with children under provision. He has published widely on treatment for juvenile offenders and on in-service training of group workers.

Evert SCHOLTE (the Netherlands) is currently a senior researcher at the Department of Educational Sciences at Leiden University. His major research interests concern the psychological and socio-ecological backgrounds of emotional and behavioral disorders in children and adolescents, as well as the effects of prevention and intervention programs for juveniles 'at risk'.

Monika SMIT (the Netherlands) is a researcher at the Department of Special Education, Leiden University. Her main fields of interest are quality issues in (residential) child care. She is also involved in research concerning single minor refugees in the Netherlands.

Benedikte VAN DEN BRUEL (Belgium) is a research assistant at the section Orthopedagogics, University of Leuven. She has published many articles about the Special Youth Care system in Flanders and about quality of child care. At present, she is involved in training and supervision of inspectors and administrators of the Flemish Ministry of Welfare working in Special Youth Care Committees and Juvenile Courts.

Margaret WILLIAMS (Great Britain) is a researcher at the Department of Social Policy and Applied Social Studies, University of Wales, Swansea. Her major interest lies in evaluative and research studies in the field of child care. Recent publications include a research textbook, *Research in Social Work: A Primer* (Peacock, Itasca, Illinois, 1990), a number of articles in North American journals, and a series of self-help manuals on how to develop evaluable child sexual abuse treatment, education and investigation programme models.